the Unofficial Guide™ to Dating Again

Tina Tessina, Ph.D., MFT

Macmillan • USA

Macmillan General Reference
A Simon & Schuster Macmillan Company
1633 Broadway
New York, New York 10019-6785

ISBN: 0-02-862454-8

Manufactured in the United States of America

10 9 8 7 6 5 4 3 2 1

First edition

*For my single friends
and clients.
May this help
all your dreams come true.*

Acknowledgments

No book is ever written without a tremendous amount of help, and I have many people to thank:

Laurie Harper, my agent, who is always there to make sure I have what I need to get the job done.

Nancy Gratton, my Development Editor, and Nancy Mikhail, the Acquisitions Editor, who knew what they wanted, and helped me to accomplish it. Thanks also to John Jones for his careful copyediting and to my Production Editor, Andrea M. Harris.

My secretary, Ruth Campbell, who always does her work to top standards, pleasantly and efficiently, and without whom I would be found buried under a sea of paperwork.

My beloved Richard, who is now a veteran writer's husband, and who has a sense of humor about seeing "the back of my head backlit by the computer screen" for weeks on end. He is my soul mate, my partner, my dearest friend, and we are unbelievably fortunate that our Dating - Again resulted in finding each other.

My "friends network" who support me, cheer me on, love me to pieces, and make me laugh when I really need it: Isadora Alman (my home away from home), Maggie and Eddie Bialack (and their daughter, who is my goddaughter, Amanda), Bonnie Booth (whose 8 year old, Helia, is the ray of sunshine she is named for), Victoria Bryan and Carrie Williams, Ron Creager, David Groves, Larry Kern, Deni Loubert, Sylvia and Glen McWilliams, Joan and Bill Mueller, and Riley Smith. Hey, gang, I'm finally done with this—let's have lunch!!

Cindy Cyr, Shawn, Barbara, Sienna, Rito, and everyone else at The Coffee Cup, my home away from home, where I go to be fussed over and restored when I can't look at the keyboard one more minute. Beverly Terwillig and Stephen, who soothe me with incredible gourmet teas and sympathy at the Vintage Tea Leaf.

My Utne Cafe online cohorts, who cheered me on and gave me material about online dating. Especially, dear friend and cohost Jim Challis, and the impressively well-informed John Burik.

And I can never forget those who gave me my start: My mom and dad, of course, and my first publishers, the late Al Saunders (the unconscious agent of the Aquarian Conspiracy) and Jeremy Tarcher (the gentleman publisher, who pampered his authors), Jean Marie Stine (who taught me what editors are all about), and again, Riley K. Smith, coauthor extraordinaire. These people have made "the impossible dream" easy for me.

You are my angels, my family. I am grateful beyond words that you all are in my life.

The *Unofficial Guide* Reader's Bill of Rights

We Give You More Than the Official Line

Welcome to the *Unofficial Guide* series of Lifestyles titles—books that deliver critical, unbiased information that other books can't or won't reveal—*the inside scoop*. Our goal is to provide you with the *most accessible, useful* information and advice possible. The recommendations we offer in these pages are not influenced by the corporate line of any organization or industry; we give you the hard facts, whether those institutions like them or not. If something is ill-advised or will cause a loss of time and/or money, we'll give you ample warning. And if it is a worthwhile option, we'll let you know that, too.

Armed and Ready

Our hand-picked authors confidently and critically report on a wide range of topics that matter to smart readers like you. Our authors are passionate about their subjects, but have distanced themselves enough from them to help you be armed and protected, and help you make educated decisions as you go through your process. It is our intent that, from having read this book, you will avoid the pitfalls everyone else falls into and get it right the first time.

Don't be fooled by cheap imitations; this is the genuine article *Unofficial Guide* series from Macmillan Publishing. You may be familiar with our proven track record of the travel *Unofficial Guides*, which have more than two million copies in print. Each year thousands of travelers—new and old—are armed with a brand new, fully updated edition of the flagship *Unofficial Guide to Walt Disney World*, by Bob Sehlinger. It is our intention here to provide you with the same level of objective authority that Mr. Sehlinger does in his brainchild.

The Unofficial Panel of Experts

Every work in the Lifestyle *Unofficial Guides* is intensively inspected by a team of three top professionals in their fields. These experts review the manuscript for factual accuracy, comprehensiveness, and an insider's determination as to whether the manuscript fulfills the credo in this Reader's Bill of Rights. In other words, our Panel ensures that you are, in fact, getting "the inside scoop."

Our Pledge

The authors, the editorial staff, and the Unofficial Panel of Experts assembled for *Unofficial Guides* are determined to lay out the most valuable alternatives available for our readers. This dictum means that our writers must be explicit, prescriptive, and above all, direct. We strive to be thorough and complete, but our goal is not necessarily to have the "most" or "all" of the information on a topic; this is not, after all, an encyclopedia. Our objective is to help you narrow down your options to the best of what is available, unbiased by affiliation with any industry or organization.

In each *Unofficial Guide* we give you:

- Comprehensive coverage of necessary and vital information

- Authoritative, rigidly fact-checked data

- The most up-to-date insights into trends

- Savvy, sophisticated writing that's also readable

- Sensible, applicable facts and secrets that only an insider knows

Special Features

Every book in our series offers the following six special sidebars in the margins that were devised to help you get things done cheaply, efficiently, and smartly.

1. "Timesaver"—tips and shortcuts that save you time.

2. "Moneysaver"—tips and shortcuts that save you money.

3. "Watch Out!"—more serious cautions and warnings.

4. "Bright Idea"—general tips and shortcuts to help you find an easier or smarter way to do something.

5. "Quote"—statements from real people that are intended to be prescriptive and valuable to you.

6. "Unofficially..."—an insider's fact or anecdote.

We also recognize your need to have quick information at your fingertips, and have thus provided the following comprehensive sections at the back of the book:

1. **Glossary:** Definitions of complicated terminology and jargon.

2. **Resource Guide:** Lists of relevant agencies, associations, institutions, web sites, etc.

3. **Recommended Reading List:** Suggested titles that can help you get more in-depth information on related topics.

4. **Important Documents:** "Official" pieces of information you need to refer to, such as government forms.

5. **Important Statistics:** Facts and numbers presented at-a-glance for easy reference.

6. **Index.**

Letters, Comments, and Questions from Readers

We strive to continually improve the *Unofficial* series, and input from our readers is a valuable way for us to do that.

Many of those who have used the *Unofficial Guide* travel books write to the authors to ask questions, make comments, or share their own discoveries and lessons. For lifestyle *Unofficial Guides,* we would also appreciate all such correspondence, both positive and critical, and we will make best efforts to incorporate appropriate readers' feedback and comments in revised editions of this work.

How to write to us:
Unofficial Guides
Macmillan Lifestyle Guides
Macmillan Publishing
1633 Broadway
New York, NY 10019
Attention: Reader's Comments

The *Unofficial Guide* Panel of Experts

The Unofficial editorial team recognizes that you've purchased this book with the expectation of getting the most authoritative, carefully inspected information currently available. Toward that end, on each and every title in this series, we have selected a minimum of two "official" experts comprising the "Unofficial Panel" who painstakingly review the manuscripts to ensure: factual accuracy of all data; inclusion of the most up-to-date and relevant information; and that, from an insider's perspective, the authors have armed you with all the necessary facts you need—but the institutions don't want you to know.

For *The Unofficial Guide to Dating Again*, we are proud to introduce the following panel of experts:

Tim Haft is the author of five books, including *Erotic New York, a Guidebook for Lovers in the Big Apple*, and is currently collaborating on a book about romantic spots in the city that never sleeps. In addition to his literary pursuits, Mr. Haft also works as a personal trainer and resume consultant, and holds a B.A. in history and an

M.A. in sociology. He is the veteran of many a long- and short-term relationship, and is still in pursuit of his soulmate.

Sara Dulaney Gilbert, M.D. Dr. Gilbert is the author of 25 self-help and useful-service books, including *The Complete Idiot's Guide to Single Parenting, How to Live with a Single Parent (For Teenagers)*, and *Trouble at Home*. She has become an expert at helping readers of all ages find their way through career changes, personal development stages, and major life events.

Introduction

Here you go again.... For the first time in a long time, you're revisiting the dating scene.

You have picked up this guide for one reason: you are contemplating dating again, and you want to know what to expect. You may be facing the wonderful world of dating for any number of reasons: you're recently out of a relationship, or you're thinking of getting out of one, you're recently divorced, or perhaps even widowed. There are lots of reasons you may be dating again, and many special circumstances in your situation. The *Unofficial Guide to Dating Again* will tell you what you need to know. This guide's for you if you are:

- dating as a grownup

- dating after a relationship disaster

- dating as a single parent

- dating as a widow(er)

- dating as a senior

- dating after giving up on relationships

- dating after years alone

In the pages that follow, you will find what you need to know no matter what circumstances brought you back to the dating scene. We'll cover all the basics, some things you already know, and many things you never thought of.

You're not alone

If you are not currently married, you are certainly not alone. According to the U. S. Census Bureau 1996 report, half of American's adult population (that's 77 million people!) is single, and the currently divorced population is the fastest growing marital status category—it has more than quadrupled from 1970. In 1996, the Census notes, 44.9 million adults age 18 and over had never been married, more than twice as many never-marrieds as was reported for 1970.

In 1996, never-married adults accounted for 23 percent of all adults. They constituted the largest share (59 percent) of the unmarried population in 1996. The next largest group were divorced people at 24 percent, followed by widows and widowers (18 percent).

The census report goes on to note: "Sharp increases in the proportion never married have been primarily seen among men and women in their late twenties and early thirties. Between 1970 and 1996, the proportion of 25- to 29-year-olds who had never married more than tripled for women, from 11 percent to 38 percent, and more than doubled for men, from 19 percent to 32 percent. Among the 30- to 34-year-olds the proportions never married tripled from 6 percent to 21 percent for women and from 9 percent to 30 percent for men." (Saluter, Arlene and Terry Lugaila. "Current Population Reports, Population Characteristics" Bureau of the Census, website: www.census.org)

While (and to an extent, because) the number of unmarried people has risen dramatically, social mores have also changed drastically. Women have far more social approval and freedom today for doing what they want than in 1965, and, as we have seen endlessly in the media, social attitudes toward sexuality, living together, relationships, and courtship are much more relaxed than they were three decades ago.

For instance, the 1996 Census Bureau statistics show that "the number of unmarried-couple households (couples of the opposite sex) has grown sevenfold since 1970, and the proportion of children under 18 years living with two parents has declined from 85 percent to 68 percent between 1979 and 1996." This marks a significant change from the household and family structures of the 1960s.

These dramatic changes in the census counts have been accompanied by equally dramatic changes in what we expect from relationships, how long they last, and how we find them. So, if it's been any length of time since you last dated, there are a lot of changes you'll need to know about. That's where the *Unofficial Guide to Dating Again* comes in. Here you'll get the information you need to smooth your re-entry into the singles world. We will give you the information you need to find suitable people to date, an effective dating process to follow, the current attitudes and etiquette about dating, and the know-how to feel confident about your dating skills.

Coping with life's unexpected changes

For many years, dating was something done mostly by young people, during high school or college, and the expectation was that they would find partners and settle down before too long. But, as the Census Bureau quotes show, more people than ever are waiting longer to marry, or becoming single later in life, after a long-term or married relationship. So, for more and more individuals than ever before, the dating phase has been extended into adulthood, through middle age, and even into the senior years. Adults who are dating again are often parents with minor children. Whatever stage of life you are in, if you have found yourself single, and want to date again, this is the book for you.

One of the main differences between you and a teenager who is dating for the first time is experience. Your experiences can have a positive effect, in that you already have learned a lot of social and relationship skills that will be very helpful in dating again. On the other hand, there can be a downside to experience. If you are dating again because you have lost a previous relationship, you may have baggage: leftover anger, hurt, fear, or grief that will cause you to react differently in the next relationship. Or, your baggage may be left over from a difficult family situation or a poor self-image. We will show you how to "unpack" your baggage, and get a fresh start at dating again.

How does an adult find a date?

Unlike when you were dating for the first time as a teen or young adult, coming back into the dating scene after years away generally means that you can't just rely on your environment (school or college) to provide opportunities to date. Everyone has some trouble figuring out how to meet suitable people. You are probably not often in an environment that automatically surrounds you with eligible dates. Even if you are, dating people from your work and your neighborhood can present problems. Singles bars and activities aren't always the most successful places to go either.

The truth is that to date again successfully as an adult, you need well thought-out plans, and strategies that work. As an adult with responsibilities, a career, and bills to pay, you probably don't have the time to spend learning to date again by trial and error. And that's no fun, anyway. We will show you what kinds of dating plans succeed, and how to develop one that suits your personality and circumstances.

Because you are an adult, the dating tips and information you will find here will help you draw on your own life experience and know-how and apply these skills to the dating process. And while much of the advice in these pages can be used by just about anybody, the fact is that each of us comes back into the dating world for our own particular reasons. So this guide provides specific counsel regarding a variety of scenarios that may have brought you back to single life:

- If you are dating again as a result of a difficult ending to your previous relationship, such as a divorce or an acrimonious breakup, we will show you how to avoid repeating old mistakes.

- If you are a single parent, we will help you handle the issues of when and how to introduce a new date to your children, and how to handle the reactions of both your children and your date.

- It is very difficult to begin dating again after the loss of a beloved spouse. The grief and disorientation associated with being widowed can make the whole thought of dating seem impossible. We will show you how to complete your healing and move on into a comfortable connection with new people.

- If you fear that you are too old to begin dating again, let us help you find appropriate, dignified, and fun ways to open up to new experiences with old friends and new connections.

Sometimes relationship experiences can be so difficult that you may have given up on relationships altogether, thinking that living alone is your lot in life. If you are not completely happy with this choice, we can show you how to come out of isolation and make a new, much more successful start. And if you've been on your own now for a span of years, opening yourself up to new experiences can be frightening. The information, facts, and how-to's we have collected for you here can get you past your fear and into a more satisfying social life.

What you can learn from this book:

Briefly, this *Unofficial Guide* provides you with information about:

- What to do with the baggage from your past

- How to find the right kind of person to date

- Dating etiquette for today

- How to handle friends, roommates, parents, children

- What to do if it becomes a relationship

- What to do if it doesn't work out

- What to do the night before

- What to do the morning after

- What to say in person, on the phone

No matter which of these issues you need to know about, or what questions you have, you'll find the answers in here are timely, helpful, and fit the world you face as a single person dating today.

Re-entering the world of dating can be a little intimidating if you've spent a lot of time out of the scene, but it doesn't need to be. In fact, it can be a wonderful, exciting, exhilarating adventure. It all depends upon your attitude, preparation, and—yes—your sense of humor. *The Unofficial Guide to Dating Again* is your handbook for making this new adventure fun, and safe.

So let's get to it!

PART I

What Brings You Here?

GET THE SCOOP ON...
Re-learning the ropes ▪ Unpacking
emotional baggage ▪ Confronting your
fears ▪ Taking chances

Dating Again: Exciting—and Terrifying!

The thought of dating again is exciting, and you spend time daydreaming and deliberating about it, but every time you think of actually doing something about it, you're terrified. The few attempts you have actually made—blind dates set up by friends, meeting someone in a bar, attending a singles event, or seeing your ex again—have all been awkward at best, awful at worst.

Your fears are understandable. They are created by society's prevalent fantasy about dating: You and some person you don't know will meet, make an instant and 100% accurate evaluation of each other, decide to go out, and spend an evening together falling in love.

With expectations like that, you're bound to feel intimidated. It may happen in the movies, but it's just plain impossible in real life. And if you've ever dated according to that plan, you've probably had some miserable evenings. At first sight you just don't know enough about the other person to be able to declare your interest and expect that extended, pleasant, one-on-one contact will result. There have to be better ways to accomplish meeting and getting to know people.

Re-socializing as a single adult

You may not have thought about it this way, but successful dating requires skill, and the various skills it requires have to be learned somewhere. You can learn them by trial-and-error, but that's painful and time-consuming. Unlike teenagers, you don't have a lot of time to spend fantasizing, comparing notes with friends, and making mistakes. And as a single adult alone in the grown-up world, dating strangers can even be dangerous.

In effect, there's a "technology of dating" that works, and you can learn it here.

What's expected of me?

It was only normal when you were 13 to feel inadequate and insecure about dating, but at least then everyone else you knew had similar trepidations. And no one expected you to know the ropes already, anyway.

Things are different today. Not only is dating something you haven't practiced for a while (or maybe a very long time), but much more is expected of an adult in today's world. In your own mind, you've got to compete with examples set by movie stars, models, and smooth characters in TV sitcoms who usually wind up with a date in the end.

When you're constantly inundated with images of beautiful people as we are today, it's only natural to want to compare yourself (or your date) to some of today's most successful singles:

- George Clooney, People Magazine's "Sexiest Man Alive"

- Clint Eastwood who, even as an older man, still gets young women

- Leonardo DiCaprio, the rags-to-tuxedo heartthrob from "Titanic"

- Clark Gable, everyone's ideal rake as Rhett Butler

- Sidney Poitier, handsome, urbane, charming

- Jerry Seinfeld, the lame nerd who's attractive anyway

- Madonna, still buff in her 40s, smart, tough and rich

- Princess Di, tragic beauty and Cinderella/Joan of Arc combo

- Elizabeth Taylor, gorgeous at 19 and still a knockout in her 60s

- Whitney Houston, slender, lovely, and can sing her heart out

But keep in mind that these and other stars benefit from lighting, scripts, makeup, direction, cosmetic surgery, costuming, and constant retouching. Sometimes, in fact, we do get a glimpse of their "ordinary" side in the tabloids: grubby clothes, wild hair, looking more like we do.

Unlikely as it seems, on the inside, the idols we mentally compete with are as insecure, confused and imperfect as we are.

Haunted by old mistakes and bad experiences
In addition to feeling like you have to live up to a

Unofficially...
Even mega-success Dustin Hoffman, a happily-married man, has his moments of self-doubt. He burst into tears on the American Film Institute's "100 Years of Great Movies" TV special when being interviewed about "Tootsie" because he said the role (cross-dressed and not beautiful) put him in touch with how many intelligent women he has ignored because they weren't attractive.

mega-star image, you may be suffering some wounds from past relationship problems. Relationships that don't last, especially the ones that end badly or that were painful, can undermine self-confidence (especially if it was not too solid to begin with) and make you fearful of trying again.

A wonderful relationship that ended only because your partner died can be especially scarring. If you're recovering from this situation, the prospect of bonding with someone new may seem insurmountable because you're faced with the possibility of going through the searing pain of loss, or the terrible ordeal of watching your beloved die while you stand by helpless, all over again.

Once you've suffered problems, pain and loss like this, it takes great courage to begin all over again. The information and methods in this book will help you recover from your past pain and loss and gain the courage to bounce back and try again.

Whatever route brought you here, if you're reading this book you are contemplating dating again, and that means you're ready to get started.

Figuring out the fearsome singles scene

The first hurdle you'll encounter is figuring out how the *singles scene*—that social milieu known only to the uncoupled—works, and what you must do to succeed within it.

As adults, we are used to being in charge and competent in the things we do. Plunging into a new dynamic undermines this competence—beginners are, by definition, not good at what they're doing. Allow yourself to have what the Zen Buddhists call a "beginner's mind."

Allowing yourself to be in a learning mode, to be a beginner in dating, gives you several advantages:

66

If your mind is empty, it is always ready for anything; it is open to everything. In the beginner's mind there are many possibilities, but in the expert's there are few.
—Zen Master Shunryu Suzuki (Quoted in Winokur, Jon. Zen to Go, Penguin, NY, 1989)

99

- You can be open to new experiences

- There's no pressure to be perfect the first time

- You might invent a new, better way of doing something

- You can more easily correct old, bad habits

You can be open to new experiences. Being a beginner, new to dating (this time around, anyway), means you can take it slowly, allowing yourself to scope out what others are doing and learn by the examples (good and bad) of those around you. When you are in learning mode, you are more alert, pay more attention, and actually experience more than if you are operating by a tried-and-true, set system. The tentative feeling of being in a new situation helps you to be alert to things you wouldn't otherwise notice. For example, in a singles bar for the first time, if you're worried about looking "cool" and knowledgeable, you'll be focusing on what everyone thinks of you. But, if you are intending to learn, your attention will be on what others are doing, and you'll evaluate how successful their approaches are.

There's no pressure to be perfect the first time. As a beginner, you don't have to impress anyone with anything other than your openness to learn. Be willing to say to people you meet, "I'm new at this." If you are coming out of a long-term relationship, they'll see this as an asset: "This person knows how to have a relationship!". Also, being "the new kid on the block" motivates others to be helpful and to show you the ropes. You are not a threat or a challenge when you're a beginner.

You might come up with a new, better way of doing something. Many of the world's great inventions were mistakes made by someone fumbling

Bright Idea
The first time in a new singles event, club, or other social situation, don't expect to meet anyone. Go with the intention of observing, and watch what goes on from a comfortable corner. You'll be more relaxed, and you'll get a better feel for the culture of the place.

around with the unknown. Modern rubber, for example, was invented in 1839 when Charles Goodyear accidentally spilled a concoction he was "cooking" onto a stove. Who knows what naive mistakes you could make that will revolutionize dating, at least for you? Don't be afraid to get a little creative in your methods—if they fail, you'll have something to laugh about, and if they succeed, the results could be well beyond your wildest expectations.

You can more easily correct old, bad habits. Opening up your mind to learning new things makes it easier to bypass old, automatic behavior. Discarding old habits, playing with the situation, and making it fun for yourself could cause you to make a social faux pas or two, but it is more likely to make the experience interesting educational—vital qualities in a successful dating experience.

Putting yourself on the line

Part of what's so intimidating about dating is that the minute you express interest in someone, no matter how casually, you expose yourself to the possibility of rejection. Ironically, one of the techniques taught in many "how to date" workshops is actually to try and get rejected as many times as possible. This little mental trick makes getting rejected the goal, so either you meet your goal, or you *don't* get rejected, thus turning the process into a win/win situation.

"Does he (or she) like me?" is the first question most of us ask upon being attracted to another. But it's much more appropriate to ask yourself, "Do I like him (or her)?" What this new person thinks of you is his or her responsibility, not yours. Your job is to find out what *you* think about this stranger. There will be many more techniques for how to do this in later chapters.

> 66
> Every situation we face in life is different, and learning from each one requires... mindful learning, which involves taking in new information in a way that allows us to use it in different situations... to vary the basics to allow each of us to use our unique physical skills, mental abilities and personalities to the fullest.
> —Harvard learning researcher Dr. Ellen Langer (*Bottom Line Personal*, Oct. 15, 1997)
> 99

In today's atmosphere of changing roles and lifestyles, answers to questions like "Who asks first?" are varying more and more. Does the woman wait for the man to ask? If so, how does she let him know she would welcome an invitation? There are lots of these questions today, from etiquette such as holding doors to buying drinks and dinner. The key to these problems is to know what message each approach sends, so you can choose what impression you're making. Dating etiquette, body language and social skills are all areas we will explore in depth.

Regression: Youthful feelings and fears resurface

When you approach a stranger to try and get to know him or her (or when someone approaches you) you encounter that "beginner" feeling again. No matter how cool-headed you may be at work, with your friends, or in front of strangers you *don't* want to date, if you're meeting a potential date you may stammer, get tongue-tied, blush, fidget, and look at everything but the person. In short, you may find yourself breaking out in all kinds of mannerisms that remind you of being a teen. Psychologists call this *regression*—feeling younger than your actual age. It happens under stress, in new situations, and when some problem from your childhood seems to be recurring. In this case, what you're regressing to is a need for approval and acceptance.

Take this in stride—it's going to happen the first few times, and then you'll calm down. After a couple of successful connections with the people around you (even just friendly smiles or "hellos"), you'll find you begin to feel more like your normal self, and your fear will transform itself into excitement and optimism.

Watch Out!
If you decide to try out the "get rejected" approach, be careful not to overdo it. You don't want to create rejection for yourself where it wouldn't otherwise exist. Your goal is simply to meet as many people as possible and introduce yourself to them, even if you think you might be rejected.

ALL YOU HAVE TO DO

To get a conversation going with someone new:

1. Remind yourself not to compare yourself or your potential date to screen idols or supermodels. You are both "just plain folks," and you may be equally unsure and nervous.

2. Take a slow breath and take your time.

3. Smile.

4. Look over the other person to become aware of what has caught your interest. (The outfit? A nice accessory or watch? A lovely smile, striking blue eyes, a pretty color of hair or clothing?)

5. Say "Hello," or respond to whatever he or she says.

6. Give a compliment.

7. Ask a question. For example: "That's a striking pin you're wearing. Does it have a special meaning?" Or, "My, your eyes are an amazing color. Does it run in your family?" Or, "I love your watch. Is it from Switzerland?"

Your conversation will be off and running.

> **"**
> The only difference between sex and death is, with death you can do it alone and nobody's going to make fun of you.
> —Woody Allen
> **"**

Taking risks, making mistakes

When you're just starting up again in the social singles world, you're accepting the risks of feeling a little foolish, being disappointed, and being turned down a few times. But when you overcome these risks, dating again can be a lot of fun. Finding the right person to date, and hopefully even fall in love with, is well worth taking a few risks. As they say in aerobics, "no pain, no gain."

You can learn to maximize your fun and minimize your difficulties with a little information, some pointers and some careful planning. What can make dating miserable is blundering around without a plan and learning by trial and error. Those unplanned errors can be very costly! The risk involved in dating should be *calculated risk*, well-thought-out and planned-for, so the consequences aren't too drastic. Every chance you take in dating should have pretty good odds of being successful, and the pain should be only minor emotional discomfort.

Am I paranoid, or is this as risky as it feels?

Dating, especially if you are not used to it, presents three possible types of risk:

- emotional pain
- financial expense
- physical risk

One of the aims of this guide is to teach you how to avoid any serious risks at all.

Emotional pain. Unless your past was unusually traumatic, either in your childhood or your previous relationships, the emotional pain you risk can be limited to disappointment, not tragedy, if you know your vulnerable areas, take the time to find out who the other person is, and go slowly into commitment. For example, if, for you, sexual intercourse is equal to commitment, it's very important that you make sure what having sex means to your partner *before* you go ahead. Or, if you're seeing someone who becomes critical of you, you need to pull back until you find out what's going on.

Financial expense. It's smart to budget your dat-

> **"**
> Love's blindness consists oftener in seeing what is not there than in seeing what is.
> —Peter DeVries
> (Winokur, Jon. *A Curmudgeon's Garden of Love.* Penguin, NY 1989)
> **"**

Watch Out!
We live in a very mobile society, so it's easy for people to be dishonest with one another. Treat your emotions, your body, and your money as equally precious and worthy of protection: Don't let yourself "fall in love" with someone until you are sure they're genuine. Don't let someone else drive unless you're sure they're sober. Practice safer sex. Don't loan money or sign financial papers because you are "in love."

ing expenses and stay within the limits you set, managing them just as you manage the rest of your finances.

Also, don't let the excitement of a new connection or the desire to impress tempt you to spend more than you can afford.

Physical risk. We would all like dating to be romantic and have a happy ending, but any newspaper will show you that dating can be dangerous. Protect yourself by meeting new people only in public places (such as at a local coffee house for a chat), by being alert to the signs of dangerous people (like reckless driving, drinking too much, angry outbursts, being too controlling), and, of course, by protecting your health with safer sex practices.

Many guidelines for personal safety are included in the chapters of this book. By following them, you can minimize the dangers of dating and maximize your fun.

Who's in control—of whom?

Most people feel more comfortable being in control of the situations they're in—so much so that we often pretend we're in control when we're really not, or try to control situation^{a}s that we cannot reasonably handle.

Remember, you are never in control of another person, even if it seems that you are, and that they wish you to be. You can't control who you'll meet, when or where you'll meet them, how anyone else will feel, or what they'll do.

Self-control is the only real control you have. However, it is all the control you'll need. By taking responsibility for your own actions, words, and reactions, you can greatly stack the odds in your own favor. I think of responsibility as *response-ability*: the ability to respond to life, people and events. While you may not be responsible for most of what happens, you are completely responsible for your reaction to what is happening. For example, if you are out with a new person and that person acts in some frightening or unacceptable manner, you have the ability to respond in many ways.

You can react without thinking, and perhaps make the situation worse; you can leave (even if it means paying for a cab or leaving your date in a restaurant at dinner); you can ask someone (such as the restaurant manager) for help. You can also respond by deciding not to date that person again, even if feelings have been developing in the relationship. Being responsible means taking care of yourself, even if it's difficult.

Learning as you go: Mistakes are okay

Dating is just another learning process. You have learned a lot in your life: How to dress appropriately, how to drive, how to use a computer, how to play tennis. This is no different. It's a series of skills and information you can master, with some practice, as you have other skills.

Even cartoonist Matt Groening, creator of "The Simpsons," had a difficult time learning to date. "I didn't know anything about love back then. I was completely screwed up on the subject. I'd had a few relationships here and there, but for some reason they kept blowing up in my face. I couldn't figure it out. A few women did agree to go out with me anyway, but they didn't last too long. Sooner or later I'd show up at their apartments, ready for another cheap night out, and they'd say the meanest, most vicious things you can say to another person. Things like: 'We have to talk.'" But even he learned. He and his wife Deborah have been married for 14 years.

And as *you* learn and explore, there will inevitably be a few social blunders. Accept this fact: You will make mistakes, and you will learn from them.

Don't expect to be Ms. or Mr. Cool. "Cool" is one of those vague ideas we're encouraged to aspire to. Since "cool" trends are driven by a combination of advertising, celebrities mimicking social outcasts (as with the "gangsta" look), and personal creativity, it's difficult to keep current on them.

One current "cool" trend is the so-called grunge look. Keep in mind that even though many of our sex-symbol movie stars are into looking unkempt these days, those looks are carefully contrived, and a result of *extra* grooming, not a lack of it. To be successful at dating, you need to be well groomed. Even the trend toward casual clothes is misleading, because that look is as carefully contrived as any formal or business outfit. Looking good is important, and takes some effort. Being well groomed is much more effective than being "cool."

Stepping into the unknown—and it's always unknown. Every date will be a brand-new experience, no matter how much mental and physical preparation you've done. The whole point of dating is to meet *new people*. In the process, you are likely to make some friends of both genders and to have a lot of interesting and thought-provoking experiences.

Since everyone you meet will be a unique individual, there's no way to be completely prepared for what will happen. If you allow yourself to experience each date with a beginner's mind—prepared to learn and to be surprised, seeking to control only

Bright Idea
You can use your business skills to improve your odds in dating. If you hire or manage people in your job, for example, use the intuitive skills you've developed there to "scope out" the person you've just met. Without being obvious, you can "interview" this person and draw out information about them. If what you hear would make you want to hire him or her, then a date might be a good experience.

your own responses, and prepared to make realistic plans and decisions—you'll enjoy the experience.

If you accept that dating is venturing into the unknown, exploring and learning, you will be in the best possible frame of mind to enjoy the adventure, and you'll get the best results.

Confronting your emotional baggage

As we mentioned in the introduction, because you are an adult, and not dating for the very first time, you have a lot of life experience, or baggage. Some of your experience will be helpful, and some will be problematic. If you take the time to examine your history and experience, you'll find you've learned a lot.

The skills you've learned in your life, in your work, with friends, in team sports and social events, and at school are very powerful and flexible tools. Many people, especially if they're nervous about dating, don't realize they can transfer other life skills into dating situations.

On the other hand, some of your life experiences have probably been painful, and that may add some problems.

The baggage of your past

Emotional trauma we bring with us from childhood and past relationships is called baggage, because it's extra "stuff" we carry with us into all our relationships, and it affects how we perceive our relationship interactions.

Beginning (or even contemplating) a relationship activates these memories and brings your old fears and insecurities to the surface. Old issues that have not been resolved, such as fear of abandonment, fear of intimacy, or fear of rejection, will surface.

66
[A] relationship is like a mirror right there at the tip of your nose. It constantly reflects... your stuff.
—Author and psychologist Ken Keyes (*A Conscious Person's Guide to Relationships*, Living Love Publications, Coos Bay, 1979)
99

Even though this may feel like a problem when it happens, it isn't. It's an opportunity to prevent your relationship problems from recurring. Let's look at how to unpack this baggage and keep it from causing you to repeat your old patterns in these new relationships.

A course in emotional growth

Dating again, to be successful, must be a course in emotional growth. Here is a helpful way to think about dating and relationship problems which will make focusing on solutions easier, and increase the odds that your relationships will improve.

You are probably quite practiced in taking courses. If you sign up for an algebra course you know what you'll face: many weeks of learning new material, and homework assignments consisting of more and more complex problems based on the material learned. You may have the urge to grumble about the homework load or complain about the teacher, but you're never inclined to think you've been given the problems as punishment. Problems are a natural part of the educational process.

Life is just a huge classroom with many classes, one of the most rigorous and daunting of which is Love 101. It's a required credit: You can't escape it, you can't drop it, you can't even just audit it. The syllabus for this class includes love of self, family, and friends. The *advanced* syllabus includes love of enemies and those who disappoint, hurt or frustrate us. All of the problems presented as homework for the class are to help us stretch and grow emotionally.

Every relationship you have is a learning lesson in love—both love of yourself and love of the other. By keeping in mind you are a student and problems are to learn from, you'll find that dating will be

---

ALL YOU HAVE TO DO

When a problem arises,

1. Be aware of your internal reaction. Are you anxious?

2. Look for what you can learn about the problem.

3. If your date has a problem or is upset, say, "Tell me more."

4. Listen carefully.

5. Don't focus on who's at fault, focus on what will fix the problem.

---

more fun, emotional growth will happen faster and be easier to recognize, and everything will make more sense.

Dealing with your fears

Chances are that even before dating was a part of your life, during your childhood and adolescence, you learned a basic truth about relationships. A serious problem in a relationship that's very important to you—whether with a best friend, an immediate family member, a mentor, or other peer—can have devastating consequences on your *basic ability to form relationships*. It's very easy to become *phobic*—intensely afraid—of being hurt or rejected.

To overcome the fears you may feel about forming relationships, you need to learn to look at dating from a new perspective—one that is rational, fresh, open-minded and optimistic.

We've already looked at several techniques for

taking care of yourself:

- having a beginner's mind
- seeking to learn
- paying attention to the character flaws and assets of the other person
- keeping your distance from hurtful people
- taking responsibility for your actions and responses

In the chapters that follow, you'll learn more details about these techniques, plus useful information and tips to eliminate fear and pain and make your dating experience fun.

The fun of dating is misrepresented by movies, TV, commercials and other media. From these representations, it appears that dating is for "beautiful people," and the scenes depicted often have a hyperactive quality that looks attractive on the surface, but feels subtly scary. You recognize that such a high level of energy would not be comfortable in real life.

That, coupled with past painful experiences, may contradict the "fun" image, and make dating seem more like a potential for misery. If you feel that way, it's natural to approach dating with a certain amount of dread.

There are a number of aspects of dating that might cause you to have these fears:

Because you can't control it. As we saw earlier, because each date and each new person is a new experience, you may feel out of control. And it is true that there is no way to completely control what will happen, or how the other person will act or respond.

However, knowing that you can control your own

actions and responses, and having information and techniques for successful dating, will put you in control of what really counts—yourself.

Because you don't know how it will end. When you're dating, there's no guarantee of a happy ending. In fact, that's what you're dating for—to check out a new person, and find out whether a partnership will work between the two of you.

Not knowing how it will end, along with being worried about rejection and hurt, can really increase your feeling of dread. But it's important to keep in mind that the unknown ending could be a happy one. Be careful not to focus on only the negative possible outcome.

Being informed about successful dating techniques will maximize your chances of having a happy outcome, and teach you how to have a good time even with the people who won't be around long.

Because it ended before. Prior pain is often a reason why people dread a new experience. If the last relationship was painful, hurtful and a disaster, it's natural not to want to try it again.

This guide will help you develop a new way to date, one in which the possibility of pain is minimized and the fun is maximized. The relationships that did not work out become an accepted part of your past life when you begin a great relationship in the present.

Because it will change who you are. Yes, dating will change who you are, and most of us don't relish change.

If you keep in mind, however, that the "new you" you are creating will have grown emotionally and will be happier, more socially confident, and very likely in love, you can overcome the dread and get enthused.

> 66
> Most of us are comfortable in the environments we have created. We identify with our sets of habits, attitudes and activities. . . Change creates the anxiety of *ambiguity*—an uncomfortable feeling that causes us to feel as if we don't know exactly who we are.
> —Psychiatrist and author Martin Groder, in an article called "All About Change" (Bottom Line Personal, May 15, 1996)
> 99

Dating again doesn't have to be dreadful. By following the suggestions here, you can create a dating style which is practical and realistic for you. Part of this process will be to discover what can make dating fun for you, and to learn how to implement that information.

The thrill of it all

Once you have examined and dealt with all the fears and negative expectations that come up when you consider dating again, you can get on with the planning and the process.

Being afraid is natural, and a healthy response to facing a situation you've had trouble with before. Your fears are saying, in effect, "We've had a bad time with this before—I don't feel prepared to do it again." Respect this message, and help yourself by getting prepared and informed. The more competent you feel at dating again, the less fearful and more enthusiastic you will feel.

You are about to learn a number of new ways to date. Careful planning will eliminate most of the problems you fear before they even come up. The whole point of this guide is to help you with that planning—to give you the information and techniques you need to make dating again an enjoyable and successful process.

My objective is to help you to feel confident. When you are secure and confident, you will also begin to get enthused, excited and ready to have a good time.

So go ahead—dig in! The information and methods presented in this book will help you to feel encouraged and intrigued. Armed with this information, you can let yourself be excited, enthused,

,and even giddy about re-entering the dating scene.

Just the Facts

- Dating again can be daunting but exhilarating.

- Avoid measuring yourself—or your potential dates—against impossible fantasy figures.

- Everyone's a little nervous out there in the dating scene. You're not alone.

- Don't ignore your emotional baggage—but don't bring it with you on your dates, either.

- Self-confidence is key.

GET THE SCOOP ON...
Obstacles to dating ▪ Healthy dating attitudes ▪
Dating myths ▪ Emotional preparation

Chapter 2

The Problems, and How to Overcome Them

If we were to believe the movies, dating is either a cinch—the person of your dreams walks in, you're instantly intrigued, you flirt expertly while the steam and the background music rise, and you're off to a beautiful, romantic, sexy beginning— or a disaster, as in the Mr. Goodbar girl-meets-killer or Fatal Attraction boy-meets-lunatic scenarios.

Real-life dating actually falls in the enormous middle ground between these two fantasies. It's not a snap, it takes some work, but, with some inside information, it can be done right, and it can lead to lots of fun times and dating success. What makes the difference is understanding what the potential problems of dating are, and knowing the skills to overcome those problems when they arise.

The quibbles and the waffles

If you were a movie character, you'd be sure of yourself, clear on what you want, beautifully turned out, and ready to go. But, you're you—a human being,

Timesaver
Do research before you go out looking for places to meet people, just as you would in shopping for a new computer or appliance. Ask your friends for recommendations, call for information, and look in local newspapers for resources, so you know where you want to go, the hours, the open days, what to wear, and what's likely to happen before you waste time acting on wrong assumptions.

with some confusion, some doubts, and some insecurity, like all the rest of us.

When you sincerely prepare to date again, and think about what to do first, you're probably going to have some quibbles—things you give yourself a hard time about—and some waffles—things you can't decide about. The most common fall into four categories:

I'm not ready

These are all the reasons you cook up about not being ready to begin dating again:

- I'm not emotionally healed from my last experience.

- I haven't a thing to wear!

- I don't know how to: talk, flirt, behave, stay safe.

- I have to lose some weight, grow some hair, get a nose job, get my Ph.D….

- I don't have any time.

All of these quibbles are just excuses for not getting started, not good, solid reasons. If you are still hurting from your last experience, you may want to attend therapy, but you can still go out and begin meeting new people. Dating again, as we present it here, is not an instant process, and going through the process can be part of your healing process.

While looking your best is indeed an important part of dating, excuses about clothing, weight, hair,. and other aspects of your appearance are not a reason to postpone dating. Actually, getting your appearance together is one of the first steps toward dating again.If you are insecure about dating behavior, flirting, and so on, learning how to do that, too, is an excellent beginning toward dating.

If your schedule is so busy that you cannot manage an evening a week, or some weekend time during which to date, you have some organizing to do in your life to be prepared to have a dating relationship. As you'll see, meeting new people and dating can be integrated into things you already do, and you can organize your life so you'll have enough spare time.

No one will like me

This quibble is related to concerns you may have about your appearance, but it goes much deeper. If you find that what's stopping you from dating is your own insecurities and lack of self-worth—feeling so bad about yourself that you can't imagine anyone else would like you—getting help is vital. Group or individual therapy, a twelve-step program, or self-esteem classes will help you confront and overcome your inner struggle with yourself.

All of these quibbles indicate aspects of dating for which you feel unprepared, and by paying attention to your insecurities, you can discover what information and skills you need. Preparing by learning these things is the beginning of your dating process.

It's going to be a disaster right from the start

It's easy to frighten yourself with negative predictions and "what ifs"—your anxieties projected into the future. Dating again *is* an unknown, and bound to produce some anxiousness, but you're not helping yourself by dwelling on what could go wrong and scaring yourself even more. Instead, focus on what you will do if any of your scary future scenarios come true. For example, suppose your dire prediction is "I'm going to go to this party, no one will talk to me, and I'll be miserable all night." Neutralize the fear by figuring out what to do if the worst happens. "If no

Moneysaver
If you don't have insurance that covers therapy, it can become quite expensive. Group therapy, classes, and twelve-step programs are all much less expensive, and you can use them in conjunction with therapy to cut down on the number and frequency of visits.

one talks to me, I'll ask the hostess to introduce me to someone, or ask if I can help pour drinks, to keep myself busy."

If you discourage yourself before you begin, you can make dating truly difficult, even if the problems never happen. If you know you can handle whatever comes up, you can have fun even when you don't meet the love of your life on a particular occasion.

If you've had a difficult time in a previous relationship, or if you've gone through a divorce, or if your partner has passed away, it's common to shy away from new relationships for fear that what hurt you once is bound to happen again.

It's not surprising, if you were hurt before, that you would be wary of going through it all over again, but it's also not necessary to give in to this fear. Treat this quibble like the others in this section—as a signal that you need to know more about the subject. In the case of broken relationships, understanding what went wrong in the first place will go a long way toward assuaging your fears.

For example, if you were shocked and surprised by a partner who lied, cheated, or who just announced one day that the relationship was over, perhaps you need to learn more about creating open communication and choosing people who will be honest with you. When you know you can do something to reduce the odds of a previous problem recurring, you will feel more secure.

Another variant on the "disaster" theme is telling yourself that love doesn't work for anyone at anytime. The only good thing about this attitude is that you won't feel bad if it doesn't work for you— because it doesn't work, period. But the whole idea is just plain wrong—there are lots of happy couples

> **"**
> Some of your ills you have cured
> And the sharpest, at least you've survived.
> But what torments of Hell you've endured
> From evils that never arrived.
> —Goethe (1749-1832)
> **"**

out there, and you can be part of one too. But negative attitudes like this one just increase the odds that you'll be miserable and even more nervous, and therefore, make mistakes.

Look around you. We live in a time of relationship turmoil, when every couple seems to break up almost before they get started—but, if you look, you'll find that there are lots of couples who are doing fine. They seem happy. Look for these success stories and focus on them, and you'll feel more encouraged and motivated to pursue dating. Love can work, if you choose the right partner and you know the skills required to make it work. And when it does, it's great!

Even if you don't find the love of your life right away, successful dating is an enjoyable way to fill your time while you're looking. It certainly beats sitting at home and eating pizza for one while watching old Seinfeld re-runs. While you may, indeed, be a person who prefers solitude and likes living alone, you still need social contacts and friends—and that's what dating is all about.

Savvy dating is making good connections with desirable people—and all of us can use as much of that as we can get. You can learn to balance your social life with your privacy, so you get enough of each one.

I can't do this to the kids, the cat, my roommate, my ex, myself

This may be the ultimate in dating quibbles. There is bound to be someone in your life you can use to hold yourself back. But what this quibble really assumes is that if you go out and meet new people, the people already in your life will suffer. But how would meeting new people be a problem for your kids, your cat, your roommate, your ex, or anyone already in your life? There is no limit to the number of people you can care for in your life, unless you insist on setting that limit. Repeat after me: "I am not interested in *replacing* anyone already in my life; I do not intend to neglect them or to ignore them. I am simply looking for some new people with whom I can have fun." Keeping that thought firmly planted in your mind will ensure that you don't cause problems in the relationships you already have.

Facing the unknown

We all want happy endings, and we want to know it's coming in advance—like reading the last page of a novel when the story gets scary, to see if it comes out all right. But, dating, like the rest of life, doesn't work that way. You won't know the end until you get there. By following the advice and guidelines given here, however, you can make sure you have good results. And, after all, *you* get to decide when you reach the ending—if you don't give up, you can meet your goals.

There are no guarantees

The best way to guarantee you *won't* have a happy ending is to avoid, procrastinate, and put off getting out there and dating. Unless you have a crystal ball that works, you'll have to take events as they come along. If you take your time, and approach dating in a logical fashion, there's not too much that can go wrong. You'll meet some nice people and some strange ones. You'll have some great times and some times that are not-so-great. There's no guarantee that you'll meet Prince or Princess Charming and live happily ever after. But, by following the sensible suggestions laid out for you in this book, you *can* guarantee that you will meet good people, have a great time, and thoroughly enjoy dating again.

Worst case, you'll live

No matter how badly a particular dating experience goes, if you make sensible choices and take some simple precautions, you'll be safe. The worst thing that will happen is occasional disappointment, a boring evening, being interested in someone who doesn't return the interest, or some other minor problem. The whole point of this book is to help you avoid more serious problems, and greatly increase the odds of having fun and being successful.

Yes, people do get emotionally and even physically hurt while dating—we hear the stories on the news all the time. But, we are not always told the circumstances of these horror stories, or how rare they are. Many of the problems are caused by one or both parties drinking too much, getting intimately involved too fast, and other lapses of judgment. Following the cautions and guidelines set forth here will help you avoid the problems and maximize your chances of success.

Time is on your side, if you let it be

No one knows how long it takes for people to make a solid connection with someone to love, because the answer is different for each one of us. The only thing you can bank on is this: the sooner you get started, the better. If you're having a good time in what you're doing, making new friends, and enjoying yourself, it will be fun no matter how long it does take.

And speaking of how long "it" will take, what goal do you have in mind? If you use these recommended guidelines, you'll be connecting with people within a few weeks, and not long after that, you'll find someone to date. Where you take your relationship (or relationships) from there is up to you. And if your goal at the outset is to find your one true love, your mate for life, that will take a bit longer.

Don't rush it—it's going to take a while

Most of the horror stories you may have heard about dating occur when you rush the process. Getting intimately involved with someone you don't know, allowing strangers into your home, or being all alone with someone you just met is just asking for trouble.

Dating successfully is an organized process that will take some time. You'll begin with carefully looking for the right people in the right places.

Squirrel hunting—how to do it

This search for dating partners is much easier than it may sound to you. I like to compare it to squirrel hunting:

There are two ways to catch squirrels. One way is to run around and try to grab them or pounce on them—but you'll only scare them away, and they'll run faster than you do every time. In the end, you'll be very frustrated and exhausted, and you'll have no squirrels.

Second, you can go to where the squirrels are, offer them something attractive, like walnuts, and wait quietly, just enjoying the day and the place. It will take a while, but if you are very relaxed and quiet, they will begin to get curious, and soon they will begin to check you out. Stay relaxed and let them know you are safe and have goodies. Before long, they'll be all over you, and eating out of your hand. You'll have your choice of several squirrels. A little patience is all it takes to guarantee success.

Finding a lover isn't much different. How you feel about yourself and your own life, and taking steps to make yourself interested, interesting, and happy, means a lot more than how rich or handsome you are. Physical looks and outer attributes fade in importance very quickly—your personality and self-esteem are what a true lover values.

Handling the hurts

Despite all precautions, you can still get hurt dating. The question is, how much hurt is unavoidable, and are you willing to risk it? Even when you are careful, you can still be disappointed, frustrated, hurt, and upset. But life is full of frustrations and disappointments. The ones connected to dating can seem to be the most painful, but that's because they involve your self-esteem and your sense of emotional well-being. And the uncertainties inherent in the dating process can make for a great deal of stress, unless you're prepared for them in advance.

On again, off again

Dating can be stressful because it involves a lot of new and unknown circumstances. Your whole goal is meeting new people, and this often involves trying new activities in new settings. Anything unfamiliar is stressful, because it calls for a lot of on-the-spot decision making. When we're in a situation we're not familiar with, we tend to be extra alert, a bit anxious, and to use more energy than normal. We are trying to size up new people and situations, and we're thinking about every word we say. All of this is tiring so, in order to keep dating for enough time to be successful at finding a partner, and to avoid burnout, you will need to learn to pace yourself.

To pace yourself, learn to follow your energy:

pursue a lot of new adventures when you feel energized and enthused, but don't worry if you feel more
reclusive from time to time. If you take regular
breaks from dating, you'll actually be able to do
more than if you keep pushing.

A change of environment can be energizing and
refreshing. If you're in a non-dating "rut, " dating
will be exciting and new. If you're tired, stressed, or
over-stimulated with the new experiences of an
active dating life, retreating to familiar friends and
surroundings will be restful and restorative.

Set up a support system

As with any change you want to make in life, having
a support system will help keep you focused and
enthused. Let your best friends and closest family
members know what you're doing and enlist them to
be your support team. They can help in all sorts of
ways:

- **Fellow adventurers:** Single friends can go out
  on some of your new adventures with you; for
  example, if you want to take a class, you and a
  friend can go together. Or you can enlist a
  friend to accompany you to the first meeting of
  a non-profit group you want to join.

- **Cheerleaders:** Your support team can also be
  there to comfort and commiserate with you
  when you're rejected or hurt, and to remind
  you how much they all care (especially when
  Prince or Princess Charming turns out to be a
  troll). When you're successful, they can cheer
  you on. You'll get a lot of energy and
  motivation from sharing your ups and downs
  with sympathetic caring people.

- **Advisors:** There's no expert like a friend who's

Bright Idea
To give yourself
a break from
the unfamiliar
territory of dat-
ing, spend time
with good friends
or family
members, doing
familiar things, or
retreat totally—
stay home and
pamper yourself
with favorite
foods, music,
and a well-known
movie or book—
you'll be surprised
how refreshed
you feel.

been there, done that. If your support team includes people who successfully dated after losing a relationship, don't hesitate to ask for their experience. Their experience can be helpful even though they differ from you, and have different needs. Even if what worked for them may not work for you, their ideas can spark more fitting ones of your own. Just as a parent who's been through it all and lived to tell about it can give reassurance and advice to a nervous first-time parent, so your friend with more recent dating experience can be equally helpful and reassuring to you. It's great to hear, "Oh, don't worry about that—I went through that a bunch of times before I got it right." It's both comforting and supportive to hear someone who succeeded tell you you're doing OK.

Mastering your mistakes

OK, OK, we all know you're cool and suave—but we also know you're going to make some mistakes. This is new territory, by definition, and you are not an expert but an experimenter. Keep that fact firmly in mind, and don't sweat the small stuff. A mistake is very small stuff; it simply gives you a chance to try again. Correcting a mistake can lead to better places with people than if you do it right the first time. Everyone admires you when you can take responsibility for whatever you did wrong or neglected to do right. "I'm sorry, I know I should have called sooner, but it took me a while to get the nerve up" is far more endearing and impressive than a lot of denial and excuses. It also provides you with an opportunity to continue the relationship, while giving up in self-disgust or self-criticism ends it. Finally, acknowledging your mistakes lets the other person know that you are capable of admitting an error and working out a mutual solution, which is not a bad quality for a potential "steady" to have.

If the mistake is more serious, like drinking too much and driving, or really hurting someone's feelings or insulting them (intentionally or unintentionally), or getting caught in some kind of lie, then you're going to have to confront *yourself.* Your behavior, and perhaps your thinking process, needs adjustment. If you can't make the adjustment by yourself, call on your support team for help or referrals to experts.

Dating again means you have a history

Unlike the teenager dating for the first time, you have experience, which can be valuable if you know how to draw on it. But if your past experience overwhelms you and prevents you from doing what you want to do, it becomes a problem. To date successfully, you need to acknowledge your history, positive and negative, and use the experience you have gained to help you know what to do today.

Memories can help or hurt

Dating again will bring up painful and happy memories of your past, which can also be useful. Noticing and analyzing memories when they come up rather than trying to ignore them will give you a lot of information. Even a relationship that did not work out can teach you good things. If you list and compare the qualities of each of your past relationship experiences, you can create a composite of desirable qualities you would like to find in the next situation, and the undesirable qualities to watch out for.

Watch Out!
Advice from experienced friends is great—just make sure it's the right kind of experience. Seek out friends who have succeeded in dating the way you want to—not the ones who have created disasters for themselves. Just as you wouldn't ask someone with a DUI for driving lessons, don't ask a relationship disaster expert for advice.

You thought your mourning was over?

One of the things that happens when a relationship ends is that the hopes and dreams you had for that relationship die with it. No matter how bad the relationship is, as long as it lasts, there's a possibility that things will change and your hopes and dreams will be realized. When the relationship finally ends, even if you're relieved, you may be confused to find yourself grieving for the lost possibilities. This can be quite disconcerting, especially if the relationship was very difficult, because your emotional reaction doesn't seem to match your experience.

If, in addition to losing these hopes and dreams, you have also lost a partner whom you still loved and still felt attached to—whether your partner died or ended the relationship unilaterally—you'll also be grieving for that.

To handle your grief properly, you'll need support. Family and friends may be able to give you the support you need, but often that support is not enough, or it fades before you have finished grieving. Individual therapy and grief groups offer more expert and lasting support—you can express as much grief as you need, and your therapist or group will help you resolve it, rather than saying you should be over it by now.

If the current source of grief connects to a more complex issue, such as childhood abandonment, your emotions will be powerful and possibly frightening to your family, friends, and yourself. A therapist or facilitated grief group will be more equipped to help you express and resolve these feelings without reacting negatively.

Even after completing grief therapy, however, you won't be completely grief-free. If you have a dif-

Bright Idea
When memories arise in the middle of having fun, take a moment to yourself to acknowledge your grief. Allow yourself to feel the sadness and loss and it will pass rather quickly. Then you can get back into the event and go on with the day. If you have trouble getting alone, consider going to the bathroom for a few minutes. There's almost always a bathroom available— it's a place you can easily retreat to and be alone.

ficult evening out, or a disappointing encounter, you may find your grief suddenly re-emerging. Also, doing things that remind you of a past relationship or a missing parent, child, or sibling can flood you with grief at unexpected moments, in the middle of your fun.

For example, if you lost a spouse with whom you often went skiing, and you go on a skiing trip with some single friends, in the midst of the fun and laughter, you may find yourself feeling very sad. This is entirely normal, especially after the loss of a person you've been close to for a long time.

Debunking social expectations and myths

A lot of the problems that come up in dating again are generated by *social expectations* (how other people think you should behave or things should happen) and *myths* (common beliefs which are not based on fact). Having such expectations and myths can shape your behavior and reactions in ways that create dating problems. Here we will examine the most prevalent of these myths.

Myth #1: There aren't enough eligible partners to go around

Our fears often cause us to imagine the worst possible problems, and often the media comes up with pseudo-facts that corroborate those fears, as in the news article that temporarily electrified the country (especially women) by claiming that there were not enough marriageable men to go around. The statistics showed in the article were later disputed, but the myth persists, because it corroborates our fears.

You only need one at a time. One thing we have a tendency to worry about is whether there are

THE WORRIER'S GUIDELINES

If you're prone to worry or anxieties, the following steps will help you overcome the worries and keep your spirits up:

Step 1. When you're feeling anxious or worried, take a few moments to write down whatever is worrying you. Pinning the worries down and making them clear will stop the free-floating sensation of vague, unresolvable anxiety.

Step 2. Look at the first item on your list. Ask yourself "Is there anything I can do about it now?" If there is, do it. If not, make a reminder note to handle it at a later, perhaps more appropriate time.

Step 3. If you're having trouble finding a way to handle a particular worry, use the following set of guidelines:

IF YOU'RE WORRIED ABOUT . . .	THEN DO . . .
An event that will happen tomorrow or next week	Make a list of things you need to do, or items to get, or people to call.
Sexual safety	Look it up on the Internet, or call your doctor, or call a sex hotline and ask some questions.
Cooking dinner for a date later in the evening	Write out the menu or list of ingredients. If you're at home, get out a cookbook and plan the meal.
How to dress for a party	Call a friend for advice and lay out your clothes, clean and ready, in advance.

Step 4. When you've done what you can, or made your lists or notes, then distract yourself: get busy doing something else, or read, or take a walk or a bath.

Repeat the above steps every time you catch yourself worrying.

enough suitable people out there. No matter how much you hear about how few eligible men or women there are for your age range, or that all the appropriate ones are already taken, take heart. You are an individual unlike any other, and you have an advantage if you are following the dating process outlined here.

Out of all the people in your town or city, you only need one, and *if* you do what is suggested here, going to the appropriate places where you can meet suitable people, as outlined in the following chapters, your chances of meeting a suitable partner are excellent, and making new friends is a sure thing.

We all get somebody to love. If your family history was difficult, and you don't know what healthy relationships are, you can feel that you're doomed—relationships will never work for you. While you may need to do some extra work to correct the damage, you can still enjoy the dating experience, make some friends, and even find a suitable relationship.

If you grew up in a problem family you may worry that you don't know what normal family interaction looks like. If there was an alcoholic, a depressed parent, a volatile or violent relationship, a missing parent, or even a foster situation, you may not have witnessed enough normal discussion, decision-making, problem-solving, and affection to know how to do it in your own relationship.

Relationship difficulties caused by your lack of healthy role models might be one reason you are dating again. If your past relationship repeated your early family problems, you may fear you'll never be able to love or be loved. But if you follow the steps set forth in the following chapter, you can avoid repeating those old patterns. Keep focused on your goal of meeting someone with whom you can create a loving relationship. If your problem is difficult, learning to date successfully could cause you to seek counseling or therapy. If so, good for you. You'll learn what you need to know to date again successfully.

You've got what it takes to beat the odds, anyway. If you're worried that the odds are against you, and that you won't succeed because few people do, you need to re-direct your thinking. Remember: you have been through difficulties before, you have learned new things before, you will survive this, and it will be worth it.

Each of your life experiences has taught you something, which means you know more now than you did the last time you were actively dating. You are following expert advice, which will increase your chances of success. The fact that you're reading this book shows that you care about the results, you're thinking carefully, and you want to approach dating again from an organized, informed point of view, which will make you more effective and successful.

In my experience as a relationship counselor, I find that people who look for a relationship after losing one, *if they do it thoughtfully and with a plan,* almost always find someone who suits them better than the last person, because they've grown in wisdom and learned from experience.

If nothing else, you'll make new friends. The best way to guarantee a good outcome in the dating process is to seek to make friends. If you set a goal to meet new friends and have good times, you'll succeed. When you approach your search as a search for friends, you can relax the stringent requirements you would have for a lover/partner. Suddenly you're free to notice *everyone*—because anyone could turn out to be a good friend. When you relax and open up your criteria in this way, you will be open to meeting more of the people you encounter, and to finding out about them. Who knows, one of them may have a sibling or a friend who could turn out to be your soul mate.

Remember that "birds of a feather flock together." In this context, that means if you find good quality people you enjoy, and if you make the effort to become friends with them, you will meet their other friends—who will be "birds of a feather." Most of the people you meet and like will know other people who are quite similar. Thus, every new friend can bring a network of new people, as desirable as the original friend, into your life.

Myth #2: You only get to love one person in a lifetime

In this day of a 50% divorce rate, it's getting harder to believe there can only be one person in the world for you, but the myth still persists. There are lots of songs, poems, and movies about the "one true love" you "can't survive without."

Anyone who has loved someone for a long time and then lost them naturally feels that there's no way they can be replaced. Of course, no one who is dear to you and now gone can exactly be replaced. There are many ways to love people, and a number of people you can love. Just as you can love various members of your family differently, and just as you can care deeply about several dear friends, in different ways, so you can also find more than one person who is compatible enough to fall in love with and create a workable relationship.

As much as you loved your last partner, you may be surprised to find that a new person has attributes

Unofficially...
50% of people now married or living together were introduced by good friends or family members. 32% met by introducing themselves to another person, according to research by Edward Laumann, Ph.D., University of Chicago sociology professor.

and qualities you really enjoy; things you never knew were missing before.

It's fortunate that we are able to love more than one person, because it's so easy to be attracted to someone with severe problems. The point of dating is to find several people who are attractive to you, so you can sort through their character traits and foibles, until you find someone who is not only attractive, but also healthy for you. For this reason, later in this guide you'll find out how to choose a relationship "from the neck up" as well as "from the neck down"—that is, using your judgment as well as your sense of chemistry and attraction.

At the turn of the last millennium, when social mores were more restrictive, and people didn't move around as much as they do today, meeting a new partner was more difficult. Today, we have more personal freedom, and neither gender has to wait for the other to make a move, or for a proper introduction. Everyone has more mobility, and a bigger population and more social outlets make meeting new people a lot easier. So, today the big question is not "Can I find the one and only true love of my life" but "How, out of all these people, do I choose the one with whom I can really be successful this time?"

Myth #3: Dating is only for the young

You can hear the age myth stated by people from 25 years old to advanced senior citizenhood. I personally know of three ladies who met suitable gentlemen and got married at the ages of 78, 85, and 87. It's never too late to meet a mate.

1. Rose was taking a world cruise. She would be on the ship for over three months of luxury and adventure. At 87, she had been widowed for

If I, after four wretched marriages... could arrive at a marriage as happy and terrific as I've got, anybody can do it... If I can be happy, anybody in this universe can be happy.
— Harlan Ellison

many years, and her children were not only grown, but middle-aged. She was still active and healthy, and she wanted to take this cruise while she was still able to do it.

One day, the cruise held a party for all the singles on board, and Rose decided to go—perhaps she'd meet some new friends. As people were introduced, she was astounded to hear a man's name which recalled her past. She went up to him, and introduced herself. It was true! Robert was the very man she had dated as a young woman. Things had not worked out when they were younger, but this time they were not going to lose each other. After getting reacquainted on the ship, they were married six months later.

2. Claire had spent her entire life in obedience to her parents. She stayed home after her father died, to care for her elderly mother, who eventually became demented and difficult. Claire even ran the local post office in the small town she lived in, because she could do that from her home. She almost never went out. When her mother finally died, Claire was 60 years old, and the federal government closed her small post office and transferred her to a post office job at the county seat.

Here, she met George, another postal worker and her contemporary. They began having lunches together and developed a friendship. After a number of years, they both retired and continued their relationship. At age 78, Clara became a bride for the first time in her life, and the ladies of her small town threw her a wedding shower. Seeing her opening gifts and holding up lovely, lacy lingerie was truly the picture of a dream come true.

3. Vera, 85 years old, had been married to a military officer and lived all over the world. She and her husband raised several children, and had many grandchildren and even great-grandchildren. Her husband had died a few years ago, and she had moved to California to be close to her younger sister, who was also now widowed. The sisters lived close together and traveled often together. One day, the phone rang, and when Vera picked it up, a voice on the other end said, "Do you remember me?" It was Ed, whom Vera had been engaged to when she was 18. He had tracked her down through people who knew her in their old hometown. They hadn't married because Vera had discovered that Ed had a drinking problem. He had long since become sober, married, and raised a family of his own, but his wife had died a few years before.

Vera decided to go to the nearby city where Ed lived, just for a couple of days, to meet him and talk. Her sister got a call. She was not coming home right away. In fact, she didn't come home for two weeks. She and Ed were married six months later.

If you ask your friends, co-workers, and family members, you'll hear many more stories of people who met and fell in love at advanced ages. It's obvious from these stories that age does not have to hold you back from meeting someone to love.

It's true that when you're a teenager, an age difference of 10 or more years makes a vast difference in your experience and your outlook on life. Such a difference can interfere with communication, life goals, outlook, and relationship experience. In addition, the social reaction to such a relationship is often very negative. If one partner is underage, a sexual relationship is even against the law.

But, as we get older, our life experiences and emotional growth even things out. A ten-year or more difference in your ages makes little difference in how well you can conduct your relationship.

Don't focus on an arbitrary numbers difference in your ages. If you are getting along, have good communication and problem-solving, and love each other, that's a precious thing, and far more important than any age difference could be. And if other people have a problem with it, let it be *their* problem.

Myth #4: They're all losers—or I am

Many myths are based on a negative view of life and love, often because the people who promote them had negative experiences themselves. As we have discussed before, difficult family or relationship experiences can affect your view of relationships and the possibility of being loved.

This is the very reason why I stress:

■ finding *quality* people to date

■ looking in appropriate places

■ taking your time before getting emotionally involved

■ interviewing new dates, and paying attention to the information you get

■ using your friends' network for support

■ checking up on the people you meet

Anyone can meet a person with problems—they don't wear warning signs so it's not your fault if you meet someone who doesn't have his or her act together. However, if you stick around someone who obviously can't function well enough to be a good partner, you can fix that problem by learning to let go of bad apples. Difficult people aren't usually a problem if you keep them at a distance. They're a giant problem if you let them into your life.

Look for *people*, not perfection. You can be led astray if you are too concerned about categories such as wealth, education, good family, impressive career, fancy car, and designer clothes. To find a quality person with whom to share your life, you must look beyond those surface clues and deeper into the person.

Con artists of all types know very well how to exploit appearances to lure you in and take advantage of you. If you follow the guidelines which are fully explained in the succeeding chapters, you will not be vulnerable to people who want to take advantage of you.

Scaring yourself about molesters, rapists, alcoholics, narcissists, and other kinds of dangerous types is just another needless worry. Each person you meet presents an opportunity for you to find out who he or she is, and there are more good people than bad people out there. With a little know-how, and proper caution, it's pretty easy to recognize the difference.

Celebrate individuality. To get to know a new person, and be known, takes a little time, because each of us is unique. We can't just say "Oh, he's a Category A, or a Category B," because people don't fit into neat, tidy classifications. You can observe someone and think "Oh, she has good manners, she must be educated," and then find out she has a problem with rage or alcohol. On the other hand, some perfect gems come in rough clothing. Many clients who are in good relationships with wonderful partners have told me "I wouldn't have looked twice at him if we hadn't gotten to know each other first." Or, "She wasn't 'my type,' but after I saw her in action volunteering in the political campaign, I realized she was an extraordinary person, with great ethics, and very caring."

Each person you meet along the dating path has unique personality traits, desirable and undesirable. Giving yourself the time to get to know them enables you to sort them out.

Don't blame a new friend for old miseries. No matter how bad your history has been, you don't have to re-create it. You can learn to interact in different ways, and to correct problems that come up. This guide is about dating correctly and successfully. If you feel out of control and unable to follow the guidelines here, you may need to work with a counselor to make the necessary changes, just as you might work with a personal trainer to correct and improve your workouts, or a nutritionist to evaluate and correct your diet.

If your background was dysfunctional and toxic, or your previous partners have been abusive or addictive, you may need to be suspicious of your first choices. That is, because of your early experience, you may be "conditioned" to be attracted to a particular character flaw. The people you automatically are drawn to, and feel comfortable with initially, may be exactly the people you should stay away from. If you know this about yourself, and can resist the pull of the dysfunction, you can meet other, better people to date. If you have trouble changing this focus, counseling can help.

We're all in the same boat. Everyone who faces dating as an adult has similar worries and insecurities. It's that return of adolescent feelings I discussed in the last chapter. If you're beating up on yourself, it's probably because you're feeling:

- Vulnerable

- Like a loser

- Afraid of rejection

- Awkward, unacceptable

If so, here's a simple truth to keep in mind: You are not alone! Everyone feels equally insecure about dating again. Some hide it better than others, some have been dating longer and have become less nervous, but everyone has been through it.

If you present a friendly, pleasant demeanor and you are open to getting to know people, they will be relieved and pleased. Here is the perfect place to practice the Golden Rule—treat others exactly as you would like to be treated, and you will have plenty of good responses.

Each new situation will produce the above list of qualms, but keep in mind you're there to make friends. Find the safest-looking person in the room, and chat with them. You'll feel better, and then you can move on to greeting others. After a few minutes of pleasant conversation with new acquaintances, you will relax, and your anxieties will be forgotten.

Where do we go from here?

Our goal in this chapter was to confront some of the common qualms and quibbles people face when they're confronted with the prospect of getting out into the social whirl again once a long-term relationship has ended. Once you've faced some of the issues that may be standing in your way to having a happy, successful dating life, you're ready to take that next step—making your first few forays into the dating scene. In the next few chapters you'll learn some of the skills that make for a successful dating experience. Before you know it, you'll wonder what all your worries were about. You'll be making new friends, exploring new interests, and maybe—just maybe—you'll be finding a new love, too.

Just the facts

- Many of the reasons we give for avoiding dating are based on a fear of change.

- Minimize the potential for getting hurt while dating by adopting a positive attitude.

- Treat your mistakes as learning opportunities and you can enhance the quality of your dating experiences.

- Social expectations and myths about relationships can be damaging.

- The best way to develop good dating relationships is to concentrate on making friends first.

Developing Your Dating Skills

GET THE SCOOP ON...
How to be "irresistible" ▪ What are you project-
ing/receiving? ▪ Notice what's here: set your
scanner to "on" ▪ Meet friends of friends ▪
You're going to have more fun than you think

PART II

Preparation

Okay: Ready, Set... Oh, you don't feel quite ready? Well, that's the first step—getting ready. Setting up your dating process to be successful right from the first will make the whole thing easier and less anxiety-producing.

Since you're probably going to be dating for a while, the point is to make dating a fun experience and a successful one at the same time. People will be most attracted to you when you are having a great time, and enjoying a lifestyle they would want to join. So, let's set this up to be fun, not only because you'll enjoy it more, but because you'll be more attractive that way.

Be "irresistible"—don't resist it

The best way to be irresistible to others is to let go of whatever resistance *you* have to them. Don't begin your dating process focused on what you *don't* want —rather focus on what you're looking for. Even where safety issues are concerned, your focus should be on the desirable, quality people you want to meet, rather than on what you're afraid you'll find. Focus

51

on the kinds of fun times you want to have, not on what awful things you're afraid might happen.

From here on, every decision you make will be based on the question "Is this going to get me closer to my goal?" And what is your goal? To meet new good-quality friends, to have a great time, and to eventually establish a healthy, lasting relationship.

Let it be a learning process

Don't be worried about not knowing what to do. You're a beginner at this, and letting people know that is fine. It's not important that you look like an expert—in fact, if you look like you've been dating forever, you'll be less desirable to most people.

> **"**
> The people who are most successful have laid the foundations for their actions well in advance of the moment of challenge.
> —"Everyday Tao," Deng Ming-Dao (p. 73)
> **"**

As we said in Chapter 1, having a "beginner's mind" works great here. Accept that everything you're doing now is new to you, and open yourself to learning about it. Wide-eyed wonder at whatever happens is very attractive. I'm not talking about being brainless or thoughtless. On the contrary. A beginner's mind is alert, observing, and open to new ideas. Your objective is to learn—about what people are doing, who they are, what the possibilities, are and how it all fits in to your goals.

Everything you've learned about relationships and dating in your past is certainly useful, and you'll draw on it as we go along, but your general approach to this process is as a beginner—"I'm new at this, I want to learn." Because you are a beginner, you can open lots of conversations by simply asking questions about what's going on.

Have fun with it

Instead of focusing on how nervous you are, look around you for what's going on that you might enjoy. For example, when you're attending an event (a private party, a class, a workshop, a charity or political event) you haven't experienced before, I recommend finding a "job" to do. Volunteer to greet people and take tickets, or keep the food table replenished, or hand out name tags. It will give you a feeling of belonging, a great excuse to meet everyone, and you'll be busy enough to keep your nervousness at bay. The hosts (generally the most influential people) will get a great impression of you and remember you later. As an added bonus, volunteering often gets you a discount on the cost of attending the event.

The most desirable and emotionally healthy people will be doing fun and fulfilling things. Most so-called "singles events," unless they're organized around activities that are interesting in their own right, create a deadly mix of desperate people who have nothing in common except loneliness. Don't go there. Stick with activities that are fun, healthy, challenging, and stimulating. That way you'll enjoy every event, improve your health and outlook, and make friends, even if you don't meet the person of your dreams this week.

A positive approach

Motivation, as I have said in several of my books, comes from appreciation and celebration. That is, if you feel positive about what you are doing and the people you are with, you'll be more motivated to continue in that activity. It won't be necessary to force yourself to attend things if they feel great, and you'll be a lot less anxious.

To enhance your positive experience, do the following steps before every new activity:

1. Make a mental note of the possibilities: Can you learn something there? Can you meet a new

Bright Idea
Rather than focus on the "meat market" approach, choose the kinds of activities you'd enjoy to begin with. Take classes in cooking, sports, dancing, yoga, automotive mechanics, great books or current movies and other activities that appeal to you. Join teams, get involved in church, charitable or political activities, or participate in hiking, biking or bird watching.

friend? Will just getting out of the house and around new people feel good?

2. Remind yourself of your goals: You're there to meet friends, to have fun, to eventually make a connection.

3. Review your positive personal qualities: What do your friends like about you? What do you like about you? Your intelligence, your sense of humor, your style, your conversation skills? Are you a kind and caring person? Reminding yourself of these qualities means you will enter the event radiating that positive energy.

The tennis match... he hits one, you hit one

Once you are at an event and meeting people, you need to create the proper energy level to attract people. This does not mean being hyper-active, giddy and over-the-top. Too much energy makes you look anxious. On the other hand, if you appear lethargic and passive, people are not going to be attracted either.

Match your energy to the energy of the people at the event. Obviously, if you're dancing or playing sports, the energy level will be pretty high. If you're having quiet conversations at a cocktail party or on a planning committee, or stuffing envelopes for a charity event, the energy will be more mellow and focused.

Conversations at events you attend should be like tennis matches. That is, the other person "serves"— he or she asks a question or makes a statement. Then, you "volley" back—you answer the question with the kind of answer that invites a response. For example:

She: "How do you know our hostess?"

You: "I met her at a class, how do you know
   her?"

Or: "I met her at class, doesn't she throw
   a lovely party?"

This invites your companion to respond and keeps the "volley" going. If the conversational thread ends, the next "serve" is yours. If you have to re-start the conversation too often, excuse yourself and move on. That person is not interested enough. If you force the other person to do all the conversational "work," he or she will move on pretty quickly. One-syllable answers are a pretty clear indication of lack of interest, even if you didn't mean it to be that way.

What are you projecting? What are you receiving?

We all give off lots of information in addition to what we are saying. How we are dressed, our posture, whether or not we're fidgeting, where we are looking, our facial expressions, and our general energy all communicate feelings, attitude, status, and other information.

If you are in your "beginner's mind," you will be alert to the information coming from the person you are meeting—what impression are you getting? What about the person interests you? Is your response to this person positive or negative?

Be aware also that the other person is picking up "vibes" from you. This is one reason preparation for dating is so important. If your mental attitude is positive, if you are focused on your goals and maintaining a "beginner's mind," the unintentional signals you are giving are more likely to be inviting. If you are thinking negatively, criticizing yourself, or worrying about what everyone thinks of you, your subconscious energy will be unattractive.

The deadpan model vs. the lively plain girl

As a perfect illustration of this, a TV news magazine did an experiment. They hired an actual, gorgeous model, and one of their staffers who was moderately attractive, slightly overweight, and no match for the model's beauty. Both were dressed tastefully. They took the women to a popular singles bar and gave them the following instructions. The model was to be unresponsive, give one-syllable answers, and generally appear uninterested and cold. The "plainer" woman was to be her normal, vivacious self. A hidden camera watched the action.

As you might expect, the gorgeous model got more initial attention. But, within ten minutes, there was a lively, interested group around the non-model, and the model sat alone. It was a graphic depiction of how much more important personality is than looks.

While women and men may be attracted to a stereotypically handsome or gorgeous face and figure, most will be won over by an open, inviting personality pretty quickly. Whether you're male or female, if you're bright, alert, friendly, and interested, you will attract plenty of people.

Seek friends—not lovers

By now you know my emphasis on making friends—it's the real key to successful dating. Making friends accomplishes several things:

- New friends make your activities fun

- Seeking friends will make you less anxious

- When you do choose someone to date, it won't be a total stranger.

- It's much safer

- It takes the pressure off you and the other person

- You'll already know your date is interested in you.

- You will have a lot more fun without the "performance anxiety"

I don't believe in dating strangers. Why waste all that time, money, and energy on someone you may not even enjoy? Like it or not, asking for a date is usually interpreted as a statement of intention, and expectations tend to rise. Therefore, wise people date selectively, with forethought.

Before dating someone new, spend some casual time together. Going out for coffee, to lunch, to a group activity, or going "dutch" keeps the expectations, and the pressure, lower. Making friends is easy—dating strangers is too hard.

To maximize your fun, reserve special evenings out:

- for people who have established a good reason to get closer.

- for lovers who want to spice up their lives with romance or celebrate a special occasion.

- for old friends when you want to show them they're special.

Don't be afraid to try

Even though dating sounds daunting, the process we're talking about here is not. If you're willing to try, and take a few baby steps, you'll find it's easier than you thought. Check out some activities, some classes, some social events, and volunteering opportunities. Try some events at your church if you are connected to one, or try attending a new church if you're not.

Sometimes, it only takes a phone call to realize the activity is not for you, sometimes it takes a few visits before you feel comfortable enough. Remember, when you're checking out options, to look for several things:

1. Is it something you'll enjoy doing? If you're an outdoor enthusiast, check out local nature and hiking groups. On the West Coast, for example, hikes and camping outings with the Sierra Club are a great way to meet people.

Unofficially...
Think about it—
Dating—what a terrifying word! What a grueling ritual! The setup is this: you're supposed to go out with someone you hardly know, usually pay an expensive tab, have a wonderful time, and fall in love forever. Does this sound realistic to you? It doesn't to me, either.

2. Are enough appropriate people there? Are there people of your age range, or a good gender balance? Are the people interesting to you?

3. Have you tried all the options? For example, if you're a senior, and the local Senior Center seems really boring, have you tried it on its busiest afternoon or evening? If your own branch of a particular church denomination or synagogue is mostly the wrong age group, have you checked out the other branches in your town?

4. Have you asked people for a personal recommendation? For example, if you take a ballroom dance class, ask the other dancers where they go to dance and meet people.

Try new things with an open-minded attitude. If you don't like the group or event, you don't have to go again.

Your relationship with you—how do you feel?

The most central relationship in this process is the one you have with yourself. Keep checking in to see how you feel about what you're doing. Are you going too fast? Too slow? Are you feeling uncomfortable with the place you're visiting right now? What do you think of this person you're talking to? Are you bored? Excited?

Getting this kind of feedback from yourself can make a profound difference in your experience. If you frequently evaluate how you're doing, you won't get too far from your main objective. And you'll know when you need to change what you're doing to have a better time.

In my 20 years of counseling people who have survived relationship disasters, I find that, looking back, my clients can always recognize the warning signs in their earliest encounters with their ex. Because of their excitement, they ignored what they suspected. Staying in touch with your own feelings will keep you safer.

Set your scanner to "on"

Another way to enhance your dating experience is to be observant. The first time you go to a new setting, or meet new people, hold back a bit and spend the first half hour or so just observing what's going on. See who knows who, how people behave with each other, and where the action is. By observing people before you meet them, you can determine who you would most like to meet, and perhaps even learn some things about your choice. Remember, you're here to learn—about other people and about yourself.

Notice the people around you

By observing the people in attendance at any event, you can learn a lot. If you're in a class, watch who seems to be most knowledgeable, who helps others, who tries to impress the teacher. If you're at a party, watch who seems to be genuinely liked, who clowns around, who is gregarious, who is shy.

Timesaver
Good communi-cation saves time. If you are willing to ask a direct question, give an honest answer, and speak or hear the truth about where you stand with someone, you can stop "beat-ing around the bush" or being confused, which wastes your valuable time.

Notice what people are wearing and anything unusual about them. You can use it to begin a con-versation later. What interests you about different people?

Remember, too, what you're looking for. In the next chapter, you'll explore what the ideal mate would be for you. Armed with that information, you will be able to observe people to see who seems to have the proper characteristics.

Conversation is available anywhere

You don't have to be at an organized event to prac-tice your conversational skills. Standing in line at the bank or supermarket, waiting at the laundromat for your clothes to dry, or sitting at the local coffee bar on your lunch hour are all good opportunities to begin a conversation.

If you have been observant, you will have plenty of ideas to talk about. If you're in the grocery store, for example, and the person in line in front of you has charcoal, hot dogs, buns, and sodas in the cart, you can observe that it should be a great weekend for a cookout. If you see the person in front of you staring at the tabloids, you can make a comment about the "Martians who landed the back yard," or the latest movie star scandal.

The weather, an attractive accessory (tie, belt, shirt, pin, earrings, shoes), a current news item, the book someone is reading, a headline in the newspa-per rack: all these can stimulate a conversation.

It is a risk to begin a conversation with a total stranger—you may get a glare, or no response. But, that is not the usual case. While the conversation may end when the line moves, it still will be good practice, and an interesting experience. And who knows? You could make a new friend.

Stay in your own head—not hers (or his)

Wherever you have a conversation with a potential friend or date, remember to stay focused on what *you* think about the encounter. It is very easy to worry about what the other person is thinking about you and forget what you are observing about him.

I call this getting into the other person's head— projecting your insecurities onto the other person and pretending to look at yourself through the other person's eyes.

There are two things wrong with this. First, there is no way you can accurately guess what the other person thinks. Second, you're wasting time, when what you should be doing is paying attention to your own opinion of the other person.

I advocate staying behind your own eyes, in your own head, and using your powers of observation and evaluation to gather information about this person. Your job is to know what you think of her (or him)— not to worry what she (or he) thinks of you.

Invite interest by showing interest

Susan, 35, and I were discussing her dating experiences. "It's like the school lunchroom," she said. "If you have a baloney sandwich, and your friend has a great-looking PBJ, and you want some of his, you have to offer to share half of your sandwich first."

It's a great image for the way you let someone know you're interested, and to return that interest. A big smile, and eye contact held for a couple of beats, toward someone who is nearby will signal "come on over, I want to know who you are."

Keeping the "tennis match" of the conversation going; asking questions or making observations that invite an answer (you can say almost anything and add "what do you think?" to the end of it); and including the new person in the conversation if an old friend shows up, signals that you're interested.

Compliments on what someone is wearing make it clear that you're paying attention. But, compliment people only on clothing, intelligence, good ideas, and clever comments. If you comment on personal attributes such as beauty, weight, facial features, or being in shape, you'll sound shallow. Such comments, though meant as compliments, can easily sound insulting.

Questions about what she thinks, how he feels, what she likes to do, what kind of friends he has, are very flattering and invite people to stick around and get to know you.

When your new friend states an opinion, it's more inviting to ask some follow-up questions that say "tell me more" than to immediately counter with your own opinion. Everyone wants to be understood, and nothing is more fascinating than being the object of someone else's interest.

You can either invite or exclude with your body posture, too:

- Turning away excludes, turning toward invites.

- Crossing arms on your chest, or putting an arm on the table between you as a barrier excludes; relaxed, open posture invites.

- Looking beyond someone to watch others is rejecting. If you're interested in the person you're talking to, you won't scope out the other people in the room. This is a great reason to

Watch Out!
When complimenting someone and asking questions to find out more about him, don't be too inquisitive about how much money he makes, what kind of car she drives, or other economic and status indicators. Undue interest in someone's income or financial status can make you appear mercenary.

look around for a while before you begin talking to anyone—you can get this search out of your system.

- Leaning toward the person shows interest, but could get too invasive and intense. If the other person leans back, you're leaning too close.

- Leave enough space between yourself and the other person. Don't touch total strangers—once you know each other a bit, then being close and touching are inviting; before you know each other, they're threatening. If the other person moves away, you're overdoing it.

- Nod your head occasionally as the other person talks, to let them know you're agreeing, understanding, paying attention. Smile a little to reassure them that you're enjoying the time. Be aware of your facial expression. Don't frown in concentration or anxiety—it will look as if you don't like what you're doing.

Drop the right hints

Keep in mind that your conversation, mannerisms, and reactions are like "cue cards" that tell the other person how to respond to you, and what to talk about. If you don't like talking sports or business, then be very careful not to bring them up, and change the subject when they do come up. The brand-new acquaintance you're talking to is looking to you to supply the clues about what you want to discuss.

If you are interested in politics, drop a hint: say "I've been following the news, and I think Congress is on the right track with the new tax laws." If you're a movie buff, mention the latest picture you've seen, or a classic you just rented or watched on cable TV. The other person will usually pick up on it, if he or she knows anything about it. If she or he lets it drop, that is also a communication.

In addition to letting other people know what you want to discuss, you can also let them know what you're interested in knowing about them. The more you can draw a new person out, the more you learn about her character and lifestyle, which is also how you'll tell if he's a suitable partner.

Interviewing

What most people don't know is that, to be successful, you can, and should, interview everyone you talk to. People give tremendous amounts of information about who they are, how emotionally and mentally healthy they are, their likes and dislikes, and their relationship histories.

In my workshop on How to Meet New People, I teach interviewing. I explain to the whole group how to interview, and then I set a scene. "You're sitting in a Laundromat, waiting for your clothes to dry, and someone is sitting next to you. Interview that person, *without being obvious about it,* for five minutes." When the time is up, I ask people to stand up and introduce each other, telling what they learned.

It is always astounding to the entire group, including both introducers and introducees, how much people can learn about each other, without interrogating, in just five minutes.

Here's how to interview:

- Have a mental list of topics you want to cover (for example, friends, family, past relationships, favorite activities, current events, movies).

- Conduct a "tennis match" conversation, tossing

the conversational "ball" back each time you get it by inviting the other person to respond.

- Pay close attention to everything the other person says. Do not let your mind wander.

- Look for clues in the conversation. For example, the person makes several references to drinking: "we went out for a couple of drinks—we were having a drink—I had a couple of glasses of wine." It could be a danger signal. If he or she describes past relationships and puts all the blame on partners, it could be a warning sign. On the other hand, if he or she talks fondly of good friends and fun times, that's a positive signal.

- Focus on your companion—be very interested and intrigued by what he or she is saying. Your friend will feel understood and cared about, relaxed, and positive about your talk and about you. Don't avoid talking about yourself, but try to say just one small thing, and then "toss" the conversation back to your partner by asking a question such as "Have you ever (done, felt, seen, thought) that?"

- Try not to repeat meaningless stock phrases, such as "you know what I mean?" It sounds as if you're not really thinking and not entirely present.

- When the conversation is over, carefully review everything you learned. If it's a person you won't see again, do this just for practice. If it's someone you're interested in, make some notes, so you won't forget.

It will take some practice before you feel com-

66
...history is important. If Madge was a real bitch who took him for all he was worth, and Heather was a total basket case who just used him and abused him, and Fiona, well, she was one crazy lady—he wouldn't be surprised if she were a drug addict or worse—then I'll hide under the house until this guy leaves.
—Columnist Cynthia Heimel in *Playboy*
99

pletely comfortable interviewing. Try it on some willing friends first. (Someone in your dating support group would be ideal. You can learn together.) Then, try it on new people you meet just for practice (don't worry about whether you want to date them, just practice interviewing them). Once you have done it a few times, you will be amazed at what you can learn, positive and negative, about the person you interview. That person would be equally astonished to know what they revealed.

Attentive speaking

To conduct your subtle interview successfully, use *attentive speaking,* a simple and highly effective technique that will help you communicate better with everyone you know.

Attentive speaking simply means paying attention not only to what you are saying, but also to how the other person is receiving it. If you watch carefully as you are talking, your listener's facial expression, body movements, and posture all will provide clues. Looking interested, fidgeting, looking bored, eyes wandering, attempting to interrupt, facial expressions of anger or confusion, or a blank, empty stare will tell you a lot.

The following guidelines will teach you how to observe your listener and gather information. This is especially effective if the other person is not very talkative, is reluctant to disagree or object, is the strong, silent type, is easily overwhelmed in a discussion, or is passive.

- Avoid monopolizing the discussion or boring the other person (if he or she looks overwhelmed, bored or distracted, you're talking too long).

- Keep your listener's interest in what you have to say (ask a question if you're losing his or her attention).

- Understand when you are misunderstood (the facial expression is not what you expect.)

- Gauge your listener's reaction (notice facial expressions, body language, and attentiveness).

- Know (by facial expressions, body language, and attentiveness) when your listener is distracted, stressed, or preoccupied.

Paying close attention to how your words are "landing" can give you lots of information about the person you are getting to know.

Conversational openers

Starting a conversation is often intimidating, but you need to learn how—you can't always wait for the other person to approach you.

This is where your first half hour of observing comes in handy. You can make a comment about what people have been doing, the food, the music, or just "It's a lovely (party, evening, house, picture) isn't it?" Or compliment something about the person: "What a great (tie, pin, dress, shoes, T-shirt, color, design)—I like it because..." He or she will probably say "thank you," but also respond with some information. If the answer is, "Thank you, I got it in Paris," you've hit paydirt. You can keep him or her talking all night about Paris....

Your opening comment shouldn't be a "line" like "what's a nice girl (or guy) like you doing in a place like this?" or "what's your sign?" These sorts of clichés don't make a good impression. Keep your statement simple, and as relevant to the time, the

GUIDELINES FOR ATTENTIVE SPEAKING

1. Watch your listener. Don't get so engrossed in what you are saying that you forget to watch your listener. Keep your eyes on your listener's face: It indicates you care if he or she hears you, and increases your listener's tendency to make eye contact and listen.

2. Look for clues in facial expressions (a smile, a frown, a glassy-eyed stare), body position (upright and alert, slumped and sullen, turned away from you and inattentive), and movements (leaning toward you, pulling away from you, fidgeting, restlessness). Rejecting body language may mean you have talked too long.

3. Ask, don't guess. If you get an unusual or inappropriate response (you're giving a compliment, he looks confused, hurt, or angry; or you're stating objective facts—she appears upset), ask a gentle question. For example, "I thought I was giving you a compiment, but you look annoyed. Did I say something wrong?" or just "Do you agree?"

4. Give your listener a choice. If your listener looks distracted or bored, invite opinion: "What do you think?"

5. Be aware of confusion. A blank or glassy-eyed look means your listener is overwhelmed. Again, ask a question: "Does this make sense?" Sometimes, just pausing gives your friend enough room to ask a question or make a comment.

place, and the person you're talking to as possible. Ask a question about where something is, or who someone nearby is, or what's been going on.

If your companion gives you any information at all, respond to it. Let him or her know you're listening by making an interested comment. If the person doesn't respond to your first or second try at conversation, move on to someone else.

If you're at a party or gathering where groups of people are having conversations, it is OK to go up to them, listen a bit, and if you know something about the topic, join in. If you know someone else at the party, you can ask for information about someone you don't know, or even ask for an introduction.

Try on a persona: Practice being the femme fatale, the hero

If you have trouble being comfortable in a group of people, try on a persona. Pick a character you saw in a movie, or a stereotype like the femme fatale, the Superspy, the diplomat, or corporate raider, and get into that character before you go in. Acting as if you're someone else won't work for long, but it may be just enough to get you past your initial anxiety, and into the mood for a party or social event. And it can be fun.

Imagining your Mr. or Ms. Right

Nothing will motivate you better before going to a new event than spending some time before you leave home visualizing the relationship you want to have. Picture yourself surrounded by good friends, happily dating, falling in love, spending your evenings and weekends with someone you enjoy being with. Take the time to remind yourself why you're doing this, and you will feel a lot better about trying new things.

Your ideal lover

If you want to find the right person, it definitely helps to have an accurate picture in your mind. If physical appearance is important to you, make that part of your picture, but don't forget that the most important qualities you are looking for are internal. Take the time to do this effectively with the following guidelines:

1. Set aside some time when you can be undisturbed for about half an hour. Sit in a comfortable place, with soft background music if you wish, and have a pad of paper and a pen nearby.

2. Close your eyes, and picture an ideal partner. He or she may be a composite of the best of your former relationships, favorite story characters, movie heroes, TV stars, members of your family (your dad, your Aunt Sara) or other people you have known in real life. Take your time picturing exactly what this partner would be like, and change the picture as many times as you want, until it feels right

3. Use all your senses—sight, smell, touch, hearing, taste—in the picture. What scent does this person wear? Does he or she simply smell clean, like soap? What does he or she look like? How is this person dressed? What does this partner's voice sound like? How do the kisses taste?

4. Picture you and this ideal mate doing things together. What are you doing? Where are you?

5. Do this a few times, until the image of the kind of person you consider ideal becomes clear.

6. Once the image is clear, open your eyes and

write down the most important characteristics of this ideal mate. Fix the image in your mind, so you can remember it even when you are not doing the exercise.

Once you take the time to create a clear image, you can bring it up in your memory to remind you of the reward you are aiming for when you're dating. If you have found yourself in difficult relationships, this is one way to re-program your radar.

Make a relationship map

Visualizing the relationship you want with this ideal partner is the next step. Making a relationship map will help you focus clearly on your goals for dating, and also encourage and motivate you.

Don't worry about how artistic your finished map is—it is strictly for your own benefit, and it is only necessary that you understand what it represents. You can change it as much as you want, until you get your picture exactly the way you want it.

1. You'll need a large piece of paper and colored markers, pens, paints, pastels, or other art materials, and several magazines full of pictures and advertisements that you can cut out, paper, paste or a glue stick, several photos of you and others in your life, and enough space to work on. If you enjoy drawing, you may want to dispense with the magazine pictures and draw your own. If you're a computer whiz, then computer art may be the way you do this. You can also add solid objects, pieces of cloth or jewelry, tokens, and keepsakes that are meaningful to you. Colorful, graphic pictures are powerful subconscious stimulants, and the point of this exercise is to help focus your subconscious on your ideal relationship.

2. Look through the magazines, or the computer graphics, and find pictures that represent your ideal relationship. If you'd like to do outdoor activities, choose pictures of couples biking, hiking, swimming, etc. Find a picture that represents a comfortable home life, such as a roaring fireplace or a lovely table setting. Find symbols of love, laughter, good communication, teamwork, sexuality, and happiness. Find as many pictures as you like, to represent what you want to create in your relationship.

3. Arrange or draw these pictures on your paper in a way that suits you. Place a picture of yourself front and center of the page. You can even put your own face on one of the pictures you cut out. Arrange and rearrange and adjust your collection of pictures until the final result pleases you. When you are finished, the picture should be a clear enough visual representation of your relationship that you are reminded at a glance of what it means.

4. Don't hesitate to redesign your picture, if you get better ideas of how it should look. When you have it complete, or when you have your pictures arranged but not yet pasted down, stand back and take a look to see if it is the way you'd like it to be. If not, play with it some more; if it is, paste things down, and find a place to put it where you can look at it when you want to.

Birds of a feather—meet friends of friends

Nothing can help your dating process be more fun than making friends. Doing things with friends makes everything more fun. And, as the statistics show, more people meet their mates through friends.

There's good reason for this. Once you make friends with the kind of people you want to bring into your life, you will gain entry into their social circle also. People tend to socialize mostly with people who are of a similar type; educated people socialize with other bright people, friends tend to be within the same socio-economic level, and friends often have work and activities in common. This is so often true that people often say "Birds of a feather flock together."

You can take advantage of this, if you keep in mind that every new friend you meet is not only valuable as a friend, but also brings a whole network of possibilities.

Never miss a party

In order to take maximum advantage of the "Birds of a Feather Network," take advantage of every party invitation you get. Anything from a pool party to a formal dinner at a friend's house is a great opportunity to meet even more friends. Somewhere in this haystack of connections is the needle you are searching for—your perfect relationship

Everyone you know, especially those who are coupled, will be eager to help you find a great partner, if you let them know you're willing to accept their help. Put out the word about what kind of a date you're looking for. If a relative or friend of one of your friends appeals to you, let your friend know. He or she will either save you time by letting you know the appealing person is off limits or has problems, or they will arrange for you to meet. What better way to meet someone than if you're both invited to a party at a good friend's house?

Watch Out!
If you do meet and date the friend or relative of someone you know, be a bit careful. Make certain you treat this particular date with even more courtesy and care than usual, even if you decide you're not interested. For example, don't say you'll call and then forget. If you anger your date, you'll upset your friend.

If a co-worker you like goes out to lunch with someone interesting, ask a few questions. You may find out that person is available.

Make new friends, keep the old

The point is to *add* to your circle of friends, not to *change* friends. The old adage "Make new friends and keep the old; one is silver, the other is gold" applies here. No one can replace your long-time friends; and there is no need to. They can still occupy the same place in your life they always have. Hopefully, some of these new friends will stay around and become old friends, but some will not.

Visualize the people you know circling around you as planets revolve around the sun. Some are very close by, some are more distant, yet all of them can be in the same system. In the same way, you can be closer to some friends than to others, but all of you are connected.

It can take a long time—sometimes many years—to create a deep and lasting friendship. This is why they're called "gold"—they are a valuable and precious resource. Newer, less well-known friends can be valuable also, even though they may come and go. You can still have good times with them and meet others through them—they can add lots of fun to your life. They are "silver"—not quite as precious, but still to be valued.

Network like crazy!

Any time you are around one other person, you have access to a potential network. Don't hesitate to connect with that network, if you have any opportunity. Invite your friends to invite *their* friends when you're going to coffee, a movie, out to brunch, or over to your house. Ask everyone you know for their favorite places to go for fun, and for recommendations to classes, organizations, church groups, and sporting activities. See if you can join in when you hear a group of people are going camping, on a picnic, or to a dance.

One way to get to know someone slowly, or to indicate you're interested in a person strictly as a friend, is to do things in groups. That, too, is a great chance to network.

All your friends are part of your social network, and they connect you to many more networks. It is said there are only six degrees of separation between you and anyone else on the planet. That means that someone you know knows someone else, who knows someone else, etc. until that chain connects you with the person (for example, a movie star or the President). So, perhaps to find your ideal mate somewhere on the planet you have to form a chain or a network of at least six connected people. The bigger your network is, the easier it will be. If you network, you'll find your true love and have fun doing it.

You're going to have more fun than you think

We discussed all the reasons to dread dating and to feel insecure when you think of it. But when you actually get out there, if you follow the instructions and guidelines here, you'll find that dating is not difficult or unpleasant at all.

Because you are following a successful process, you'll meet a lot of new friends, and date some very nice people. The guidelines will keep you far away from *dating disasters*, and will maximize your odds of being successful.

Moneysaver
The Internet can be a way to travel without leaving home or spending a lot of money, and also a way to meet people. Internet dating services may charge a fee, but there is no charge for most Bulletin Boards, Chat Rooms, or online discussion sites, such as the Utne Cafe— http://www. utne.com

Not just looking for dates but enjoying life

You can make this process simple and pleasurable or difficult and painful, simply with your attitude and outlook. If you strain to meet your goal, focusing on one narrow definition of success, and are impatient and disappointed when you do not meet it immediately, you will have a struggle.

If you resolve to enjoy the process, and have a sense of humor about your mistakes and about the things that don't turn out as you wanted them to, you will have fun, and you will find what you're seeking more easily.

In short, approach dating again as an exercise in enjoying life and getting out of your own way. Spend some time every day being grateful for what you have, and balance that with some time focusing on the most efficient and enjoyable way to get what you want, and you will succeed and have fun in the process.

Exotic places to look

Another way to maximize your fun is to find innovative and unusual places to meet new people. Read your local newspaper, listen to the radio, and when you hear of something that interests you, don't be afraid to check it out.

For example, in Long Beach, California, the brand-new Aquarium of the Pacific opened, and it uses lots of volunteers. For people who are interested in the ocean and ocean life, volunteering at the Aquarium is a great way to meet other people with similar interests, have fun doing it, and have a great subject for conversations!

Travel can be a good way to meet people, also, if you don't mind running the risk that your new friend may live far away. Joining a ski club which has ski trips, or a kayaking group which does whitewater trips, an archeological dig for a summer vacation, or even a gourmet cooking group which travels to exotic locales to focus on the food, can be both a great travel experience and a wonderful way to meet and get to know someone. Are you a train buff? Would you love to pet a koala, or ride an elephant? Fulfilling these wishes can also be an exotic way to meet new, potential dates.

Becoming the person you want to meet

To get the greatest possible benefit from dating again, use it as an opportunity for personal growth. If your intention is to become the kind of person you'd like to date, or better yet, the kind of person you'd like to fall in love with, you'll use your mistakes and disappointments as sources for growth.

While this may not be the sort of fun you have in mind, it can be extremely rewarding and satisfying. Psychiatrist Abraham Maslow, the founder of Rational Emotive therapy, studied man's happiest and most memorable moments, which he called *peak experiences.* He said that they occurred most often in people who were *self-actualized,* meaning they had worked on and learned how to be the best people they could be.

A more recent researcher, the University of Chicago professor Mihaly Csikszentmihalyi, calls his study of "the psychology of optimal experience" *flow.* He says achieving flow "...means paying attention to what is happening around you so that you notice things, care about what happens, and forget yourself in the process. Whatever you are doing becomes very absorbing and interesting."

Bright Idea
To change your focus from negative to positive, whenever something goes wrong or you make a mistake, take the time to learn from it by analyzing it. Write down what happened, and come up with three things you could have done to avoid or correct the problem.

This kind of absorbed interest is the same state of mind you use when you're learning. So having a beginner's mind, focusing on learning whatever you can, and paying attention, as this book recommends, also increases your chances of enjoying and feeling good about your dating experience.

You'll miss this single life when you're mated, really

Above all, remember to appreciate your life today. Don't fall into the trap of thinking you'll be happy later, when you find the person you're looking for. Dating is not all wonderful, but a lot of it is fun. You are single, and you have the freedom to do whatever you want, without having to take a partner's feelings or wants into consideration. It's that freedom that long-time married couples miss.

This is your chance to meet everyone you want to meet, to do whatever you want to do, to try out your fantasies, to make sure that when you do finally settle down you won't regret it or miss dating any more. Date enough people to be sure you know, when you choose one, that it's the right choice. Learn everything you can about yourself as a single person, so when you have a relationship, you'll know what you like and don't like as an individual, without your partner's influence.

Make the most of every day and every opportunity while you're dating again. The following chapters will present more step-by-step information to help you be successful, to keep yourself safe, and to get the most fun out of the experience.

Just the facts

- Successful dating is based on certain skills, particularly communications skills.

- The "tennis match" conversational style generates interest because you're *showing* interest.

- Take time when you first meet someone new to learn about them, their interests, and their goals.

- Networking is a great way to increase your circle of friends—and your pool of potential dating partners

GET THE SCOOP ON...
Setting priorities ▪ Dating motivation ▪
Acquiring ammunition ▪ Keeping it light

Chapter 4

Let's Get Out There and Have Fun!

OK, so you've explored your anxieties, you've prepared yourself, you're ready to go... do what? Dating is about accomplishing something in addition to simply meeting friends, having fun, and meeting a partner. It's about something very specific and special to you. What you need to know is, what do you want to create in your life with dating?

Hopefully, you're not dating simply because you think you should, or looking for just anyone to date. Like any other activity, to be successful, dating needs to have a purpose—to suit who you are, and to accomplish one or more specific goals. Now's the time to decide just what your goals might be.

What are you looking for?

Of course, you want your time spent dating to be fun, rather than a drag, but what is fun to you? How will you know how to have fun with someone else, and how will you know if they're having fun with you? In this chapter, we'll explore what makes things fun for you, and how to find or create an atmosphere that helps you have fun. But while it's important that you keep the dating process fun, most people have other goals as well. Here are a few of the more common reasons people date:

Seeking a serious relationship. Are you looking for a committed, serious relationship? What does one of those look like? Do you know if that's what you want? Does it sound like an impossible dream, or too scary to think about? The kind of relationship that works well for you now might be different from the ones you've had before. You've changed and grown, and hopefully, you've learned from your experience. I don't recommend that you commit to any relationship that will not make you happy. If you discover what kind of relationship you require, and how to recognize another person who wants the same thing, you don't have to be afraid of being trapped or disappointed. This chapter shows you how.

Looking for a sexual partner. It's entirely possible that you're happy with your solitary life, and you want to date strictly to find one or several sex partners. The euphemism for this is usually "I just want to date—I'm not ready for a relationship." That's a legitimate thing for you to want, if you're clear about it. The danger is that you won't really be certain this is what you want once you are dealing with actual people. On the other hand, most people who date are hoping for some sort of sexual connection, with varying degrees of commitment implied.

It's essential to know how much sex and commitment are involved in what you are looking for, and whether sex implies commitment to you, and at what point you consider sexual contact OK. Thinking it's OK to have sex after a date or two, and thinking that you should wait until you have a monogamous commitment or are married, are vastly different conditions, and need to be clearly understood by both you and your partner.

Companionship. Perhaps what you really want is a companion, someone to do things with and spend time with, and commitment and/or romance are decisions you'll make later. "Having friends has been of major importance to me since high school, when I had virtually none", writes Suzanne in an Internet chat. "My community of friends is even more important to me than a lover..."

Friendship is not only an essential support system for you as an individual; friends also enhance and support your relationships. Knowing what kinds and degrees of companionship are most satisfying to you will also help you know what you're looking for in dating.

Alleviating boredom. Whatever the reason you are single and dating again, you have probably spent some time alone, recovering from your loss. At first, the only thing you want to do is hide out at home, but after a while you'll get restless. Feeling bored is a sign that "the bandages are coming off," you're healing, feeling stronger, and getting ready to try some new things. Heed your boredom and get out there. You'll feel better doing new things, even the ones that don't turn out, than you will sitting around doing nothing.

Establishing your dating priorities

Who needs dating, anyway? You do! Dating is far more important than just the search for a relationship. Through dating, you'll accomplish several

> **"**
> Each friend represents a world in us, a world possibly not born until they arrive, and it is only by this meeting that a new world is born.
> —Anais Nin
> **"**

things:

- learn how others see you

- make new friends

- practice communication with a variety of people

- sharpen your ability to evaluate people you meet

- have fun

- cultivate some new interests

- practice your relationship skills

Unofficially...
Average amount an American earning at least $250,000 would pay to find "true love": $487,000, according to Harper's Index.

If you never want to have another relationship, and you don't want any romantic involvement, then dating is not important for you, but making friends still is, and the guidelines in this book will also teach you how to do that. Besides, if you weren't interested in dating again, you wouldn't be reading this book, would you?

Gauging your dating needs

The issue is not whether you need dating, but exactly how important it is to you. The importance you assign to dating and to finding a new relationship will dictate how much time and energy you want to put into it.

If being in a relationship is very important to you, then it makes sense to put a lot of effort into dating successfully; if it's less important to you, having a good time and making friends may be of greater importance. The significance with which you view relationships, friends, and fun will shape your attitude and approach in dating. It's part of determining your style.

If friends and fun are more important, you will focus on meeting lots of people, getting to know them whether they're "eligible" or not, and enjoying group activities and more theme-focused events, such as sports, classes, and hobbies. Once you get your network of friends in place, you'll be content with it.

If you are clear that your goal is a committed relationship, you'll still do those things, because they're a great way to meet people, but you'll be more focused on gathering in-depth information about individuals, and making one-on-one connections.

Where does dating fit in your overall life?

The phase of life you are in will also effect how important dating is for you. If you are at a crucial point in your career, if you have younger children, if there are elders or others in your family who need your care, or if you are deeply involved in some avocation or art that requires a lot of time and energy, you will have less time for meeting new people and dating than if you're less involved.

To be realistic about your dating endeavor, you must know what is most important in your life. If your life is busy, it will probably be necessary to schedule some time for dating and stick to the schedule, or you will find that it never happens. Also, if you are feeling too stressed or guilty because you're neglecting other important things, you won't enjoy dating.

If you evaluate where dating ranks in your priorities, you can avoid stress and guilt by devoting appropriate time, not too much or too little. With a little thought, you can also combine some of your priorities with dating-related activities. For example, if you have children, you can join some child-parent activities that give you time with your kids, and also the chance to meet some new people who are also

Bright Idea
List your major responsibilities and activities. Then, rank them in order of importance. Add dating to the list, wherever you think it belongs in the ranking. You'll see how much time and effort you can spare for dating again.

parents. Or, if you like to be active, you can experiment with new sports, different leagues or events where a number of teams get together, and meet some new people.

Evaluating your relationship needs

The importance you place on a primary relationship, plus the level of responsibility in your life, indicate whether you will do better in a permanent, committed relationship, or whether casual dating, for now or for an extended time, is best for you.

In the city I live in, a singles group called Athletic Singles Association, which puts together a calendar of events for members, has evolved into a core group of friends who essentially pay their membership fees so they can attend a lot of the activities ASA organizes; but they're no longer actively looking for new people to date. They're all busy people who have found the social circle they're looking for, and enjoy each other. The organization provides a structure of things to do, and the group members can easily join in when their schedules permit, without having to make a lot of arrangements.

Some of these people will continue to connect with each other for years in this way. Others will join this core group for a while, then either find a more lasting relationship and leave, or move on to other activities.

Celebration + appreciation = motivation

The energy you bring to dating again will make a big difference in your results. You can maximize the energy you have in two simple ways:

1. Celebrate each of your accomplishments, and

2. Appreciate yourself for who you are, your style of doing what you do.

What will make this fun for you?

The first section of this chapter, exploring what dating is all about for you, can help you appreciate your style. If you look at your motives, your circumstances, and your desires honestly, without criticizing them, you will get a sense of what your dating style will be, and why. There's no need to give yourself a hard time if dating is low on your priorities; just accept that your life is busy right now, and adjust your dating expectations accordingly. You can still have a good time and be successful dating, even if you only have limited time to do it. In fact, understanding that you have a tight schedule will hopefully cause you to choose your activities wisely, and may even make your dating more successful.

On the other hand, if you haven't much going on in your life at the moment, and it feels a bit empty, use that as a chance to combine dating again with exploring activities and opportunities you want to add to your life. Either way, begin looking for the positive aspects of who you are and your style, and capitalize on them.

Celebrate the small steps

Celebration always creates motivation and energy. Every time you acknowledge an accomplishment, you are encouraged to try for more. If you have to wait for the "grand prize," you'll lose energy before you get there. Celebrating your small dating accomplishments can make the difference between feeling like a failure because you didn't meet Mr./Miss Wonderful tonight, or like a success because you went out, met some nice people, and had fun.

As you develop your dating style, break each step down into its smallest components and celebrate them. For example, if you've decided to take a class,

RACK UP POINTS

One fun way to celebrate your small dating accomplishments before your big success happens is to keep points. Develop a point system, based on how difficult things seem: 2 points for making an info call, 1 point for talking to a friend, 5 points for speaking to someone you don't know. Keep a mental record of your points for the evening, and have chart at home for tallying your score.

You'll find a point system helps you stay focused on your real goals. For example, if you go to a party, and you know you'll only get a point each for speaking to the people you know, you might be more motivated to try speaking to strangers.

you can break down the process of choosing the class and signing up into very small steps: calling for a catalog, reading the class descriptions, making a choice, finding out how to register, registering, attending the first class. Each of those tiny steps can be celebrated, if only by crossing it off your "to do" list, calling a friend to discuss what you did, or breaking open a can of soda and toasting yourself.

This may sound silly, but you'll find that if you do it, you'll be a lot more energized and you'll procrastinate less. We all thrive on recognition and rewards, even from ourselves. Of course, the bigger the step you've achieved, the bigger the celebration will be.

Think globally, act locally

The old ecology-minded slogan, "Think Globally, Act Locally" can be adapted to your dating situation. If you keep your overall goal intact (thinking globally) while you do whatever you can do right now (acting locally), you'll stay on track better, and be more efficient at seeking your goal.

The point system mentioned elsewhere in this chapter is one way to do this effectively. If you set up your points to reward yourself for doing the most effective things, focusing on the points will automatically keep you on your program. There are other ways, too. For example, reminding yourself what you are looking for before choosing an activity or saying "yes" to an invitation, or reviewing your goals just before attending an event, can prevent you from self-defeating behavior. If you know your goals are to meet new people, you won't spend the whole evening huddled in a corner with people you already know, or say "yes" to invitations that waste your time.

Acquire an arsenal

To really get out there and have a good time, you need ammunition—your own personal arsenal of tricks you can use to help you through whatever comes up.

Clothes and make-over

Your appearance is the first impression you'll make when you're meeting new people, and while your character and personality are much more important, a proper look will smooth the way. If you're great with clothes, and love to put outfits together, you're all set. But if, like most of us, you feel unsure about what to wear and when to wear what, it's a good idea to get some advice. If you have a friend or a relative who looks well put-together, ask for some help. If your friend is willing, you can go through your wardrobe and get help with mixing and matching, which clothes look good on you and which don't, and what to wear to which event. Just a few outfits, put together from clothes you already have, are all you need to get you where you want to go.

While the clothes you wear should reflect your personality, it's also important that they suit the atmosphere you're in. Dressing too casually for a formal occasion, or overdressing when everyone is casual, is not a crime, but it does make you feel uncomfortable and takes away from your fun.

Hair and, if you're a woman, makeup should be neat, tidy, and appropriate to the activity, also. Looking more or less like the kinds of people you want to meet is the best bet. If you stand out too much, you may get attention for it, but it may be the wrong kind of attention. When you know you look your best, and your appearance is appropriate to what you're doing, you'll feel more secure and more relaxed.

Support system

Your support system is a very important part of your arsenal. The people around you can help you with appearance, what to say and do, how to answer questions, and give you honest feedback about your appearance and approach. The people around you can also provide you with moral support, and sometimes even go along with you on your adventures in the dating world. And, of course, they're a wonderful source of new people that you can meet.

Communication techniques

The more you know about communication and conversation, the better your chances of really getting to know someone. If you use communication skills at work, don't forget they're in your arsenal, and use them in your social life, too.

If you feel inadequate in communicating, try

practicing with your friends—ask a friend to role play with you. You can pretend to be at the event, party, or class you're going to, and practice how to approach your friend and begin a conversation, or practice having the friend approach you. If you run through several scenes, you will feel a lot more confident when you are in the real situation.

If role playing with friends doesn't answer your questions, try taking a class in communication techniques. You will not only learn how to communicate, you'll also be creating an opportunity to meet some new people.

Don't call it dating, call it squirrel hunting

If you think of what you're doing as making friends or squirrel hunting instead of dating, it will sound a lot less intimidating, and that will make it easier to change your old habit patterns. When you imagine that you're attending an event to attract squirrels, you'll feel less anxious. If you are feeling tense, just think of all those squirrels, and you can chuckle to yourself.

Making it fun

Remember, in squirrel hunting, you find yourself a comfortable spot, relax, and enjoy it, so the squirrels can check you out and see that you're non-threatening. In terms of dating, this means having a good time wherever you are, and making yourself comfortable. Relax and talk to some people who seem easy to meet (whether you'd like to date them isn't important—they can be the wrong age, the wrong gender, etc.)

Focus on enjoying whatever is there to enjoy. If you're attending a class, concentrate on the lesson or the activity, and don't worry about dating for the moment. Instead, try out some of the following suggestions:

- At a party, talk to anyone who seems easy to approach.

- If you're playing or watching sports, concentrate on the game.

- At a committee meeting, the PTA, or a volunteer group, get the work done.

- On a hike or camping trip, watch for the real squirrels, and enjoy nature.

Once you get to a function or event, you'll have a lot more fun if you forget about the dating, and participate fully. You'll enjoy what you're doing, and because of that, you'll be far more attractive to the squirrels. Implicit in this advice is doing things you can enjoy in the first place.

What are you interested in learning?

The area of your interests is like the forest where the squirrels are. Once you find it, the people you want to meet will be there.

Aside from finding a partner, what interests you? Are you an astrology or tarot buff? Do you like to play or watch golf, tennis, basketball, or other sports? What about the theater, the arts, politics, photography, science, bridge, books, computers, crossword puzzles, model (or full-scale) airplanes, or boating? The possibilities are endless. If you follow your own interests, you'll automatically meet people you can have fun with, and who have something in common.

How you follow those interests makes the difference. For example, if you just buy a ticket and go to a baseball game, you are not too likely to meet anyone. (The love of your life could just happen to have the next seat to yours, or be standing in the hot dog line when you go, but the odds aren't good.) However, if you get involved in a booster club, or find a group of people who enjoy playing or going to games, or even meet with a group to watch games on TV, as long as there are enough of the right kind of people for you, you'll have a great chance meeting some friends and eventually making a serious connection. If you just take photos, you'll have nice photos. If you go to a photography class or group, you'll have the photos, plus a chance to meet others you can "click" with.

To turn your interest into a dating opportunity, just find a way to meet other people who love the same things. Find a group or a class on the subject, and you'll automatically find others who love it. Through them, you can also network, and learn about new resources and more people who share your interest.

What's fun about you?

Your fun qualities are the tempting bait you offer. What do your friends like to do with you? What do they seek you out for? Do they like to come to your place for dinner? To go to the beach? To talk? To go walking or bike riding? To work on projects together? Would your friends say you have a good sense of humor?

The people who know you best want to do what they have the most fun doing with you. They think of you first when they want to do that activity, because you help make it enjoyable. Pay attention when your friends seek you out, or compliment you, and remember what they consider important.

It's also important to consider the personality

qualities you like about yourself. Knowing what people enjoy about you is valuable for two reasons. First, it's good to remind yourself of those positive attributes when you're feeling anxious or unattractive. Second, you will know what qualities to display when you're meeting someone new.

How to be fatally attractive

The most attractive people are friendly and interested, but not too interested. Being relaxed and enjoying what you are doing, chatting in a friendly manner, and cooperating with the people around you are all appealing.

If you're interested in someone, smile in that person's direction, perhaps chat a bit, but after a short time, turn your attention somewhere else—give your quarry time to think about how pleasant it was talking to you. If that person is interested, he or she will find a way to get next to you again.

In the ideal situation, you'll be near this person repeatedly, in some kind of scheduled fashion, as in a class or a group which meets regularly. Each time you meet, give the other person a big smile, and mention something from the last time you met. For example, "Oho, you're in that seat today, last week you weren't so close to the front of the class." Or, "You always look so nice—I thought that (tie, scarf, vest, sweater, shirt) you wore last week was neat, but this one is even better." The person will feel flattered, noticed, and remembered.

After the greeting, go on about your work. Let your quarry make the next move, in "tennis game" fashion.

This kind of gentle, flattering interest, with no pressure, is the most attractive. It is "fatally attractive" in that it produces a positive, elusive image in the other person's mind. Behavioral psychology research shows that "intermittent reinforcement" is the most effective type. That means that giving a reward (your big smile and greeting) and then leaving a space with no reward causes the subject to become fixated on when the next reward will come. Your "squirrel" will be hooked.

Finding a dating process that suits you

Putting all these clues together, and using the information you've gathered about what you like to learn, what you have to offer, and how to hook the interest of your "squirrel," will help you decide where, when, and how your personal squirrel hunting process will work. Of these criteria, the most essential is finding the right places to go. Finding places where you can learn something of interest means finding people who share your interest. But the dating process differs depending on a lot of factors, particularly your age and your gender.

Age differences in dating

At different stages of life, we have different approaches to dating, and different reasons for it.

In their 20s most middle-class people used to be focused on finding a marriage partner and having children. Today, the younger generation of middle-class daters tend to be more focused on career and postponing marriage and childbirth. If you are in this group, you are most likely looking for a partner to enjoy time with, but not yet feeling ready for a serious commitment or a family.

If, on the other hand, you are a young single parent, you may have decided you just want an occasional companion, with no intention of co-parenting or living together, or you could be considering whether the person you're dating will be a good step-parent.

If you're in your 30s and 40s, educated and well-employed, you probably are more career-focused, establishing yourself financially, investing in property and retirement accounts. At this stage, you're more interested in commitment and partnership, and most likely you want a partner with whom to build a future. If you want children, this is when the urgency to start a family is acute.

Dating again in your 50s and 60s may mean you have lost a long-term relationship, have children in high school or older, and are looking for someone with whom you can enjoy traveling and spend your weekends with. You'll probably feel more like settling down and pursuing a healthy lifestyle.

After retirement, your dating may be less focused on creating your security and more on enjoying it. Leisure pursuits, community activism, and enjoying your grandchildren may be on the top of your list.

Whatever your stage in life, and whether your personal life journey exactly matches these, your age and circumstances will certainly influence what you're looking for in a date.

Gender differences in dating

Women may not be from Venus, nor men from Mars, but they usually do have different ideas about dating.

Women, as a rule, value emotional connections, communication, reliability, romance, and stability. Men, on the other hand, enjoy the competitive aspects of the chase, action, and having fun.

No matter what the differences between the genders are supposed to be, what is most important is who you and your date are. You can use the supposed gender differences to begin a conversation and get to know each other better.

Don't get too serious

If you find someone you want to date, give the dating a chance, and don't get too serious. By going slowly, and taking time before settling down to one person, you have a chance to learn more about yourself and the other person. When you do decide to focus on one person, if you go slowly, you'll give your relationship a chance to grow and go through stages, and reach its full development.

Give yourself a choice

In my counseling practice, the biggest single mistake I see people make in relationships, the one that results in disaster, is being too much in a rush to choose one person and settle down. Or, to just stay with the first person who seems to get along with you.

To give yourself a choice, you need to date for long enough to meet and get to know several people. The experience of interacting with several people will teach you about how you react to different situations, and which problems you bring to every relationship.

Observing yourself in relationship with several other people will give you new insight into your personal relationship dynamics. Once you have observed the differences in relating to several people, you will be able to make a more solid choice of special person.

Focus on fun and friendship

To keep things going slower, and give yourself a choice, our strategy of keeping your focus on fun and friendship is ideal.

Watch Out!
When using gender differences to open a discussion, be careful not to state them as rigid facts. Statistics may show that most men are one way, and most women are another, but the person you are talking to is an individual, and cannot be categorized.

You can get to know many people at once by attending group activities and going out with groups of friends. Seeing how the people who interest you interact in a group can tell you a lot about their character and relationship skills.

A focus on fun keeps the interaction light and allows you to learn more before the relationships get too serious.

Why the rules work for both genders

You may have read *The Rules*, a book for women about how to date men and get them to commit; it was so successful, you probably heard about it. The major message of *The Rules* was: do not appear to be desperate or waiting around for the man you want. The rules (which include things like not phoning, but waiting until he phones, and not returning his calls immediately) are designed to help overly dependent women appear to have a full life and not much free time, to impress the man with the need to make a claim.

While the rigidness of the specific rules in the book led to much criticism and even derision, the basic idea behind it was compatible with the "tennis game" approach covered in earlier chapters in this book. The tennis game approach is not rigid, but a flexible attitude that you can adapt to almost any situation.

Whether you're male or female, to keep your relationships in balance, especially when they're brand new, make sure you don't do all the calling, all the planning, all the talking, all the giving, and all the chasing. Make a move to show the other person you're interested in being friends, then sit and wait for your new friend to make a move in return. For example, make a phone call to invite him or her for coffee, or to join a group going to the movies, and then let him or her make the next invitation.

This is often difficult to do, because the natural tendency, if you're interested, is to be aggressive. But being too active in the relationship may push the other person away, or may disguise a lack of enough interest on the other person's part. Don't keep hitting balls over the net if they're not returned.

On the other hand, if you never hit the ball, but always wait for the other person to do it, you aren't playing a very good tennis game, either.

It's essential that you do your part, because passivity is easily interpreted as a lack of interest. The tennis game is a great metaphor, because if you compare what has gone on in the relationship so far to a tennis game, you will quickly see if you've been either too passive or too aggressive.

Better safe than sorry
When you meet someone who excites you and even returns your interest, you may be very tempted to focus solely on that relationship, and stop your dating process. This is neither wise nor safe. When you meet someone who returns your interest, the most effective thing you can do is continue your dating process—continue making friends and trying new things, while getting to know this new person.

Include the new person in some of your plans, but not all, and make sure, until you have a chance to really get to know more about him or her, to be around other people when you're together.

This may sound too cautious, especially if you're sexually turned-on, or eager to develop a relationship. But please keep in mind that you've just met this stranger, no matter how good it feels. Seeing this new person interact with others, getting feedback from your other friends about your new date, and taking your time to get to know each other is much safer, more sensible, and more effective.

If you find out this is the kind of quality person you're looking for, you can laugh about your caution later. But, if you find out that this person has a problem history, you will be very grateful you waited.

As I write this, I have an acquaintance who has a very impressive job, is attractive and seemingly successful, but who has a history of many broken marriages, children with several partners, and a problematic legal history. Yet this person is about to be married another time. I often wonder why the new partner hasn't found out about the history, or even worse, has discounted it.

Appearances are deceiving. If a person is unknown to you, and your friends don't know him or her either, be very careful. It's extremely easy, in today's mobile world, to hide a frightening background. And please, whatever you do, don't ignore a person's problem history, or make excuses for it. Check things out carefully before you leave yourself vulnerable.

The un-date

To keep things going slowly and smoothly, learn to have *un-dates*, get-togethers which will give you a chance to get to know new people without the commitment and interest implied by an actual date. Some examples of un-dates would include:

- going out for lunch
- going out for coffee
- a walk in a public park
- meeting at almost any place like a museum

- taking a class together

- going Dutch to a concert or movie

The old-fashioned term "going Dutch" means that each person pays his or her part of the bill. Although social mores are changing, and today it is just as acceptable for a woman to pay the whole bill as it used to be for a man, when one person invites another, and pays for the meal or activity, it is still seen as a "date," and the pair are thought to be seriously interested in each other, or at least exploring the possibility.

When a couple go Dutch, on the other hand, it means that they are going out as friends, without the extra pressure of dating—an *un-date*. To set this up, you can say, "Can we meet for coffee?" or "I'm going to the movies Friday, would you like to join me? Tickets are about $7."

After going out in this casual fashion for a while, you can always change the intent by asking your new friend on a "real" date, and paying for the meal or outing. One appropriate phrase to use is: "Please come to the movies Friday, *as my guest,*" or "it's my treat." A date is a more formal occasion than a friendly get-together.

With others around

Another way to keep expectations from getting too high, and things from going too fast is to invite your new friend to join you and other friends for a meal, a movie, or an outing.

If you meet somewhere, and there are other people along, the outing will give you a chance to get to know each other; and it will give you a chance to observe your new friend interacting with others. When others are around, especially if you don't pick up your new friend, it will automatically feel like an un-date.

Working with this new acquaintance on a class project, a volunteer committee, or a political or church event will also surround you with others, and provide a similar opportunity to learn about each other and to watch the interaction.

Un-date times and places

Certain venues almost automatically feel like un-dates because of the time of day or the setting. If the setting is very informal, and not very romantic, your companion will not be as likely to think you're on a date. Here's how the un-date rationale works:

- Lunch, because it's in broad daylight, especially if it's in a less-expensive restaurant, feels like an un-date. Be warned, however—a picnic lunch, lunch at your apartment, or in a very dimly lit place will feel more date-like.

- Coffee, because it's inexpensive, fairly brief, and around people also feels less romantic. It does not involve the time, money, or energy commitment that goes into taking someone out to dinner.

- The telephone, because it's not face-to-face, and thus creates some distance in the conversation, is a kind of contact that is not seen as a date.

- The library is an undate, because it's functional, and you probably need a reason like, "I'll help you find another book on that subject if you'll meet me at the library after work."

- A walk, because it's very informal, and out of doors, feels more like a friendly act than a romantic one.

In short, any activity that does not appear to invite sexual contact (although we are all aware that sex can happen almost any time and place) or involves limited opportunity for intimacy is a good non-date.

Providing opportunities to get together with someone you want to know better in the above ways will reduce the tension, limit the possibility of sexual involvement, and keep you safe until you're sure you have found someone you want to become more intimate with.

Flow—ease in getting together

To create a relaxed "flow" of communication between yourself and another person, demonstrate *disinterested interest*. That is, be interested in what he or she has to say, and fascinated by details of his or her life, but do not display any concern about whether those things will mix well with your needs and/or wants.

This is too soon to insert yourself into the other person's picture. You can chime in with things that are similar in your own experience—for example, if he or she says "I go walking every morning, I find it's great exercise," you can say, "I love walking—I like to walk on the beach in the evening."

Don't say, "That's too early for me," which makes you sound as though you're competing or comparing.

In your own mind, you can make those judgments and comparisons you need to make to discover whether this is the kind of person you want to be close to, but aloud, just be politely enthusiastic for some part of your new friend's conversation.

The conversation will flow better if you leave plenty of space for the other person to give you information, without halting the flow by objecting, interrupting, or challenging anything that's said. Your questions should be designed to elicit more information, as in "You went to Finland? I've always been curious about that part of the world. What is it like?" which encourages the flow, rather than "You went to Finland? That's too cold for me," which stops it.

Don't be a drag: Following, not leading

Here's the place to begin following the relationship, and not leading it, as we discussed in the last chapter. Allow things to develop any way they want to, as long as you're taking care of your basic safety and not doing anything that feels like a bad idea. Do give yourself a chance to find out what your partner likes, wants to do, wants to talk about, and wants to spend time with. Don't insist on doing it the way you want to do it. For the time being, go along a little bit.

Make your own suggestions, but also go along with your partner's suggestions (as long as they fit your criteria for going slow). By doing things your friend likes, and seeing how your friend responds to your suggestions, you will learn a lot about how a relationship would be with that new person.

Above all, take your, time and observe carefully who it is you're dealing with. Be aware of making assumptions (he's well dressed, he must be a good guy; or she's lovely, she must be emotionally healthy) because you'd really like them to be true.

The more you relax, go slow, and allow your partner to relax and reveal as much as possible. This is the best way to be safe and not sorry.

Just the facts

- Establishing a clear-cut sense of your dating priorities simplifies your dating decisions.

- If you concentrate on making friendships, you remove the stress from the whole dating process.

- Un-dates are great ways to get to know someone without the pressure of a regular date.

- Dating needs, attitudes, and experiences differ according to your age and your gender.

- Keeping your early dating experiences light and stress-free minimizes the possibility of getting hurt.

GET THE SCOOP ON...
Personal dating style ▪ Knowing
yourself ▪ Opening up to others ▪
Defining the ideal mate

Defining the Dating Players

Chapter 5

W hat do you want in a partner? Most people don't know. They want "someone nice." The same person wouldn't buy a car, a new outfit, or a head of lettuce with such vagueness. I see so many men and women choosing people to date with less thought than they'd put into choosing a turkey for Thanksgiving dinner. At least for the dinner, you know you're getting a turkey!!

A person you're initially attracted to can turn out to be ineligible because he or she is not verbal enough, too verbal, too assertive, too passive, uncooperative, addicted to some substance or habit, dishonest, unreliable, uncaring, demanding, not intelligent enough, or any number of personal quirks or traits you cannot manage to live with. Many of these traits can fall within normal ranges, yet be unacceptable to you.

Couples fight over smoking, eating habits, money, sleeping habits, religious differences, pets, children, friends, holiday and family traditions, house cleaning, and time schedules.

Know yourself: Who are you?

Finding the proper match in a person to date begins with knowing clearly who you are. As a unique individual, you need more than a cookie-cutter idea of who you want to date. Are you gregarious or shy? Physically active or more sedate? How much sex do you want? How much closeness, how much space? Are you a loner, or a people person? These traits point the way both to where you meet people and which of them to focus on.

If it seems premature to examine your life in such detail when you haven't even met a suitable person to date, remember that being clear about your goal will affect each decision you make throughout your dating experience.

The following information and exercises will help you define who you are, and then who you would like to be with, more clearly.

Selective attention: How it works

As human beings, we are equipped with a miraculous bit of brain acuity known as *selective attention*. This mental marvel allows us to unconsciously focus on whatever we deem important to us. For example, if you have a crush on someone who drives a blue Ford Escort, you will probably notice similar cars driving by, whether you want to see them or not. It can be quite distracting. This same ability shows up when you scan a page and your own name, or a bad word, "jumps" out at you.

What you may not know is that selective attention governs which people you notice, also. If your father was an alcoholic, you may find yourself able to pick out the one alcoholic in a room full of peo-

> **"**
> One of the pleasures of being a grown-up is that you can now pick your own friends on the basis of your own choosing; wanting an outgoing gregarious friend while you are shy and withdrawn is not an impossibility. Such a balance might well be to the liking of both of you. The point of any good relationship is that both people in it enjoy and benefit from it.
> —Sex columnist Isadora Alman in *Ask Isadora.*
> **"**

ple. You naturally seem to gravitate to that. If your mother was angry, or passive, that's who you'll notice today. This can strongly affect the kind of people you are drawn to. Selective attention can cause you to notice people who feel familiar, who remind you of family members, and who have similar patterns of behavior—even if your parents, siblings, or other relatives were not particularly good to you or for you.

What you are doing in such cases is continuously searching for resolution to past problems. If you felt unloved, you'll search for love; if you felt unheard you'll seek someone who will listen; if you felt unappreciated you'll try to find appreciation; if you felt smothered you'll seek lovers who will give you space. By fixating on early sources of frustration and hurt, you keep attempting to relate to the same toxic personality types.

This search is a natural healing process, a chance to correct what was misunderstood, mishandled, or deficient in our past. The dilemma inherent in this is that as long as you subconsciously fix on the type of person with whom you had a past problem, you'll keep repeating the struggle rather than resolving it. Psychologists call this kind of phenomenon *projection,* which means that you project onto someone else the persona of a parent with whom you have unresolved issues.

The good news is, you can change this selective attention to focus on the kind of person you actually would like to meet. To do so, it is necessary to let go of the familiar as a criterion and to develop a new awareness of what really works for you.

If you have had a series of relationships that have all resulted in similar problems, or that have just not made you happy, then you're probably operating on old programming. You've never taken stock of what a healthy person is; you've just been blindly looking for someone who would love you. The way you re-focus selective attention is to get a very clear picture of your new objective, your quarry, which begins with knowing yourself accurately.

Know-yourself exercise

Mentally step back and look at yourself as objectively as you can. Keep in mind that this is a fact-finding, not a fault-finding mission. Imagine a typical day in your life, and think about what you do: morning/evening routines, meals, work, play, and general lifestyle. Answer these questions as though you are responding to Barbara Walters, who is hanging on every word!

Waking up. What are you like when you wake up in the morning? Are you slow and groggy, cheerful, or quiet? Are you organized or haphazard? Do you have a regular routine that never varies, or do you get yourself ready differently each day?

Are your clothes laid out the night before, or do you have a sleepy interlude at the closet deciding what to wear?

While you're getting ready, are you relaxed or tense? Are your movements slow or fast?

Do you follow a routine in the a.m., such as exercising or meditating?

Do you like to sit and read the paper, or do you pare your morning time to the bare minimum, and sleep in?

Do you eat breakfast at home, on the run, at work, or not at all?

Mornings can be crucial in a relationship. Most of us are more natural and less rational first thing in

Timesaver
You may have already done a lot of work on knowing yourself clearly. If so, you can skip this exercise. I recommend skimming it to make sure you can answer all the questions. Then skip on to the next section. You can skim-and-skip any exercise in this book—some you may want to come back to later.

the morning. You express your personality in your morning routine, and it's vital information for you and your potential partner to have. Couples who begin their mornings in harmony have a better chance of continuing to enjoy each other throughout the day.

Work style. Is your work creative, challenging, stressful, artistic, boring, detail-oriented, or technical?

Do you work with the public, co-workers, or alone? Is teamwork required? Do you supervise others?

What is the mix of people you work with? Is it comfortable for you?

Do you like your job or profession? What do you like best about it? If you don't like it, what would you rather do?

The work you do, and how much you like it, says a lot about your preferences, your strengths and weaknesses. For example, if you enjoy a people-oriented job, you may be very outgoing and want to have many people in your private life. Or, if contact with the public is stressful, you may prefer lots of time alone when you're not working. Your stress level, travel schedule, work brought home, and other factors will also impinge directly on your relationship.

How important is your work? If it's more important to you than your relationship, or periodically takes precedence, you need to acknowledge this. You could easily be at a point in your career, or your career could be so satisfying to you, that it occupies a primary place in your life. If personal time is something you only get when your career permits, you'll need a different partner than if you make your home life a priority.

Knowing this beforehand can save a lot of struggle and disappointment.

After work. What do you usually do after work? Do you come right home and relax? Do you take a nap so you'll have energy for the evening? For dinner, do you cook a special meal or microwave a frozen dinner? Are you active—that is do you run off to classes, meetings, rehearsals, or workshops? Or are you quiet, preferring to spend your evenings watching television or reading, then relaxing in the hot tub?

Do you usually pursue creative hobbies, like writing, painting, building things in your workshop, rehearsing with a little theater group, or playing an instrument?

Do you work out at the gym, play a pickup game of basketball, jog, go to softball practice, rollerblade, or do some other type of exercise after work?

Do you get together or go out with friends on weeknights? Do you spend time with your children, your family, your pets?

Weekends (or days off). When do you wake up on weekends? What is your weekend morning routine like?

Do you eat differently on weekends? For example, do you barbecue with the neighbors, eat out more? Cook at home more? Take the kids out for burgers? Go on picnics?

Are you involved in organized weekend activities, like sports or group events, or is your activity more individual and spontaneous?

Do you attend church, synagogue, temple, meditation sessions?

Do you volunteer time at political, social or charitable events?

Do you putter around the house or yard a lot?

Like evenings, weekends are usually considered "couple time". Look at your current weekend and evening lifestyle to see what activities you want to share with a partner.

The following quiz is designed to help you develop a general, overall picture of who you are, and thus it should help you define your wants and needs in a relationship.

GENERAL LIFESTYLE QUIZ

Are you more organized or more spontaneous?

Are you a very neat housekeeper, who cleans regularly and thoroughly, or are you sloppy and haphazard about it? Do you pay someone else to do it for you?

Do you like a busy environment, with lots of stuff on the walls and knickknacks and mementos on the tables and shelves? Or do you prefer a spare, clean, uncluttered environment? Do you like decorative frills or straight clean lines? Danish modern or early Victorian?

Are you around people a lot by choice?

Do you spend more time with your own gender, the other gender, or with mixed groups? With one person at a time, or several? With old friends, family, new acquaintances, your children, former lovers?

Do you spend much time alone? Do you like solitude?

(quiz continues) ⟶

Do you have pets? How much of your time do you spend with them? Will a partner have to like pets, too?

Do you have children? Do they live with you, either full or part time? Are they grown? How often are they around? How close are you to them?

Are you artistic? Do you often have a creative project going? Do you spend a lot of time at it?

Do you have a sport or hobby that consumes lost of time, energy, and/or money?

How are you with money? Are you responsible? Are you very detailed, or more casual? For example, do you balance your checkbook every month, to the penny, or do you get a vague idea of how much you have left from the instant teller balance? Do you ever bounce checks? Are you meticulous about paying bills, or do you sometimes get late charges? Do you like doing the accounting chores (paying bills, balancing checkbook) or do you wish someone else would do it?

Is food important to you? Do you like to cook? To entertain? To dine out? Do you follow a special or vegetarian diet?

Do you like intense conversation? What about?

Are you careful or casual about your appearance?

Are you spiritual or religious? Do you attend a church, synagogue, temple, retreats, or meditation sessions?

Visualizing yourself in a relationship

What do you want to do in your relationship? It should be somewhat similar to what makes you happy now. Examine your fantasies of being in a relationship to see that they actually suit your lifestyle.

If you spend lots of time home alone, a fantasy of being coupled with someone who is the center of a social circle could be very unrealistic.

To get an accurate picture of what really would work for you in a relationship, examining your history, and comparing it with your wishes for the future, is a good place to begin.

Where you've been: Analysis of history

Make a list of your major past relationships. Go back through the "know yourself" exercise, and make notes about what you did in these relationships about each of the categories: how you spent weekdays, weekends, mornings, etc.

Divide these notes up into what felt good and worked well and what didn't. If there's something you did, such as read the paper together in the morning, that you really loved, make a note of it. If there's something you did, such as have to wait for your partner every night to eat dinner, or always get stuck doing the dishes, or have to be quiet on the weekends while your partner slept late, or be wakened earlier than you wanted to be by a noisy partner, make notes of that, too.

Where you're going: What will be different

Using the "know yourself" exercise information, plus the analysis of your history, condense the details into a list of the kind of activities you want to do in your new relationship.

This list should include the most important

things you want to do, for each time of the day and week.

Choosing your target: Your ideal mate

Now that you have clarified your idea of who you are and what you like to do, it's time to focus on who you want to be with. Doing this will set your selective attention.

Using the following information will help you figure out if the attractive individual you're considering is a good match. This research is precisely the reason I suggest you focus on friendship and take your time. It takes a while to know the deeper attitudes and values of someone new.

Beauty is only skin deep

When thinking of the kind of partner you wish for, it's easy to let your focus be on what the person will look like. There is a great emphasis on looks in our society, especially in the media.

Keep in mind that you're looking for a person with whom you'll spend a large portion of your time. What he or she looks like will fade very quickly—you won't even notice it very often.

Your partner's deeper characteristics such as personality, intelligence, values, integrity, warmth, sense of humor, little quirks, and ability to cooperate and solve problems will soon come into sharp focus and be much more important than mere surface looks.

It is these characteristics, rather than hair or eye color, stature, or appearance, that you need to focus on to be successful.

Your basic requirements—the 'tudes

I like to call these deeper characteristics the 'tudes, because all the categories can be summed up in words that end in that syllable.

Attitudes: Your partner's attitudes will be central to the question of whether you and this person are compatible. You have examined your own attitudes and temperament—what kind of person will be compatible with who you are?

Are you a relaxed person? If so, would you do best with someone as relaxed as you are, or do you need someone with a bit more energy, to offset your calmness? Opposites often attract: that is, if you're very verbal, a quiet person might be appealing at first. But, after a while, opposites can be grating—when you've been together a while, the other person's quietness may be irritating to you.

One way to see what kinds of attitudes are most compatible is to look at your past relationships, your friendships, and your family relationships. Which kinds of people do you tolerate better for long periods of time? Which do you enjoy being around for a short time, but soon want to get away from?

Take a look at these relationships and evaluate the temperament and attitudes of the people you most enjoy being close to. What do they have in common? Do you tend to enjoy warm, talkative people? People who are quiet and allow you plenty of space and privacy? Fun people who are always ready to go out? Solid people you can trust and count on?

Taking the time to examine these relationships can open your eyes in terms of who you could really manage a long-term relationship with, and who would be initially attractive, but soon become irritating or boring.

Aptitudes: But as important as *attitudes* may be, *aptitudes* can be equally important. By aptitudes I mean intelligence and sensory awareness—verbal, tactile, visual, and auditory skills in both yourself and your partner. The match between you and your partner in terms of intelligence and communication styles will have a large effect on the ease of your problem-solving and teamwork.

You can certainly learn to communicate with someone who has a different style than yours, but ease of understanding comes with similar styles. Again, look around at friends and relatives and evaluate who feels easiest for you to understand and who seems to understand you best. Familiarize yourself with these traits so that you'll recognize them when you see them in a stranger.

People use their senses differently, which affects perception and communication. Just as you have your style of living, and your preferred way of dress, you also have certain ways of absorbing information. There are three ways we acquire information: auditory (hearing), visual (seeing), and tactile (touching). Most of us learn by using a combination of these avenues, and your particular combination becomes your perception style. People receive information in different ways: we are auditory, visual, tactile, and imaginative in different proportions. That is, words (sounds), pictures (sight), touching, and imagination are more or less important to you depending upon your perception style. Sensory preference refers to the senses you primarily use to receive information with the deepest understanding. For example:

- **Auditory/verbal:** If you absorb information mostly through listening to words, and you think in words rather than pictures, your style is more verbal and auditory, and not very visual. You will be more likely to think in words than in pictures, and you know you have understood a new idea when you can explain it clearly. You enjoy talking, lectures, and audiotapes, you listen for the words of popular songs, and you may enjoy listening to the radio. You'll probably use a phrase like "I hear what you're saying" or "It sounds like..." to mean you understand someone. Sexually, an auditory/verbal person is turned on by talking and be talked to.

■ **Imaginative:** Are you a daydreamer? Do you often practice "scenes" in your imagination, such as running over a job interview or a discussion in your head several times before actually doing it? If so, you are used to understanding via your imagination. For you "I wonder, " Let me think about it," and "I can see it in my mind's eye" would be common statements. Sexually, fantasies are big with the imaginative person, and lots of play-acting.

■ **Visual:** If you understand better when you see things, and you tend to picture ideas rather than think them in words, you probably know you've understood something only when you can picture it. If someone tells you about their vacation, and you've been to the same place, you'll get a visual picture of the whole discussion. Such visualization videos, watching someone else or seeing diagrams and pictures, are probably the most effective way for you to understand. You may say visual things like "I see" meaning I understand, or "see that?" meaning, do you understand? Turn-ons here include clothing, mirrors, videos, etc.

■ **Tactile:** If you lean toward the physical, and

you are a tactile (touching) person, you understand best by doing, "tinkering" with things, and you know you've understood when you "feel" it more than see or hear it. "Walking through" a new idea, acting it out physically, using things you can touch, work well for you. For you "I feel it", or "I've got it" are ways to say you understand. As lovers, tactile people are usually sensual, like to touch and be touched, and are not very verbal or visual.

Knowing your own sensory preference, and observing the styles of others, will help you communicate more effectively. For example, if you're asking someone to feed your cat, and you're verbal, but they're visual or tactile, take them through your kitchen, open the cupboard where the cat food is, and let them do it themselves while you watch. If their style is auditory, you can write instructions, or just explain, and they'll get it.

If this sounds too picky and detailed to you, just try it a few times—you'll see the difference it makes.

Beatitudes: A further 'tude category is what I call "beatitudes"—a person's spiritual orientation and ethical stance. While similar religious backgrounds or belief systems aren't required to make a relationship work, they are also basic things that can aid your understanding of each other.

You should at the very least be able and willing to talk to each other about the deeper meaning of things. If a spiritual point of view is very important to one of you, the other must be able to respect and listen to that point of view, without dismissing or ridiculing it.

Spiritual differences are one of the things that are easy to ignore and gloss over when the relation-

Moneysaver
Nothing is more expensive than marriage, moving in with, or even going steady with a financially irresponsible person. In your observations, look out for money clues. Does he live at home at age 27? Does she constantly get money from Dad? Are there signs of unpaid bills, ignored parking tickets, late rent, or borrowing from friends? If you see irresponsibility cues ... look out!!

ship is new, but become more and more difficult over time. If one of you has a spiritual point of view, it will affect many things you do, and decisions you make. You must be able to come to an understanding about these matters.

For example, Sue is not willing to watch violent or very negative movies—she believes they are unhealthy for her emotional/ spiritual well-being. Her husband loves action/adventure films, although he doesn't like gory movies. He goes to see the violent ones with other people, because he respects that it's not something she wants to do. They have different but compatible religious beliefs—they can discuss how they feel about a matter and come to a mutual understanding. He meditates differently than she does, but they both understand the value of meditation.

Similarly, Tom is Jewish, and Jane is Protestant, and they were married in a mixed ceremony with both a rabbi and a minister. They have mixed the two religions: Tom has learned to cook some of the ceremonially significant foods he loves, and Jane helps. They light Sabbath candles, but Tom goes to temple on Friday nights, and Jane to church on Sunday mornings.

They often attend each others' services, and special functions, and they enjoy teaching each other and comparing notes. They plan to teach their children the basics of both faiths and allow them to choose when they get older.

In these ways, a couple with different beliefs can blend, but it takes thought and effort. Similar spiritual beliefs can give you a mutual understanding and also provide structure to your relationship that requires less effort.

Plenitudes: Most of us don't consider it very "nice" to care about the financial status of a person we're dating, and indeed it's inappropriate at the beginning. But, if the relationship is going to become serious, your different money situations and attitudes will rapidly become a big issue.

You have looked at how you are with money in the know yourself exercise. Now, look at your imaginary partner. Do you want someone who is very careful, invests wisely, plans for the future, and doesn't want to spend much today? Would you do better with someone who is less concerned, and more willing to be spontaneous with money? Are you looking for someone who does money the way you do, or someone to balance you? That is, if you're thrifty, do you want someone as thrifty, or do you want someone who, while responsible, will help you loosen up and enjoy spending a bit from time to time?

I don't recommend looking for a partner to rescue you from money woes, because often the price you pay is very high, but, if that's really what you want, at least you can be honest with yourself about it.

Money is one of the top three things couples fight about, along with sex and power. Money, in fact, can often be used to control a partner in a relationship. Couples who fight about big money issues are not happy. Take the time to sort out your money issues before you get too serious.

> 66
> Love seems blind to personal habits, and people who can't tell the difference between a house and a hamper inexplicably manage to attract people who alphabetize everything short of their children.
> —Miss Manners (Judith Martin)
> 99

The frills

The following traits are "frills" because they are often attractive, and they don't get annoying until you've been around the person for a while. Usually, differences of this sort are easier to work through and accommodate than the 'tudes.

Similarities/differences. Neither similarities nor

differences in themselves will make or break your relationship. The challenge and stimulation in a relationship arise from the places where you're different, and the trust, comfort, and security between you grows from your similarities. Neither differences nor similarities are bad in themselves. But, if you get too much difference your relationship will feel like lots of work, and if you get too much sameness, it will feel smothering and boring. Understanding how different you are, and which similarities and differences you want, will help you achieve the proper balance.

Neatnik/beatnik. Ah, housekeeping! Many a relationship has foundered on the shoals of clothing tossed on the floor, or cluttered table tops and funky bathrooms. A neatnik (immaculate housekeeper, very tidy) with a beatnik (couldn't care less, sloppy) is not a good match, unless you both have a great sense of humor about it and can negotiate well. For example, the beatnik-type may love gardening, working on the car, and tinkering around, while the neatnik does the housecleaning and the dishes. The untidy one may even love to cook, if you will clean up. Often, sloppy partners are great with children, pets, and in bed. So, there can be many compensations. But, if you get together with one of these, don't expect any transformation. The housework will be yours, or you'll pay to have it done.

Physical/mental. People tend toward physical expression or mental expression. While many people achieve a balance of both, you'll want to have an idea whether you and your partner are physically and mentally well-matched.

A computer "nerd" or a bookworm who likes being inside and values mental stimulation may have

> **"**
> We're wearing ourselves out trying to have it all.
>
> No is a two-letter word that can free up many hours a week.
>
> —Elaine St. James, in *Living the Simple Life*
> **"**

difficulty being matched with a physical person who has to have vigorous exercise on a daily basis and can't sit still for long.

Think about how much and what kind of physical and/or intellectual activity you'd like to share, and discuss your preferences with potential partners. Like most differences, these can be worked out, if you're both flexible enough about what you want. But, if your preferences are too different, you might be disappointed later on.

For example, if you're a physically active man who loves hiking and camping, be wary of being attracted to pretty, dainty women with perfect makeup, hairdo, nails, and impossible shoes. That look requires lots of attention and pampering, and doesn't hold up well in the outback. Find out how she feels about "roughing it." Her idea of wilderness may be anywhere out of reach of room service.

On the other hand, if you're a very bright, intellectually focused woman who loves reading classics and listening to opera, a man who's focused on Monday Night Football and playing basketball on the weekends may not be able to relate to you.

Social/quiet. One reason the "opposites attract" dictum arose is that social butterflies and quiet "corner sitters" are often mutually attractive. The social life of a gregarious person can be very seductive to a shy one, and the quiet, composed space of a reserved person can be very refreshing to the party person. Again, the differences can be worked out, but you must be aware that you are different, and that your differences, charming now, may become less acceptable later on.

A gregarious person can feel stifled and trapped by a quiet one, and the shy person can feel overwhelmed and highly irritated by the more social one.

Activities/preferences. Although you've covered most activities in the know yourself exercise and this above section, you may not have thought about how much activity is enough, and how much is too much.

If you're both active people, combining all your activities may be overwhelming, and deciding which ones to share, which to do separately, and which to eliminate altogether may be necessary.

Some activities may be essential to you, such as physical exercise, political action or hours of meditation, or practice of a skill or talent like throwing pottery, studying music, karate, or tai chi.

Others may be more easily let go. If you find that there is too much going on for the two of you, remember to sort through what feels vital to you and what is easily let go. Even if you disagree about how important some particular activity or involvement is, if it's important to you, stick to your guns. If you let go of something you love to keep this partner, you'll resent it later, and that will create tension in your relationship.

Your past partners

In the section on the 'tudes, I asked you to evaluate the people you are closest to, in order to discover the personality traits you are looking for in a partner.

Now we will focus on your past relationships, to discover both what worked and what the problems were. Doing this should help you become more clearly aware of how your selective attention caused you to choose, and what aspects of that automatic attraction you need to challenge.

This exercise is much like the process a therapist would do with you if you asked for help in transforming your relationship patterns.

Positives: What was good about him/her

No matter how difficult you may have thought a relationship was, in the beginning you were hopeful, attracted, and excited. Get out paper and pencil, or your journal and [Note: in chapter 1, I suggest creating a relationship journal or notebook] write down each major relationship in your past (or use the list you made in the Analysis of Relationship History, above). Under each person's name, list the most positive and attractive qualities you saw in that person. Be honest with yourself here. If the attraction was an affluent lifestyle or a hot body, list that, too—even if you'd feel differently today.

Negatives: What was not good about her/him

Now, on the same list, write down the negative qualities. What eventually led to the end of the relationship? If it ended involuntarily due to your partner dying or leaving, perhaps ill health or inability to commit would be one of the negatives.

Take your time and remember what about each person drove you crazy, or made problem-solving, having a good time, or just being together difficult.

These negative traits can be anything from a serious character flaw such as addiction or dishonesty, to a small habit, such as not putting the cap on the toothpaste, or not being affectionate enough.

Problems: What relationship difficulties did you have

What were the problems in each past relationship? If you had only one relationship, and few problems, then look back at other relationships with siblings, parents, friends, or co-workers where you had difficulties.

Be thoughtful about this, analyzing what went wrong and what part was played by you and by the other person.

These problems can be anything from money arguments to workaholism to violence to too much interference from in-laws or family.

Solutions: Were you able to solve them?

If you solved some problems in the course of your relationship, pay particular attention to how you both did that, and what each person did to contribute.

This may be a bit difficult to remember, because once a couple truly solves a problem, the whole issue tends to fade into memory and be lost. But it's an extremely important indicator of negotiation and behavioral skills you already possess, and the things you remember you can build on.

For example, did you learn how to talk things through without getting angry? To "sleep on the problem" for a day or two, until you both calmed down, and then solve it? To keep current with each other, so resentment didn't build? The skills you learned in past relationships, even though the partnership didn't last, are still useable in relationships you have now.

If you were unable to solve some problems, or if you never understood what the problems were, write that down, too, and analyze it as thoroughly as you can. Here are the clues about what you need to learn or change, or what skills you need to look for in a new partner.

How does the next partner need to be same/different?

Look at your written examples carefully. They represent your relationship patterns until now. When you take the time to analyze and compare them, you can see the patterns emerge.

Once you see both the good and bad patterns, make a list of the qualities and characteristics you want in your next partner. Take the best of what you had before, add the missing qualities from your know yourself exercise, and condense it into a description of the person you're looking for.

Take enough time with this, and use your sensory preference. If you're a visual or imaginative person, visualize this partner, and picture the two of you going through a typical week, seeing the details of your time together.

If you're verbal/auditory, read aloud what you've written, or describe your ideal partner and relationship to a trusted friend.

If you're tactile, walk through your home, picturing your new partner there, and acting out what you'll do together.

You and your partner may not be the only people you have to consider when thinking about a relationship. If you're a single parent, the next chapter will help you manage the difficulties of dating in that circumstance.

Just the facts

- Before you can know the best dating partner for you, you need to get to know yourself.

- An honest assessment of your present lifestyle gives you clues about the kind of people you'll be most comfortable dating.

- While it's said that "opposites attract," it's important have a measure of compatibility with your dating partner as well.

■ It's important to take stock of the baggage from old relationships that you might be bringing into new ones.

Where to Go

PART III

Chapter 6

Squirrel Hunting

D ating, as I said earlier, is like the fine art of squirrel hunting. Where you choose to hunt makes a big difference in how good your chances are.

As long as you're going to all the trouble of looking for someone to date, maximize your odds of getting the right kind of person by making informed choices about where to look. Most relationship problems can be avoided by finding and choosing the right quality of person to date in the first place, so take some time in deciding how you're going to go about finding people to date.

Where do most people meet potential partners? According to University of Chicago researcher Dr. Edward Lauman, here's how the statistics break down:

- 23% meet at school
- 15% at work
- 10% at a private party
- 8% at a bar

- 8% at a church or synagogue

- 4% at the gym

- less than 1% at the gym

- less than 1% through personal ads

The best odds

So where do you find the right person? In the right place, of course. People gravitate to certain places according to what is going on in their lives and who they are. Healthier places, places where something productive is going on, will attract healthier people.

The odds are better that you'll find people you'll enjoy in places where people who share your interests congregate. Take a look at your favorite activities, and begin by exploring the singles scene at places where these activities occur. This approach not only gives you a better chance for success, but it's also safer than looking in places where shopping for companions is everyone's primary activity. At non-specific singles events or bars, you'll find a bigger percentage of people with emotional or drinking problems.

Let's take a look at the right places.

Intrinsically interesting places

Intrinsically interesting places are places you would like to go because the venue's activity itself appeals to you, whether you can find people to date there or not.

People who are in relationships and busy with their work and personal lives often talk longingly about all the things they'd like to do. The list of things people would take part in "if I only had the time..." abounds:

> 66
> Friends will get you through times of no lovers better than lovers will get you through times of no friends...
> —Unknown
> 99

- go back to school

- pursue a hobby

- try out for a play

- take up a sport

- get in shape

- learn to dance

- join a hiking or camping club

- be a community activist

- volunteer

If you have ever dreamed of doing some things like these but didn't for lack of space in your schedule, then now is the time: Combine your search for potential dates with fulfillment of those wishes. Think back to all the things you have fantasized about getting involved in. Perhaps the time is right to dive into something like one of the following activities.

Sport or hobby clubs. Are you a collector? Do you love horses, travel souvenirs, dancing, 30's memorabilia or stamp collecting? Are you enthused about model trains, miniature aircraft, or flying kites? Are you an avid skier, gardener, or hiker? Do you love playing bridge, chess, or computer games like Myst? Do you like the mental challenge of math or crosswords or astronomy? Do you love reading mysteries or science fiction? Watching movies, plays, operas, concerts, or sports?

Each of these activities has organized groups, clubs, and related gatherings that are full of other people who are just as interested in your favorite thing. People here automatically have a lot in common with you, and beginning a conversation is easy.

To find meetings, events and seminars, check your local newspaper, the Internet, or fan magazines devoted to your interest.

Volunteering. If you want to work for a good cause and to meet other people who want to improve their own lives and those of others, volunteering is your best bet. You can volunteer in the arts by becoming a museum docent, ushering at concerts, or building sets in a theater. Get involved in politics by joining a campaign, working for a human rights group, or spreading information on local neighborhood issues. If you're a senior, consider joining the American Association of Retired Persons. If you'd like to work on environmental issues, join GreenPeace or volunteer at a local nature center or wildlife habitiat. You can find opportunities to further animal rights by working at the local animal shelter or for an activist group like PETA. For spiritual support and fellowship, volunteer for your church, temple, mosque, or synagogue. If you love children, help the kids of your community by getting involved at a group home, in the schools, in a tutoring program at your local library, or with scouting or sports programs.

Volunteering for a cause you believe in not only will enrich your own life and give you a big return on your investment of time, it will also mean being close to other concerned people for long enough that you'll have a chance to get to know them well in a comfortable setting.

Classes. Education provides natural places to meet new, intelligent and motivated people. You can find classes in anything that interests you in several venues: Local colleges and universities usually have community outreach programs for adults, in addi-

Moneysaver
Volunteering at a theater or museum will not only get you involved with what interests you, it can save you money. Being an usher or volunteering to help backstage at the opera, concert hall, or community theater usually allows you to attend the performances for free.

tion to their regular catalog of subjects. Municipal parks and recreation departments have classes in sports, crafts and other activities like yoga, dancing and tai chi. Commercial "catalog" schools such as The Learning Annex offer one-session or ongoing classes, often with celebrity teachers. Consider signing up for a class to learn more about a subject that interests you or to help you develop skills you've always wanted to have. You can take classes in fitness, yoga, acting, musical instruments and performance, literature, great movies and countless other interesting subjects.

The friends network

You get the best odds of meeting desirable people when you meet them through your friends. As we mentioned in the Introduction , most people in successful marriages met their spouse through a friend.

Of all the intrinsically pleasurable resources you can have, your friends network is the most logical and natural place to begin when seeking to find dating partners. Friends provide support, companionship, and comfort, and they also can introduce you into their social networks. The friends that you already know and love are a group with whom you can share holidays, good times, bad times, and information.

A solid network of friends provides a cushion and a shield in life's difficult times—people to talk to when you need support or advice, and people to help you look out for your own emotional and physical well-being. The same network will also make your good times better by celebrating with you and congratulating you. There is nothing that feels as good in life as being surrounded by a trusted and trustworthy group of friends. More than anyone else,

Unofficially...
Eight years ago, I took a "catalog school" class on "the little theaters of Los Angeles." The class attended award-winning plays at small 50-seat theaters, and after the play we'd get to meet a member of the cast or the director, who would field our questions. Then we'd go out for coffee and a lively discussion. Through that class I developed a group of friends with whom I still see plays today.

friends accompany you on your life's journeys, and they know exactly how far you've come.

Rely on your network of friends as a resource. Even your married friends know single people they can introduce you to. It's not a good idea to get involved with someone at your own work, but people who work with your friends are fair game. If there's anyone interesting in your friend's office, have your friend set up a get-together with a group of co-workers and friends for lunch or coffee sometime.

As you form friendships with people you think you'd like to date, introduce these new potential dates into your network of existing friends so that you can see what your friends think of them. Allowing your friends to check out your potential dates will provide you with an honest and more objective assessment of their character. You'll be more comfortable developing a romantic relationship with someone that your friends also like and feel would be a good match for you.

Organized resources

Groups that already have a schedule of planned events and an organizational structure can be extremely helpful to you as a single person seeking dates, especially if your group of friends is too small or too far away to be useful as a resource for meeting new people.

Organized resources such as groups, clubs, churches, and classes are readily available in most communities, and provide the next best thing to a network of friends. In fact, if you attend meetings and events of an organization for a while, you will soon make friends within that context and thereby expand your own social network. The people you meet there will already be known to others in the group, which makes it safer for you as well.

Socializing through organized resources is similar to the "un-dating" method discussed in Chapter 4. A main objective of the un-dating process is to find a way to be in the company of new friends long enough to figure out if you want to date them. Organizations with regular meetings or events give you an opportunity to work or play with a group of new friends frequently and regularly, in a similar context each time, as you get to know them.

Why it works

All these strategies for finding compatible dates are effective because you are not solely focused on meeting somebody—you're participating in enjoyable activities and you have interests in common with the other people there. It's a much more realistic way to form a successful new friendship than going to a place solely for the purpose of finding a date. You're under a lot less pressure because you're doing something you understand, and that you know you'll enjoy.

In addition, when you're involved in something you feel good about, your demeanor will reflect that, and you'll be at your most attractive. The other people you meet there will share your interest, and you'll have a natural and easy topic for discussion that will lead on to other topics as you get to know one another better. In this way, you'll get to know each other gradually and simply. The whole process is a lot more inviting and less anxiety-producing than "singles events."

The people you'll meet there will often be mixed in age, background, and marital status, but that can be a plus. People who are not "eligible" for dating will be relaxed about meeting you, and they have friends. The "ineligible" people you meet might be a better resource for meeting new people than the event itself.

Why effective dating looks difficult

When most people think of dating, they think of singles events and singles bars. That's how it's portrayed in the movies and TV, and people talk about the "fun" they have getting drunk in a bar. There's even a special vocabulary devoted to the seedier side of the singles scene, made up of phrases like "meat market," "trolling," "bar crawling," and other equally pessimistic expressions. Going to a bar requires no research or advance planning, so in this regard it sounds easy enough. Having a drink sounds like it will make you less nervous, too.

Finding a suitable activity you enjoy, on the other hand, takes some work and advance planning, so in this way it seems a lot harder to do than simply putting on a clean shirt and hitting the corner hangout for an evening. Once you've chosen your activity based on an interest or hobby, going to the first event or meeting may make you nervous, since you can't really know what to expect until you get there. You may worry that there won't be enough single people there, or enough people your age there.

Don't fall for this line of thinking, because it's the exact opposite of the truth. Getting drunk and meeting other drunken people may seem to be fun at the time, but it seldom seems that way afterward, and it's a recipe for disaster. Likewise, a group of "singles, " together because they're single and for no other reason, has a desperate, superficial, anxious atmosphere that's not fun, either. Often, you come away thinking you've never met such shallow people. Sometimes the people there aren't really shallow, but the loud music, stilted atmosphere, and anxiety make them seem that way. It's almost impossible to get to know anyone.

The truth is that while it may be easiest to *meet* people at a singles club or bar, it is hardest to find friends in these places. And while attending scheduled events may *seem* harder because it requires some planning, it provides the easiest venue for finding compatible dates.

The worst odds

Singles settings and bars are not the only places on the list of scenes to avoid in your search for new friends. Therapy groups and work are also places where people meet, but which are unlikely to produce the opportunity for forging successful relationships. You may be surprised at the places with the worst odds for successful dating.

Bars/clubs

The downside to meeting potential dates at bars or clubs should be obvious, but so many people think they're the place to go to meet other people that the myth has yet to be debunked. What is the reason most people go to a bar? To drink, and to be around other people. What does this say about most of the people there? It says that they're lonely and that alcohol is important to them. Also, it says they couldn't find a better place to be, or better company to be with. While some of the people in the room will be completely healthy and may just be hanging out away from home or meeting a few friends after work, many of the regular denizens of bars have some problems.

While our statistics say eight percent of couples met in a bar, it says nothing about the nature of the relationships that are formed from such meetings. If you don't want to bring a lot of problems into your private life, don't bring people home from bars.

Singles events

While it's not impossible to meet suitable people at events that are specifically designated "for singles," these scenes are only slightly less problematic than the bars are. The difficulty here is that the only purpose of the gathering is to help people "meet someone"—there is no other focus, except perhaps the wine and snacks.

Once again, you are around people who don't know what else to do to meet people; in other words, to put it bluntly, a lot of the people there don't "have a life." Even the ones who do have interests and activities outside of work will be feeling anxious. It's difficult to talk to anyone comfortably under those circumstances, much less get to know them.

Also, most singles' events are "now or never" situations. Unless the get-together is hosted by an ongoing group, you'll only meet these people one time. In order to see them again, you have to set up a date. This means you have to make an instant decision, based on surface information, about whether you want to date the person.

Work

Dating at work is frequently a disaster waiting to happen. While statistics show 15 percent of people meet their spouse at work, that statistic does *not* reflect the difficulty they encountered in the process. Even worse to consider is the problems created when a developing relationship in the workplace goes wrong.

The reason so many people meet at work is that it is often the sole—or at least principal—place you spend significant amounts of time in away from home. In addition, the workplace supplies the criteria for bonding: contact, with meaningful content, over an extended period of time. You have things in common with your colleagues at work—shared deadlines, similar encounters with other co-workers, and so on. Cooperating with other people to accomplish goals gives you a mutual focus, which supplies an atmosphere where you can learn about each other.

However, although the opportunity to bond is supplied at work, the potential problems are an important reason to avoid looking around at work for dating relationships. Workplace competition—for that raise or that promotion—is only one potential problem. Jealousy from other co-workers is another, as is the fact that when you date where you work you're just asking to become the focus for gossip. And if one of you is higher up on the organizational ladder than the other, you're setting the stage for even more trouble. If the relationship doesn't work out you have the awkwardness of working with a disgruntled former partner, and you might even run the risk of accusations of harassment.

Dating someone who works with a friend of yours is a different matter. At least the person will be somewhat known to your friend, which is a plus. The only downside is, if you and your date have a falling out, it may be a bit awkward for your friend. If you're dating someone who works with another friend of yours, learn to keep friendship, dating, and work issues separate.

Recovery groups
Recovery groups are terrific places for healing, for

finding support, for growing, and for learning. They are terrible places, especially for newcomers, for finding a relationship. Any twelve-step recovery group (Alcoholics Anonymous and its offshoots) will tell you that—they strongly recommend you not date anyone in the group until you've been there at least a year.

Why? Because people in self-help groups (especially the new members) are there to recover from various kinds of addiction and dysfunction, and they're in no condition to begin a healthy relationship until they've completed their healing work. If you go to such a group and you don't need it, you're there under false pretenses, and misrepresenting yourself. If you're there because you do need it, you shouldn't be looking for a relationship in that setting—you have more important things to focus on while you're there.

If you've been in recovery for a long time then you may already know whether there is anyone else in the group stable enough to be a healthy partner. Just remember that your primary purpose as a member of a group like this is to complete your own recovery and to assist others in beginning and continuing their healing processes. You are probably surrounded by some pretty fragile people, so proceed with caution.

Therapy groups

The same caveat about recovery groups applies to therapy groups as well. These are places to heal and do honest work, not to pick up a date from among the vulnerable people there. If you're in a therapy group and another member is looking very attractive to you, "bust yourself" by talking openly about it in the group, or privately with the therapist.

Timesaver
"You have to kiss a lot of frogs to find a prince," the saying goes. By using singles events and bars to meet your prince, you up the ratio of frogs to princes, and waste a lot of valuable time. Choose your meeting places wisely and your time will be efficiently spent.

Odds are, it's a bad idea to explore the possibility of a romantic connection with someone whose biggest trait in common with you is a very serious problem. If against all odds it should turn out to be a good idea, your honesty will only help it work.

Your ex

Perhaps the most stereotypically disastrous approach to re-entering the dating scene is to begin dating an ex-partner again. Getting back together with someone who was a disaster once before represents the epitome of worsening the odds of success. However, lots of people try it, so if you're going to stop your dating process and try again with an ex, see the guidelines for improving the odds on page 146.

Why it looks easy

All of these places seem to be the likely places to meet a mate because this is what we have been told by endless advertising, movies and TV sitcoms. It also may seem easier in these settings because at places like work or a therapy group you are surrounded by people you already know and with whom contact is easily available.

Although the entertainment industry may want you to believe otherwise, you won't find your Prince or Princess Charming without doing the work necessary to make friends and get to know people in healthy social settings.

Why it doesn't work

Making friends and going slowly sounds too hard when you feel lonely and desperate to have a new relationship, but they are the real way to end your loneliness and surround yourself with new, desirable friends, and eventually find your ideal partner.

These seemingly "quick and easy" places to find

GUIDELINES FOR IMPROVING
THE ODDS WITH YOUR EX

- Get therapy first. Have an expert help you decide if you're making progress towards a healthy partners situation. Insist that your ex take part in this therapy with you.

- Slow down. If you're rushing into it, chances are that you're allowing yourself to ignore some issues you don't want to face. If it's going to work, it will work better if developed slowly and thoughtfully, and you'll have a chance to build a better foundation than the last time.

- Treat it like a new relationship—don't assume you know the things you need to know about this person already. Use the information and exercises in this book to help get your "new" relationship with your ex started on the right track.

- Analyze what went wrong the last time and consciously try to do those things differently this time. Talk about it with your ex and make sure you understand what his or her point of view is on what went wrong. If you cannot talk honestly together about what to do differently, you'll never change anything.

- Make sure your ex is as determined to correct the old problems as you are. If he or she is blaming you for everything that went wrong, or vice versa, disaster is imminent.

dates wind up wasting your time and money. If you get together with someone who has character problems such as addictions or past emotional trauma, you'll be in a painful situation of being bonded to someone with whom you cannot possibly make a relationship work. You can waste years doing this and wind up so damaged by the experience that it will affect your ability to create healthy relationships at all. That's a terrible price to pay to avoid a little planning and effort.

Resources

Beyond the conventional public venues in which to meet people, there a number of dating resources have sprung up to help you meet people to date. They range from dating services to personal advertisements, and each has its share of pros and cons. Here's a brief rundown on some of the options out there.

Dating services charge you money to help you find people to date, in much the same way employment agencies charge money to find a job or an employee. They're busy and making a lot of money, but are they successful? Will they help you? Some people have had success meeting potential partners this way—here's the lowdown on different types of dating services:

Video dating services. These services used to be very popular, and heavily advertised. In recent years, they are less visible, which may indicate how successful they were. Video dating services are very expensive, often costing more than a thousand dollars. Your money purchases is a video in which you're interviewed on camera. Your picture and bio, as well as the tape, can be viewed by other members of the service who are looking for dates, and you can see their bios, pictures, and videos.

You can find video dating services through advertisements in your local paper or in the Yellow Pages. When you call them, they'll make an appointment for you to come in and listen to their sales pitch. Be sure to ask if there are any reduced rates (student or senior) that you might qualify for. If you decide to join, they'll take your credit card and then set up an appointment for you to make your video. You'll also get a bio sheet to fill out, and you'll be asked to supply a photograph.

Figures on success rates are hard to come by—but anecdotal evidence is not encouraging. In the experience of every one I know who ever tried video dating, no one had a really successful experience, and some had some really miserable dates. Others had no contact with anyone even months after making their videos.

Beyond the issue of success (or lack thereof), there's the question of safety to consider. The service acts as a clearing center for people who want to date, but it does not guarantee that anything you read or see about another person is true. There's no way to tell if an applicant lied on his or her bio, say to conceal a prison record or a drug habit.

Still, if you're determined to go this route to dating, there are some ways to maximize the possibility of success. Since the video almost guarantees that this dating service is primarily about appearance, that's where you're going to have to focus your biggest efforts. If you're not young and handsome or lovely, don't bother. People who are very physically attractive will probably get a lot of attention, a lot of dates, but whether it's worth your investment is a big question.

Computer matching. Long before the Internet became all the rage, people found ways to use computers to find a date. Computer matching actually dates as far back as the late 1960s when companies began using computers to match data from hand-marked questionnaires. Today, it happens on the Internet. (Computer matching is different from the matching that takes place in chat rooms, although many matching services have chat rooms.)

Computer matching, whether online or off, takes the information you give on your registration form, including facts about you and the requests you have about the person you're looking for, and matches them to the answers given by other subscribers to the service. Once you've paid your membership fee, you can ask for all kinds of things in your match: non-smoker, within a certain radius of where you live, physical characteristics (age, weight, height, hair and eye color, ethnicity) and the computer will get as close as it can.

At some sites, such as http://www.Match.com, you also write a bio and send in a picture which is posted with your bio. When the computer thinks it has found a "match," you and your potential date are both contacted, and then you can check out each other's bio. If you want to, you can send an e-mail, and begin corresponding. Sometimes there are "chat rooms" (online sites where you can write messages to each other in a group or privately).

All it takes to sign up for a computer dating service is to find its website (you can do this with any web browser, such as Yahoo), and read the instructions. There is usually a questionnaire and a place where you can write a bio of about 200 words. Usually, you pay a modest fee with a credit card right on line and join instantly. Then you mail in your picture (unless they can pick one up off your own website). There may be an additional fee for answering other members, once they contact you, but you can soon get off the dating site and into free e-mail, if you want to.

The cost of computer dating services varies, but it'll run you about $50 on average to sign up, with a few extras you can purchase if you want to.

One plus of the computer approach to dating is that, as long as your relationship remains online, safety is not a big problem. However, at the point that you meet face to face, you must take the same precautions as you do with any stranger. The biggest problem is that days, weeks or months of e-mailing and phoning can make you feel as if you know a lot more about the other person than you do. Remember, no matter how sincere your new friend sounds, he or she may not be telling you the truth.

Your success will depend largely on the expertise with which you write your bio, the appropriateness of your wants in comparison to your own characteristics (that is, if you're 55 and want to meet a 20-year-old, you'll have a tougher time) and your picture. You must manage to make yourself attractive in print, not an easy thing to do. Again, most people will go according to your physical looks, unless your bio is so witty that it catches people anyway.

In a recent chat room discussion, people explained that, in a written medium like cyberspace, spelling, grammar, and punctuation count a lot. How well you write takes the place, to some degree, of your physical impression. So, if you're going to meet people on-line, learn to type and spell, or get a spell-checker on your e-mail program. Be as positive, cheerful, and helpful in writing as you would be in person, to make the same sort of good impression.

To increase your odds of success, send a good picture of yourself, preferably doing something you like to do. It helps if you have a website you can refer people to, because you get to tell a lot more about who you are on your own site. Search the web for services that allow you to list a link to your own website, if you have one. Find out if it costs extra, once you pay for membership, to contact individuals you're interested in. Find out how long your membership fee covers, and if renewals are the same price or cheaper.

Matchmakers/introduction services. This is a profession with a history that goes back hundreds of years. Matchmakers are people who introduce people to eligible partners for a fee. They advertise in every newspaper and magazine that has personal ads, and they also advertise on the Internet. If you sign up with a matchmaker, you'll fill out a form much like the ones used by computer matching services, and you'll possibly have a personal interview as well. They'll ask about your income, your physical characteristics and age, and other information such as your interests, habits (drinking, smoking), and education.

Then, they will compare your answers with others, and try to match you up, and then introduce you. The big difference between a matchmaker and a computer dating service is that there is usually a lot more person to person contact at the matchmaker's, but it is also a lot more expensive. (Some matchmakers charge more for men than for women.)

If a matchmaker seems a good idea to you, check out the personals in your local papers for ads. Once you've located a service, call up and ask a lot of questions. Find out how their process works, what it costs, how many introductions are included in the cost, and how you will be introduced to prospective partners. Also find out if any parties or gatherings are included, or if it's matching only.

These introduction services can be pretty costly, up to several hundred dollars. For that sum, there may or may not be some guarantees of how many matches you will receive, but of course, there are no guarantees that you'll meet someone you can create a relationship with. Every one of these services brags of their successes, but as far as I know, there are no reliable statistics on how often it works (that is, leads to significant relationships) or whether it does at all.

When making your initial call to the matchmaking service, be sure you find out whether they check the references of each applicant, and *how much* checking they do. Many such services do no checking at all. Your introduction could be to someone who has made up almost all their "facts." The usual cautions about meeting strangers apply here as much as in any other situation when you're meeting people for the first time. If the service has a place where you can meet a new person, use it. Otherwise, meet in a public place, or bring a friend. Before signing up, find out how other members would choose you, or you would choose other members, know exactly what information is given out, and what any extra charges are for meeting specific individuals.

The connection's made—now what?

If you connect with someone through an online, video, or introduction-type dating service, no matter whether you or the other person initiated contact, here are the basics you need to know.

- Your initial objective should be conversation— by e-mail or phone. Even if the dating service suggests you go out together right away, let the other person know that your personal preference is to get to know each other a bit first. Keep the conversations a two-way street by inviting a comment or question at the end of everything you say, and by not talking too much at one time. Once you feel comfortable enough with the other person (and don't be fooled into thinking you know them yet), *then* suggest that you meet.

- The optimum first meeting would be a group setting. If you and some friends are going to the movies or to lunch, invite this new person to join you. It may be a little awkward to meet for the first time with others around, but it puts the relationship on a more realistic footing. You hopefully will recognize each other by your pictures, posted online or sent through the mail. If you want to meet the person one-on-one, choose a neutral, public meeting ground, which provides safety and an easy escape if the meeting doesn't go well.

- Your responsibilities are to be honest, take care of yourself, and don't make promises you can't keep. Pay attention to the clues the other person is giving out, and be more worried about whether you approve of him/her than whether you are being approved.

- There is nothing you can do to enforce your date's responsibilities, but a considerate person will be kind, honest, interested in getting to know you rather than talking about him/her self, and clear about what he or she is looking for. If your new acquaintance doesn't possess these qualities, don't schedule a second meeting.

Sorry, wrong number

There are several ways that matchmaking of any sort may not work out for you. First, you may not get any matches—a good reason to ask for a refund, but don't count on getting one if it's not stipulated in your contract. Or you may get matches that simply aren't suitable when you talk to or meet them. If either of these cases apply to you, you aren't totally lacking in options.

If the matches you get don't meet your requirements, if you don't get any responses (or not a reasonable number) within a few weeks, or if the service doesn't live up to any of it's promises, make some waves. For your own sake, and for the sake of other people who may sign up, complain about anything that doesn't meet what they told you to expect. Businesses need to know they can't get away with false claims. If their behavior is particularly objectionable, be sure to report them to the Better Business Bureau, as well.

In the case where the service failed to live up to its written promises, ask for a refund. Send a photocopy of your original contract, or the confirmation letter the company sent, the credit card charge or check (never pay cash), and any other pertinent information, along with a letter explaining what went wrong and insisting that the charges be refunded. While you're waiting for action from the service, make sure you call your credit card company and tell them the charges are being disputed, and follow up by sending the credit card company a copy of the letter to the dating service. Or, call your bank and put a hold on your check, if it's not too late. Stopping the funds, even temporarily, will usually get a response from a reluctant company.

Personalizing the personals

The only difference between placing and responding to personal ads and enrolling in online computer dating groups—aside from their low cost—is that if you use a hometown paper for your classified ad you'll get responses from people who live near you, which is a definite plus. Otherwise, the ad is virtually the same as the one you'd run online (although space may be more restricted). Find out everything you can about the charges. For example: How much is an ad? What does it cost to answer an ad? Are there any hidden charges (for example, a per-minute charge for phone calls?)

You may have to try several local newspapers before you find the best one. Ask your friends if they have had any experience placing ads, and what they recommend. The more local the paper, the cheaper the ad, as a rule. Also, in a huge newspaper, you'll get responses from far away. Local papers are likely to produce local responses.

Once you've identified the paper where you'd like to run an ad, open to the personals' pages, and find the form that's usually provided for you to fill out. The paper usually provides plenty of instructions and even a phone number where you can call for help. The newspaper makes money from these ads, and wants to make it easy for you.

The cost varies widely from paper to paper, and can even be free for *placing* your ad. What usually costs money is calling or writing to respond.

Sometimes it's a 900 line that costs so much per minute to listen to the time-consuming messages advertisers have recorded. If you're not careful, your phone bill can be a shock, so keep a stopwatch or timer near the phone when you call, to keep track of how much you're spending. Ask enough questions before you place an ad so you'll know what it will cost you.

Success at getting responses to your ad relies heavily on how good you are at writing it. Read enough ads until you can tell what the best ones are like. I have known people to be pretty successful at getting responses to their ads, but whether you can succeed in creating a functional relationship is another matter. People who place ads are essentially in the same boat as people at singles functions—they are looking for a quick and easy way to find a relationship, and it usually doesn't work that way.

Assuming you don't give out your address or home phone number (use a P.O. Box), safety is no problem here until you meet someone face to face. The same cautions apply here as with people you meet on the Internet or through a dating service. Talk for a number of times on the phone before you meet, try to see the person in a group or public setting, be cautious until you know the character of the person.

Organizations for singles

Wherever you are in the country, there will be lots of groups specifically geared to singles. Advance Degree Singles (members are supposed to have college degrees); Professional Singles, Large Size Singles, Tree Toppers (for tall singles), Athletic Singles, and many other groups abound. You need to sort through them until you find out what group suits you.

No matter how good the name sounds, you need to ask a lot of questions, and probably actually attend an event, to see which group you want to join. No matter how much they say their members meet qualifications, most of them don't check very carefully, and people can fudge their applications. To see if you'll fit in, ask for the "demographics" of the group—a polite way to find out the age range, income, attitudes, gender balance, and so on, of the group. See what kinds of parties, gatherings or functions they have.

A group that runs activities with content—theater parties, lecture series, sporting events—will be easier to relate to than a nondescript "party" or "meeting", because it has a structure and a focus. It is easier to start up conversations with strangers when there is an event to discuss. Some singles groups are organized around dinner parties, with about six people at a table, and everyone getting up and changing places between dinner and dessert, so you can talk to a number of people during the evening.

Costs for singles groups can vary widely, with yearly membership starting at $50-100, and going as high as several thousand for an "elite" group. Sometimes membership fees are different for women and men. In addition to membership fees, the group can charge admission to events, and other fees. Be sure you know how costly it is before you join—there's no guarantee of success.

The plus for this kind of group is that there's safety in numbers. As long as you are at a group function, you can just relax and enjoy yourself. Do remember, however, that if you meet someone you'd

---

QUESTIONS TO ASK BEFORE JOINING
A SINGLES GROUP

- Do you have a membership fee?

- How much is it?

- What kind of events do you put on?

- How much do events cost?

- How many members attend your events?

- Is there are regular monthly calendar of events, or are they irregularly scheduled?

- What are the demographics of your membership?

---

like to get to know better, you need to exercise the same caution you would with any other relatively new person in your life. Take things slowly.

These groups give you a scheduled activity, usually on a regular basis, and if you go often, you'll get to know some of the regulars. It's a difficult way to know who you're meeting, however, and, as with dating services and personal ads, it wastes time you could be using much more pleasantly and effectively, doing something more constructive. If this is the only thing you are motivated to do, by all means try it. It's better than bars, and it is something you can do with very little advance planning.

Internet

Lots of meeting rooms, chat groups and bulletin boards exist on the Internet, separate from the dating services. These places have varying degrees of contact, content, and conversation, depending on how they were set up. They can be x-rated, fantasy-based (you can assume a persona and an icon represents you on screen), intellectually challenging or boring and lame.

Basically, they are just web sites with software that assists you in posting a message that can be read and responded to by others. There are basically two types of "chats"—bulletin board and real time.

On a real time chat, other people must be visiting the site at the same time you are if they want to talk to you. When you type a message in the window provided, there's a few seconds of delay, then your message appears on the screen.

A bulletin board site, such as the Utne Cafe (www.utne.com), provides a similar window, but once you post what you want to say, it remains on the screen, and other people (also from anywhere in the world) come by whenever they want, and post a response. In 24 hours, there might be 20 posts after yours.

The best websites for meeting people are rated and given awards. By searching on the Internet for website awards, you can find the best sites. Also, once you connect to a site and chat with the people there, they'll let you know where the other good sites are.

But keep in mind that websites vary wildly in character, so if you stumble onto an S&M or XXX rated site, don't assume that every other website will be like those. There are many differences, and it's worth your while to check out a number of sites.

When you find a site you want to try, you will probably be asked to register. It is almost always free, and usually requests your real name, your address, your e-mail address, and suggests you choose an online name and a secret password. You may choose your password, or it may be assigned to you. You'll need this password to log into the site in the future, so if you're not good at remembering such things, keep it in a notebook near your computer.

Once you register, you have to learn to find your way around the site. There'll probably be a section marked "FAQ" which means Frequently Asked Questions, and this is usually a great source of information for beginners. There is usually a section called "introduce yourself," with people who can help you figure things out. It takes a few visits to feel comfortable and understand what you're doing.

Chat sites give you a chance to get to know people on a gradual basis, discussing all kinds of topics, before you decide to focus on one person. You can observe others in relationship to each other. Some people online are quite aggressive, and how your new "virtual friend" deals with being "jumped on" can tell you a lot about emotional control and character.

However, it is quite easy to construct a whole new persona, different from your real one, when you're online. Some people even go to the extremes of changing gender, ethnic background, and education or employment. You may not be able to trust the person you're chatting with.

Still, if you feel you've made a connection with a fellow visitor to a chat room, you can take the relationship out of the Internet and into the real world. Typically, people chat for a while, move to private e-mail conversations, then phone calls, and finally to meeting live. If you reach the point where you're ready to take the relationship that extra step into a face-to-face meeting, be sure to take it slowly—meet in a public place, in the company of friends, and check out the other person before going off with him or her on your own.

Networking—or what's a friend for?

According to most studies, the most successful way to meet people for lasting relationships is through friends and relatives. The reason for this is pretty easy to understand. After all, your friends know you well, and share—or at least know and appreciate—your values and lifestyle. And they're likely to recommend people that are at least minimally compatible with you.

If you're interested in meeting new people, network with everyone you meet, everywhere you go, and make friends with people of the proper quality. Take advantage of every opportunity to attend social gatherings with the people you respect and enjoy. Meet as many new people as you can, and be open and eager to meet their friends. Soon enough and you will meet enough people to find a quality connection with a person you can feel good about.

To succeed in networking, all you need to do is be a good friend, good company, and pleasant to be around. If you are an asset at a party or dinner because you can carry on a good conversation, the invitations will keep coming. Of all the ways to meet prospective dates, this one can be the most fun! When you create a network of good friends, the good times abound. Your friends will share their favorite experiences with you, and you'll have a full, happy and rich life even *before* you meet a partner.

Where do we go from here?

So now that we've identified all the possible approaches you can take to meeting new people, it's time to look a little more closely at the actual dating process. Part 3 will take the mystery out of the dating

Moneysaver
If your budget is limited, you can be creative. Reciprocate for formal dinners by inviting people over for a back-yard cookout, or payback for a restaurant dinner out with a home-cooked spaghetti dinner. When friends invite you to expensive places, invite them to someplace fun, like a fish cookery on the wharf, or a picnic in the park.

process, and give you the tips and hints you need to make your dates fun, safe, and stress free.

Just the facts

- Networking with friends and colleagues is the best way to make lasting connections with potential dates.

- Joining a sports or hobby club, or doing volunteer work, gives you an interesting social outlet and maximizes your chances of meeting someone who shares your interests.

- Dating people you work with is usually not a good idea—there are too many complications if the relationship doesn't work out.

- Bars and clubs are not good places in which to make meaningful connections with potential partners.

- Dating services—from old-fashioned matchmakers to internet matching services—provide alternatives for meeting people.

GET THE SCOOP ON...
Types of dating venues ▪ What to do ▪
Dressing appropriately ▪ Who you'll
meet ▪ How to handle yourself

Making the Most of your Dating Venue

Chapter 7

As you learned in Chapter 6, some places are better than others for finding potential dates. But no matter where you go, even at the places with bad odds, there are things you can do to make your chances better and your process more effective. Even though I strongly advise you to stick with the places in which you will have the best odds, I will cover as many possible venues as I can in the following guidelines, so you'll know what to do wherever you are to maximize your dating potential.

Bars/clubs

Let's begin with the toughest venue in which to successfully find quality dates—bars and clubs. How do you behave in a bar in ways that will enhance the possibility that you will interest the proper person? How do you know who the proper person is? It's not easy, but it certainly is possible. I personally know people with happy and successful marriages who met in a bar, but I know many, many more who found disasters. Once again, in a setting like this, proceed with caution.

At first sight

Walking into a bar can be an anxious experience. To minimize this problem, have your plan together before you even get there. Know what you're going to do, what you'll have to drink, and what you want to accomplish on your first visit. If you drink alcohol, limit yourself to one drink, then switch to sparkling water, soda pop, fruit juice, or even coffee. This minimizes your odds of making poor decisions because of impaired judgment. When you walk in, find a comfortable place, and sit for a while just to look around.

What you want to look at is the types of people in the room and their various behaviors. Sit back and plan to spend some time looking around before you approach anyone, because if you spend some time observing each possibility, you'll be able to spot the losers by catching their negative behaviors and cross them off your list before you ever talk to them. If you really want to learn about who's here, you'll come back several times. Familiarity works as well here as any place.

As you observe the people in your surroundings, see what you can tell about their education level, alcohol consumption, and their interactions with others. Get your focus off who's cute or physically attractive, and try to observe who's kind, polite, friendly and interacting well with others.

Bar-wear

The first time you plan to go to a bar or club, find out if there's a dress code by calling the place in advance. If not, dress according to what you know about the attitude and price level. That is, if it's a very inexpensive neighborhood bar, you can probably be pretty casual. However, remember that sloppy is never attractive, so make your casual outfit a neat one. A fancier, expensive bar will probably require a jacket and tie, a nice dress, or pant suit or a business outfit. Dressing according to trendy styles such as baggy clothes or cowboy boots can be risky unless you are going to a place that reflects that style in its music and interior design. If you're not sure what the dress code is, dress simply and conservatively. If you know anyone who frequents the place, ask them what the typical clothing style is.

Squirrel hunting, bar style

While you're still observing, make an effort to look pleasant and interested in what's going on. If you began by choosing an isolated corner, once you feel a little more comfortable, you may want to move closer to where most of the people are. If anyone catches your eye, smile pleasantly. If anyone engages you in conversation, respond in tennis-game style, answering every remark with something that invites another comment.

Observe your own body posture, and make sure you don't look closed off. Even if you're nervous, with a pleasant, unforced smile and relaxed body posture you'll look at ease. Be as open as you can to anyone who seems friendly and is not obnoxious. Smiling and talking to various people sends the signal that you are approachable.

It's realistic to hope that you get to talk to several people on your first visit, and if you come back several times, it's reasonable to expect that you'll be recognized and eventually become a "regular." Whether that's desirable or not is up to you. You can hope to

Watch Out!
If you decide to get together with someone in a bar, be very careful... You're risking driving with someone who's been drinking, and being alone with a stranger. Both are terrible and dangerous risks.

meet someone you are attracted to, but only if you're very careful to pay attention to who this stranger *really* is.

It's *not* realistic to hope for an instant connection that will end your loneliness immediately and forever. Nor is it likely that most of the people you meet in a bar will be problem-free. Don't think that if you have a drink you'll be more relaxed and meet people more easily. What a drink will do is cloud your judgment and relax your inhibitions, so you're more likely to act on poor decisions. Not a good mix.

Also, don't expect that you can avoid the long, slow process of getting to know your partner. Meeting someone in a bar is likely to lead to instant sexual contact, but this can derail any possibility of an ongoing relationship.

Dating in the bar context

Because of the alcohol and the expectations of bar culture, a date here usually doesn't mean very much. It's an escape from loneliness, sadness, and real life. The vast majority of dates made in bars become one-night-stands. Each partner's expectations are set by their initial interaction with the other, and changing them isn't easy, so if you intend to develop a caring relationship, don't start it out with a sexual experience. A date at a bar can be simply one drink over the course of a conversation, and it can't be much more than that before you risk some serious side effects.

If you're in a bar you don't know, there is really no one you can trust. If there's a friendly bartender or server, you may be able to get some idea from that person of which customers are good people and which you should steer clear of. However, remember that they only know what they see in the bar, and they may be mistaken, or even reluctant to tell the unpleasant truths which could hurt their business.

If you want someone to trust, learn to be trustworthy yourself. If you really want to be in charge of making good decisions, don't drink alcohol here, and keep your goals firmly in mind. Better yet, bring a friend or two whom you *know* you can trust. Designate a driver, and go home with the same friends. If you meet someone, get your friends' opinions on whether the person seems okay.

How can you be found? If you're going to meet people in bars, it's a good idea not to give out your home phone number or address. Only give people your post office box, voice mail number, or pager number until you've seen them a few times and know they're trustworthy. In a setting like this it's important to be a bit more conservative about how much you let people know right away, for the sake of your own safety. If they're a mature and good person, they'll understand.

It's very difficult to know who you're meeting in a bar. Short of hiring a detective agency or meeting someone who's already a friend of a friend, you can't know who it is. Use the interviewing techniques in earlier chapters to find out as much as possible, but know that it will take extended contact, meeting this person's friends and family, and observing behavior and checking facts over time to really find out who you're seeing.

By now I've made it clear that I think bars are a very bad place to meet potential dates. The prevalence of alcohol, the anonymity, and the late hours all conspire to make bars breeding grounds for disaster. It's the last place I recommend spending your time as you seek new, true friends.

Classes, lectures, and workshops

Opportunities for learning or exploring something new are the best places to meet desirable people. If you can choose something that genuinely interests you *and* that attracts the kind of people you're looking for, you'll have an excellent chance of at least making good friends and a high probability of meeting someone suitable for dating.

Classes and workshops offer a better opportunity to interact with the other people than lectures do, unless the lecture is followed by a lab or a discussion. On the other hand, I know of privately-run lectures, which run for months or years, in which the people attending really get to know each other.

First day at school

Upon entering the class or workshop, look around to see who's there. Arrive a bit early, so you'll have some time to check out the situation before you have to pay attention to the instructor. If you're female and the other attendees are all women, you may want to drop the class right away, before are committed. On the other hand, if the subject is truly interesting, you may want to stay and make women friends, hoping one of them has a brother, a cousin, a friend, or an ex you'll be interested in. If you're a man among all men, the same choices apply.

If the class has educational prerequisites, you'll know that all the students have at least that much in common, as well as at least a rudimentary interest in the topic. You can learn a lot about the other people here by paying attention not only to the subject matter but also to the interaction between students and the teacher or lecturer, and among the students

Bright Idea
You can print up personal cards, including your name, post office box, voicemail, pager, and e-mail address on your computer or have them printed at an office services venue. They give people you meet the correct spelling of your name and only the contact information that you want them to have.

themselves. Who is bright, who is pensive, who helps others? Who has a good sense of humor? When you've gotten over focusing on who is the most physically attractive, pay attention to who's the most emotionally and intellectually attractive. Who seems to have a personality you could live with? And if the instructor is single and the appropriate gender, pay attention there, too.

Classroom dress code

Classes, lectures and workshops are pretty easy to dress for. If it's an academic subject or an arts topic, wear clothing that's business or casual yet neat. If it's a hands-on or physically active class, like cooking, yoga, painting, gardening, carpentry, or auto mechanics, your clothing will be more durable and casual, with appropriate protective gear (smock, apron, coveralls, kneepads)—not much chance for glamour in the traditional sense, but activity-specific clothing can be attractive in its own right and provide new tools for expressing your own personal style. Don't wear watches or jewelry that will get in the way if you're in a hands-on class.

Dress as attractively as you can within the limits of the required uniform, if there is one. Choose colors that flatter you and draw a little attention, but don't be too outrageous. Dress conservatively, whatever that means to you. After the first class session, you can get a little more experimental if you want to attract more attention.

Add a little pizzazz by bringing a very noticeable pen, notebook, purse, shoes, briefcase, apron or gardening gloves and hat. Here, you can get a little outrageous to offset your conservative clothing. An interesting scarf, tie, pin, cufflinks, lapel pin, or earrings can afford you with an opportunity to begin a conversation.

Star-pupil style

Be alert, positive, and interested in the class material. Read up a little in advance, so that you'll have some interesting things to contribute. Don't be afraid to ask questions, as active interest is an appealing quality. On the other hand, don't show off too much; you don't want to be intimidating. If you know a bit about the subject, be generous in helping others. If you're really new to it, don't hesitate to ask for help.

Bright Idea
Share your expertise with all your classmates. The ones you aren't interested in dating just might have a friend you'd someday love to meet.

Nothing attracts women more than a male in a cooking class who knows nothing and needs help. Similarly, women taking auto mechanics or electrical repair have a great opportunity to meet men. Breaking out of the traditional gender roles in the activities you choose to pursue will deliver the message to others in the course that you're an innovator and not afraid to break the mold.

If you're already advanced in the skills being taught—perhaps you're in your third year of studying yoga—then offering to help someone else (with the teacher's permission, of course) will create a helpful and generous impression. Or, if you're a beginning student in a life-model drawing class, you can ask questions of the more experienced artists. It's flattering and appealing to those you approach, and a great opportunity to ease into a conversation.

A-Plus expectations

It's reasonable to hope you'll make a new friend, perhaps several, at class. You will be together, working on the same projects, for a period of time, a sure bet for making connections with your classmates. If you cultivate these friends properly, you can hope to be introduced to their networks, and find a special person. If your stars are in the right place, and your luck and timing are right, you might just find the partner you're looking for. At least you're beginning with a common interest, in a positive atmosphere of growth and productivity.

You can also hope to learn something useful or fun, which may connect you to other resources for your dating plan. But no one can guarantee you'll meet Mr. or Ms. Right at your first class or lecture. Be prepared to attend a few different classes to make it happen. Don't just sit quietly and hope for someone to come find you. It could happen, but your odds are much better if you talk to others, ask questions, and volunteer to work together on projects. Meet other students before or after class for meals or coffee, and if you're invited to a gathering of students at someone's home, make every effort to go.

Academic encounters

If you've gotten to know someone in the class, especially if you've been for coffee and out in groups, when you or someone else initiates a date, it most likely means a lot. Remember, you've had a chance to get to know each other, and asking someone out (or being asked out) has a much more significant meaning than in the woozy atmosphere of a bar or club. Here, it signifies "I've gotten to know you a bit, I like what I've learned about you, and I'd like to explore whether we can make a connection."

Also, when you're on a date, you'll have a lot to talk about, beginning with the class topic and other people in the class, and moving on to more widespread and personal subjects. A date with someone you met here is more likely to be comfortable than a date with a virtual stranger.

I'm always cautious about trusting anyone at first, but here, if you interact with everyone, you can begin to see who's trustworthy and who isn't. Who can be relied upon to do the assignments and to fully participate? Who takes appropriate responsibility for his or her part in a project? Who is pleasant, cooperative, and easy to get along with? Who speaks fondly of friends and family?

Be a bit wary of class members who are controlling (if you work together, they want to be in charge), too perfectionistic, or negative and unfriendly with others (shy is OK, angry and hostile is not). Carefully observe anyone who is critical behind the backs of other students or the instructor — it's probably a warning sign. Listen for hints that this person has a lot of struggles with friends and family. Negative attitudes and experiences with others are warning signs.

In this situation, getting to know others is pretty easy. If you interact within the class, and in groups outside the class, you'll be safe until you learn who these new people are.

Go to the head of the (academic dating) class

In a classroom or lecture setting you have a chance to observe other people, which will tell you a lot about who they are. You can see them interact with others in the class, and you can get the feedback of others. When you find someone you want to get to know, use your interviewing techniques, introduce them to friends and later ask for your friends' opinions, and listen to your intuitive reactions.

Classes, lectures, and workshops are a very good idea—a "can't lose" situation, because you're doing something you're interested in and meeting like-minded people. Whether developing a relationship with an individual you meet here is a good idea depends on what you've found out about that person.

If your intuition is telling you something's wrong with a person, or you feel nervous or insecure about a person, don't ignore it. Check out what you're feeling, and see if it's your normal anxiety, or if there's something about the other person that you're reacting to. We all have radar, if we remember to pay attention to it.

By taking your time, interacting in groups, interviewing, trusting your intuitive sense, and doing things you know are safe until you learn whether you can trust the other person or not, you'll have a better chance of connecting with a quality person.

Spiritual venues

If you are of a particular faith, the regular organizations connected with that belief are a very good bet for finding a potential partner. Even if you're not heavily invested in one particular faith, finding a generic Protestant church (if you're not used to religion, look for an Open and Affirming Congregation—they're more tolerant), or one of the more New-Age denominations (which tend to be more open-minded), such as Science of Mind (also known as the Church of Religious Science) or Unitarian Universalist, can be a good source for meeting people with good values.

People generally go to churches because they have concerns about being spiritually healthy and doing good in the world. While some denominations define these terms in ways that might make you uncomfortable (for example, a heavily fundamentalist sect or a cult-like group), most of the mainstream denominations promote excellent values.

I knew that I was hiding facts about him from my family and friends, because they wouldn't approve. That should have told me something, and I will never ignore what I know again.
—Participant in online chat group

You may not personally like everyone you meet, and there may be a few bad apples, but generally, faith communities consist of people who get to know each other, and who can vouch for each other at least to some degree.

Entering the community

If you're new to the group, attend a few services to see if you're comfortable with the overall belief system. If you decide you want to be involved, you can attend classes in the faith, which will tell you all the pertinent details. If you already know the faith, seek out a congregation that has a number of people in your age range and an active social calendar. Social events will be in the program or bulletin and announced at every service.

Get involved. At the beginning, attend whatever gatherings they have after the service for coffee. If you attend the service, and don't stay for coffee, you won't have any chance to meet and talk to the members. As you get to know the group, find social functions or events to attend or committees to join.

At the service, sit in the back of the room so you can see the whole congregation. You'll be looking at their backs, but you can still make some observations about the demographics of this community. What are the age ranges? Are there lots of parents and children? Are there small clusters of adults in your age group? (People in clusters tend to be single.) Is it a large congregation, or a small one? You'll have a lot more opportunities to meet people in a large group, but it's easier to get to know people in a small one.

Make as many observations as you can during the service. Later, at coffee, you can begin to talk to people and ask some questions. Go to the minister, rabbi, or leader, introduce yourself, say you're brand new, and ask to be introduced to some suitable people. He or she will know all the central people in the congregation, and will be happy to introduce you. Once that happens, people will feel you're a little special, and make an effort to talk to you.

Appropriate attire is a must

Church is a formal occasion. While some congregations may be casual, your best bet is to go dressed in business- type clothing. Suits for men, dresses or nice pantsuits for women. Some religious denominations require headgear. Call in advance if you don't know. If you go to a Jewish temple or synagogue, for example, *yarmulkes* (small hats for men) are provided, but most of the people have their own. Some Moslem mosques provide head coverings for women, if women are allowed inside. Again, the experienced attendees have their own. Some Catholic congregations require women to cover their heads, but expect congregants to know this, and the congregations don't provide any. Once you get to know the place and the people, you can adjust your dress to match theirs.

Appropriate dress, and a calm, relaxed attitude are important here. Joining the group for coffee, smiling, and making "small talk" will create a good impression.

If you decide to get involved, join some social events or study classes, where you can get to know people individually. Don't worry about not knowing the faith. People will love explaining it to you.

Volunteer to help with dinners, fund-raisers, cleanups, and other events. Being part of the organizing or work committee gives you that golden opportunity to be in the company of others for

Watch Out!
While you might attend church services in hopes of meeting a date, if that's your *only* reason for going you may offend regular members.

extended time, focused on a mutual task.

Expectations in the faith community

You can hope for the best here. If you find a group with compatible beliefs and age range, you'll meet a lot of caring, ethical people who mostly have their lives in order. Some will be here in pain, looking for healing, but most will have made the religious observances a part of everyday life. Many people attend religious groups when their children are small. It's quite easy to meet single parents here, or married people who have friends they'd love to connect to someone from their church, mosque, or synagogue.

You can hope to meet people who care about relationships, family, and commitment. These are the values promoted by such organizations, and they fit nicely into your plans, if you want a lasting relationship. So, you can hope to be supported in meeting someone, once you are known to the congregation. Church and temple-goers can get really excited about helping you connect with someone suitable. You may have to beat the *yentas* (Yiddish for aunts, used to mean "matchmakers") off with a stick. While it can get a little overwhelming, these are often experts who can find you the kind of person you really will like.

You can hope to meet a very high percentage of healthy and happier than average people. Research shows that members of such organizations have longer life spans, report more happiness, and have more lasting relationships than people outside faith communities.

On the other hand, instant success is not a realistic hope here, any more than anywhere else. You must plan to keep coming back, until you make enough connections to meet the people you need to know.

Keep in mind that this is a *very* serious place to date, so do a lot of socializing in groups before you choose someone to single out. The whole group will be aware of your date, and any untoward behavior will be reported. This is a *community*, and if your date, who is a member of the community, is treated lightly or disrespectfully by you, there will be a price to pay in group feedback and censure. This works the other way, too, in that if you get to know the group, they will be equally protective of you.

If your intentions are honorable, and a pairing just doesn't work out after a date or two, as long as you and your date remain friendly, there will be no harm done. So you need to make sure the two of you are clearly communicating about what's happening in your relationship.

Whom can you trust?

If you get to know people here, you'll have a lot of people you can trust, and you'll have access to the gossip, which, just as in a small town, will tell you a lot about the history (within this group) of the person you're interested in. It's definitely worth getting connected here—it will provide you with community support and the community gossip network, which are extremely effective in curbing and reporting bad character traits.

However, just as in any other venue, you have to show up to be found. No one is going to come to your door looking for you. Make yourself available as suggested above; bring your personal cards and pass them out freely. You'll have to become a member of the group, but this is not the same as joining the religion. There are numerous members of congrega-

Watch Out!
Once you get to know the congregation, if you get interested in someone and either other members or the leader are less than enthusiastic about your choice, pay careful attention. A minister or rabbi may not be able to tell you some negative thing he or she heard in confidence, but may indicate non-verbally that there's something wrong.

tions who are not officially members of the related religion.

The structured nature of this type of group will help you a lot here. The spiritual leader (minister, rabbi, mullah, priest, etc.) usually knows a lot about the people here, and so do board members and other long-time members, including deacons, cantors, choir members, Sunday school teachers, and so on. Once these people get to know you a bit, they will help you figure out who the other people in the congregation are.

Meeting someone through your place of worship is a very good idea. The odds are maximum, in favor of meeting someone with good values and getting to know them well before you have to make any commitments. And, in addition to the opportunity to meet potential dates, you'll get other important things by being involved in this community, as well as a sense of connectedness, spiritual exploration, and a lot of good times.

Single parent dating: Child related events

If you are a single parent, you need to attend child-related events anyway, so why not turn it into part of your dating research? There are a few things you need to be concerned about, but if you have the proper priorities, this can be an easy and productive way to meet someone who understands the issues of single parenting.

There are school functions you can attend from pre-school to college, and all will put you in the proximity of other parents, some of whom are single, and all of whom have children in the same age range as yours. Plus, you can often tell from the emotional well-being and the casual chatter of the child what kind of parent you're dealing with. Children (including yours) don't keep secrets well.

First contact concerns

Your initial moments in sports, school functions, parent night, etc. will probably be absorbed by your child(ren). But, once the dragging on your arm has ended, you can get a chance to look around. If you're at a concert, play or sporting event or other sit-and-watch happening, you can strike up conversations with the people around you. Again, don't forget that even married couples have single friends, siblings, and even in-laws.

As time goes on, getting established in school activities, such as PTA, is not only a wise parenting tactic, but will put you in the proximity of other parents who care. PTA meetings are usually adults-only. So, at first, treat them as suggested above for classes, lectures, and workshops. The topic you have in common here is your children, education, and school political issues. There should be no shortage of things to talk about with other single parents, and don't forget eligible teachers.

As a parent, you'll find a great mix of teachers, other parents, and students. You have the greatest excuse in the world to get to know the parents of your child's friends—it's just good parenting to know who your children are meeting.

Depending on the activities you attend because your child is involved (such as a play or band concert and rehearsals), you may have interests (theater, classical music) in common with the other parents. So, by supporting your child's interest, coaching or scoring for teams, or getting involved behind the scenes, you can automatically find other parents whose interests coincide.

Appearing appealing

Clothing here is pretty easy, except if you have pre-teens, who will complain that you look like a "dork" no matter what you wear. Actually, your child's conservatism can work in your favor, keeping you well within acceptable ranges. Just suit your clothes to the occasion—business or slightly dressy for concerts, casual business for PTA meetings or parent night, casual for sporting events, and remember to be neatly groomed and dressed in becoming colors. If the school's color is goshawful, like orange and purple, try wearing some neutral color that looks good on you, and just wearing a pom-pom pin, or carrying a school flag... Nothing too provocative or dramatic—this is about the children, not the grownups.

Aside from what you're wearing, your attitude and facial expression are what send the invitation. Be pleasant, attentive to your own child and others, and helpful to the adults around you. As always, getting known requires getting involved, so begin immediately to volunteer for PTA committees, etc. Find out where the suitable partners for you (i.e., single parents and teachers of the other gender) are involved, and get involved there.

Gold star expectations

Expect great times for yourself and your children. Expect to meet other parents, single and married, with whom you can form the "village" it takes to raise your children. Expect to get to know families which are safe and secure places for your children to socialize, and from where you have an excellent chance of meeting someone to seriously date. Hope to meet a co-parent for your child, who understands parenting from experience.

But don't fall in the trap of expecting to break up any existing couples, no matter how tempting it is. It will ruin your chances of meeting anyone appropriate, because word will get around quickly. Don't try to force a relationship with a parent of your child's friend. If the relationship grows naturally out of sharing parenting tips and problems, car-pooling, baby-sitting and shared outings, great—but if there's no chemistry, or one-sided chemistry, stick to friendship. You'll make everyone's life miserable (including yours and your child's) if you try to force something that isn't there.

What does a date mean here?

A date with someone from your child's school means your child (and everyone else) will know about it. Be a lot more subtle than that, as discussed in Chapter five. Do things with all the children, have outings and picnics and lunches *en famille*. Don't date until you're pretty sure a relationship has a good chance, and even then be casual with the kids. "Susie's dad and I are going to see a movie that's too grown up for you kids." Or "I'm going to escort Ginny's mom to her office party, so she doesn't have to go alone." Try not to let your enthusiasm show too much. If the kids like each other and both of you parents, they will be crushed if it doesn't work out. If they don't want you to get together (perhaps because they're still wanting their original family back), they'll get rebellious and give you trouble.

If the kids are already friends, interacting as a group as much as possible will give everyone a chance to bond. However, if the children have a falling-out, don't pressure them to get along—just wait, and the problem will most likely pass. Children go through these things quickly and repeatedly. It's part of their learning about relationships, and has nothing to do with the parents' friendship.

The interaction between parents and children is very telling. If you get to know the children of the other parent, you'll know what kind of family it is before too long. If the child shows signs of stress, severe acting out, and/or depression, those could be warning signs about the parent. On the other hand, this family, like yours, has gone through divorce, desertion or death, and may be stressed from those things.

Again, making friends is the best way to find out what's going on. Also, if you get involved in a school group, there will be useful gossip.

Networking works on two levels in parenting venues:

Watch Out!
Be careful not to appear too eager to be close to married individuals of the other gender. If their spouses get concerned, you'll ruin your chances of entering their network. Rather, make friends with the spouse of the same gender. Believe me, any couple you get close to will be very eager to get you safely married off, and will work hard at it.

1. You can get parenting help, trading off having children stay over so you and the other single parents can have nights off, for example. You can also find out from other parent's experience what works in terms of setting limits, discipline, parent/child communication, and home remedies for simple ailments.

2. You can develop a circle of friends that includes resources for both your child and yourself, and will lead (through friends of friends) to meeting new people, and eventually the right person (who will not be a stranger, because your friends will know him or her).

As you spend time with these other parents, you will be able to see whose interaction is healthy and supportive, and who has struggles and fights.

If you get involved on a regular basis in school functions, you can be found there, and it's valuable to exchange phone numbers with other parents of your child's friends. PTA and other groups often pass out lists (with permission) of phone numbers of the parents involved, to make contact easier between meetings. Your personal cards will come in handy here, too.

This is one of the safer groups in which to give out your phone and address, because of the accountability. Knowing that you are well-connected at the school means people will not normally behave badly—it's not a total guarantee, but it's considerable protection.

By listening to what your child says about the other child's parent, by getting to know the other person as a friend through working for school groups, and by listening to what is said by other parents about the person, you can get a lot of information about character. In addition, you'll be getting to know this person as a friend, and using your interviewing techniques.

And meeting someone through your child's school is a very good idea. It is easy, when your child gets to interact with other children and their parents in groups, to form a friendship, to see how the other person and your child get along, and to learn about the person's character and personality before ever declaring that you care, or letting your children know. If you go slowly, and it doesn't work out, your child hasn't been dragged through a bonding experience and then wrenched away from someone they're close to.

You have a lot in common with another single parent, and you can benefit in many ways other than just meeting a partner. It's another "can't lose" situation.

Howdy, Neighbor

We often hear the phrase "geographically undesirable"—and in places like Southern California, you can easily meet people at work, classes, or other groups, who live too far away to be easily accessible. It doesn't necessarily doom a relationship, but it's an obstacle to overcome.

But what if you could walk out your front door and meet someone right there in your neighborhood? Wouldn't that be nice? Whether you can or not depends on the kind of neighborhood you live in. If you get to know your neighbors, they will trust you, and happily introduce you to their friends. If you're a young single in an established neighborhood with mostly elderly people, you have to network to see if any of your neighbors have eligible adult children, or friends, co-workers or other relatives you could meet. Similarly, if you're a single heterosexual in a gay neighborhood, your neighbors will be excellent neighbors, but not eligible—however, like the older kind of neighbors, they may very well have friends and family members who are eligible.

Knowing your neighbors can provide a lot: safety, in the Neighborhood Watch sense, and instant pet-sitters or baby-sitters in an emergency; someone to keep an eye on the house while you're gone. Neighbors who are talented at cooking, carpentry, home repairs, gardening, etc. will give you free advice. Friendly neighbors can be a great help and a safety factor, too. If you're friendly with your neighbors, and their teenagers play their "music" too loud, it's much easier to request them to turn it down without creating bad feelings. If there's a problem in the neighborhood, such as car break-ins, streets in need of repair, drugs, or an eyesore, you can all work together with your city council to solve it.

Getting to know you. . .

Whether you just moved in, or you've kept to yourself in the neighborhood, you need to let your neighbors know you are interested in them. Pause outside to say a friendly "hello," make a comment about the weather, ask when the trash is picked up, or what day the street sweeper comes by, borrow a cup of sugar, a wrench, or a lawnmower, or pick up a piece of trash from your neighbors sidewalk.... anything to get that "neighborly" feeling going. This is easier in a small town than it is in a big city, because in a small town everyone expects to know everyone else. Big city neighbors are often slow to warm up. If you live in a metropolitan area, your neighbors are the other tenants in your apartment or condominium building. You can get to know these neighbors on the rooftop in hot weather, or by the swimming pool, or near the mailbox.

Bright Idea
A smile is a great ice breaker when you're new to a community. Keep yours polished up and at the ready.

You may also meet your neighbors in local stores, especially the little grocery on the corner, or the mom and pop breakfast place down the street. If you see a familiar face, smile and say hello.

Your neighbors can be almost anyone. Sometimes the neighborhood will indicate who lives there. For example, if it's near a school, you may have a lot of families with children. If it's an older neighborhood with individual houses, you may have elderly neighbors who have lived there for years. If you're near the beach, you may have students or families with kids.

Obviously, an affluent neighborhood means most of the homeowners and renters will be upper middle class or higher, and a low-rent district will attract people with less money, such as single parents and children, young adults starting out. A low-rent area will usually be more culturally mixed, with all kinds of people represented.

Whether your neighbors seem eligible for dating or not, remember how important networking can be. There might be a lot of eligible people "connected" to your neighbors, and if you get invited to your neighbor's party or barbecue, that eligible friend or family member might be there. If your neighbor has a warm feeling toward you, that person will have a favorable impression, too.

At home appearances

What you see is what you get in the neighborhood. As long as you're appropriately covered (even if you're sunbathing in your bikini in your front yard), your dress is OK. But, keep in mind, if you want to make a favorable impression, come outside (where you can be seen by the neighbors) looking good at least some of the time.

If you live in a house, the more time you spend outside, gardening, reading in the sun or shade, and just hanging out, the bigger chance you have to meet your neighbors. If you live in an apartment or condo complex, then the pool or community room will work. But the best thing is to join the tenant's association and help run the place. You'll soon know everyone and some of the dirt on them, if there's been any.

If your complex has cocktail get-togethers, or your neighborhood has a block party, join in and socialize. Even if you don't meet your mate, you'll get acquainted with some other people and have more say over decisions that affect you, too.

Home-based expectations

Friendly relationships with your neighbors and a good support network are two pluses attached to getting to know your neighbors. In addition, becoming active in your neighborhood pretty much guarantees that you'll have more control over what goes on on the local scene. Possibly, some personal friendships, and maybe even that certain someone, will come out of the network you create with your neighbors.

But don't expect perfect harmony. Your neighbors are the usual mix of people, some good, some problematic—so, you may have to learn the hard way whom to encourage and whom to avoid. Don't waste your time hoping for Prince(ss) Charming to live next door, and don't get tangled up with married couples. When it comes to couples, make friends with the person of the same gender, and you'll be less threatening to the spouse.

Whether you find your partner or not, knowing your neighbors will be worth it.

Dating the boy (or girl) next door

Tread very carefully. As with work, if your relationship turns sour, you'll still be living next door, especially if you both own your homes. It's a lot safer to meet a friend of one of your neighbors, but if you do get connected with a neighbor, follow the *Unofficial Guide to Dating Again* guidelines of building a friendship before you get involved in dating. You can invite your neighbor to coffee at your house with other friends and neighbors, attend apartment complex gatherings, spend time out by the apartment house pool, get involved in Neighborhood Watch, and talk over the backyard fence—but take your time, and go slowly, until you know who your neighbor is.

There is no qualifications exam for neighbors, so there's no way to know if you can trust them. This is one reason to take your time and get to know all of your neighbors as a group, to promote neighborhood (or apartment complex) events. There's safety in groups. Getting involved in neighborhood improvement groups, Neighborhood Watch in cooperation with your local police department, cooperating with your neighbors in block parties and garage sales gives you a chance to get to know neighbors and become friends safely and carefully.

One reason you need to be careful as you get to know your neighbors, and the most important reason you *need* to know them, is that all of them know where you live. It's important to your safety to know the people who can keep track of your habits.

Don't worry about nosiness—it will really work in your favor. For example, if your neighbors know you through Neighborhood Watch, and they can see something unusual happening at your house or apartment when you're not home, they will report it and make notes about it. That can be a lifesaving or possession-saving kind of nosiness.

Neighbors who are home or condominium owners are likely to live in your neighborhood longer, and be more concerned about the neighborhood itself, because they have a financial commitment. On the other hand, rental tenants are a lot more mobile, although there are many who live in one neighborhood for many years; some owners buy, renovate, and move rather quickly. So find out, if you can, who owns and who rents. If you own, and live near people who rent, find out who the real owners are, in case you have a complaint.

All in all, getting to know your neighbors is a great idea, whether it leads to dating someone or not. It will enhance your lifestyle, increase your safety, and provide people nearby who can help in many ways, if you need them.

Special Interest Organizations

Special interest groups can be political, like Green Peace, The Sierra or Adirondack Clubs, the American Association of Retired Persons (AARP), a reelection committee for a politician, or a human or animal rights organization. Or, they can be focused on the arts, a school alumni association, service organizations like the Elks or Moose clubs or organizations like Boy and Girl Scouts, YMCAs and other church and civic groups. Arts organizations, such as the Pacific Corporation for the Arts, a local Civic Light Opera or Community Concert group, or a Community Theater. Museum or zoo support groups or the local ASPCA may get your vote. Joining such a group, or volunteering for it, is another opportunity to meet people.

You don't have to join most of these organizations to see what goes on and who's here. You can go as a visitor or a guest. Many of these groups are excellent for older people to meet suitable friends, since retired people usually have more leisure time to get involved. When you attend a meeting, go to find out two things: do you believe in the purpose of the group ? And who is there? You want to join a group with people you want to meet and make friends with.

As you know by now, the idea is to make friends in whatever group you attend, and network from there. In these special interest groups, however, you'll meet people with strong opinions and pas-

Bright Idea
If your walls are rattling from loud rock music, and you know the owner of a rented unit, or the parents of the children who live nearby, call and hold the phone up to give the owner or parent a true idea of how loud the music really is. You'll get results right away. If you can't find a responsible party, you can call the local police station, and hold the phone up to let them hear the "music." You'll get a quick response.

sionate involvement in various causes, and you want to be sure you're comfortable with the cause and the people in it. When you attend, listen carefully to the discussion it will tell you about the attitude of the group and the individuals within it.

Making an effective appearance

Attending a meeting of a group like this usually requires casual business type clothing, unless it's a working meeting, when clothes appropriate to the work are worn. When you call to find out about a meeting, find out what people usually wear.

At some of these organizations, you will be evaluated according to your contribution and dedication to the cause, while others are a lot more social and relaxed. That is why it is so important to observe the temperament of the group before you decide to get involved.

In general, looking good and being friendly will serve you well until you get to know the group better.

Expectations and issues

Hope to find a group whose cause or focus you are passionate about, and then meeting others who have that same passion. Out of that connection, you can develop friendships and eventually a special relationship. Many excellent marriages have been fueled by a shared passion for a cause. But don't expect to be comfortable with the people in a group whose cause or focus you do not share. Make sure the group is right for you, because that's where you'll find the right people.

Working together with people on a cause or project you are excited about can easily lead to a more personal relationship. The danger here is that the shared interests can blind you to the personal characteristics of the person you are interested in. Also, if the other people in the group know you're dating, that can lead to jealousies, etc.

As you work together with other people, especially if you're under some pressure from time to time, you'll get glimpses of the hidden parts of their personalities, and you'll learn who is trustworthy, who is vindictive, who has angry outbursts, who's cooperative, etc.

Making connections

Anyone in the group probably has access to a membership roster, but your personal cards come in handy here, too. If you are on a small committee, you will probably wind up meeting at people's houses, perhaps including yours. This is usually safe, as long as it's a group project. But keep in mind that at the point you first join the group, you will have very little information about the people in it. But, as time goes on, you'll interview, hear gossip, and observe others to gather information on what kind of people they are.

If you find an organization whose cause you can believe in, and which has people you feel good about, it's a great idea. If you work together on a cause you are enthused about with people you like, you'll soon be friends, and meeting people through friends is still the best way to create a lasting relationship.

Taking care of business—meeting people during everyday life

Unless you live in a rare, isolated spot in this country, people abound in your life. However, you may not notice them. While it's a very big long shot, with terrible odds, you could meet your dream date at the

It could happen.
—Judy Tenuta, Comedienne

Laundromat. It has happened before. So, just in case, why not practice your conversational skills whenever you get the chance.

Quick!! You only have a minute!! What can you tell about the person in front of you in line at the grocery store (look in the cart), at the bank (look at what they're wearing), or at the Laundromat (notice what they're reading).

Meeting people while you're running your usual errands and performing your everyday tasks is a totally random event. You can choose the line you want in the grocery store, if more than one is open, but you often can't choose who is with you. This is where your observation and interview techniques come in handy. Find out as much as you can from what you observe and the conversation.

Making the most of serendipity

Remember what your mother used to say when she lectured you about always looking your best? Any time you're in public, you could be about to meet your soul mate. You're smart to look as good as you can, even in the Laundromat. You're mother would be proud of you.

But whatever you're wearing, in circumstances where people don't usually notice each other, your friendliness will stand out. Be pleasant, smile, be helpful, offer to help someone understand the machines in the Laundromat, or let someone in front of you at the checkout counter. Take an interest in the people around you and enjoy talking to them.

If you do, you can realistically hope to improve your conversation and interview skills, and make your wait a lot more pleasant. Don't get too hopeful about really meeting someone you can get to know. This is a total stranger (unless you begin to see this person in the Laundromat a number of times), and you have no way of knowing about his or her character. Still, who knows? You might meet a magical someone while picking up your dry-cleaning. But just because you see an attractive person standing in line, don't let your fantasies run away with you. This is not a safe place to make a personal contact, no matter how much fun you may have chatting and flirting.

And keep in mind that a date made while standing in line means you are taking a very big risk. If you're going to see a person again, make it for coffee in a very public place, in broad daylight. Bring a friend along for safety.

Trust no one that you meet in such a casual way. There is no way to know who you're talking to. Flirt with strangers in this context only as practice, and don't assume you know anything. If, by some miracle, a relationship should begin to develop, find other people and do things in groups, and ask the new person to bring some friends along, so you can get to know something about your new friend.

Whatever you do, do *not* give out any personal information to someone you've met through a chance encounter like this. If you want the person to be able to contact you, use your personal cards. After all, there is almost no way to know who you're meeting. Your interview skills will get some information, but you won't have a chance to double-check it.

In the final analysis, talking to strangers this way can be great fun, and it can get you past some of your awkwardness in new situations, but actually dating one of the people you talk to in line is not a good idea at all.

Special event encounters

It is not easy to meet people at special events such as theater showings, sporting events, and the like unless you get specially involved in a group, such as a movie appreciation class, a little theater support group, a travel club, or a sports fan club or booster club. Just going as a passive spectator, you're as likely to be struck by lightning as you are to meet someone special. Yes, you can strike up a conversation with the person next to you, at your seat, or in line for refreshments, but the likelihood that the random seating will put you next to a desirable, eligible person, or that your conversation will continue once the event ends, is very slight.

If you're traveling in a group, or on a bus, a train, or a ship, you'll have a bigger possibility of meeting a soul mate, but only if you follow the processes outlined above for groups and classes and get yourself involved. On a ship or train, you can be seated at dinner near eligible people (you can even request that when you discuss your seating with the Maitre d'), but again it's only a random chance that you'll meet anyone eligible and interesting.

Moving to the next level

By now you've got a pretty good idea of the wide variety of venues in which you can meet new people, some of whom may become friends, and a few of whom may turn out to be worth considering as potential dates. And you should have an sense of the pros and cons of all the possible ways you can meet these new people. So now's the time to get down to real brass tacks. Part 3 will give you the lowdown on the specific dating skills you'll need to go from first contact to closer personal connections. Are you ready to take the plunge?

Just the facts

- You can maximize the likelihood of successful encounters no matter where you meet new people.

- Even negative meeting venues, handled appropriately, can yield worthwhile dating possibilities.

- The best places to meet new people are the places that reflect who *you* are—your interests, values, and personal style.

- Even chance encounters can result in meaningful meetings.

- Wherever you meet new people, be careful for your safety—avoid giving out personal information until you know the new person well enough to develop trust.

The Dating Process

PART IV

Chapter 8

Getting Connected

Now that we've examined all the places you can go to meet new people, it's time to take a look at just what you need to do to attract that special someone who catches your eye. No matter where and how you come face to face with someone for the first time, whether it's across a crowded room or right next to you, once you get noticed, you want to get and hold the other person's attention long enough to stimulate some interest. In this chapter, you'll learn the skills you need for making contact, flirting, circulating, and connecting on the telephone, Internet, or via e-mail.

First contact—generating interest

The first thing to do when you meet someone who interests you is to make direct eye contact. Research shows that holding eye contact, even from across a room, is almost irresistible. Unless the other person is with a partner, he or she will eventually respond. Your gaze should be a little longer than a glance, but don't stare. Let your eyes wander away, but keep wandering back. Each time your eyes meet, hold a beat or two, smile, and then allow your gaze to wander off again. You'll soon find the other person nearby, seeking to learn who you are.

The eyes have no equal in the world of unspoken communication, but if you're on a chat group or communicating by e-mail, you need to come up with a near equivalent to this first gaze—something that catches your correspondent's. "Emoticons" (stylized symbols produced by using characters on the standard keyboard), if handled correctly, might do it. One popularly used emoticon is the smiling face, like this one:

:-)

Another way to capture online attention is to pick a "signature" quote to use on your e-mail. Pick something that suits your personality and style. Here's one of my favorites, by Dorothy Parker:

Oh, Life is a glorious circle of song
A medley of extemporania.
And Love is a thing that can never go wrong
And I am Marie, of Roumania.

If your initial contact with a potential date is on the telephone, your best means for generating interest is a quiet, soothing, pleasant voice. If your listener has to pay attention in order to hear you, so much the better—being too loud on the phone makes your listener back away, but mumbling is simply irritating. And along with that pleasant voice, you should make an effort to provide and witty conversation.

In fact, whichever of the above attention-keeping skills you do best could help shape your dating process. For example, if you have great eyes, and a smouldering or inviting look, then organize your search process so face-to-face contact is how you begin. If you write well, then you might want to begin on the Internet. If your speaking voice is your best asset, try personal ads with voice mail.

Flirting—The ancient art

Once you've attracted someone and you have his or her attention, the next step is to increase the energy a bit by flirting. There are lots of "attraction behaviors" that influence people to respond positively. And your body language is the first place to start. Check yourself out in the mirror—take stock of how you present yourself to the world. Make sure you don't appear shut down and closed off, and don't get a leg or an arm between you and your new friend like a barrier. Don't hug yourself, as if you feel afraid. Relaxed, open posture is much more inviting.

If you don't know what to do with your hands, hold a beverage or play with your watch or your jewelry. This minor movement will call attention to the watch or jewelry, which can provide a conversation topic, and it indicates you're a little nervous (rather than anxious), which makes the other person want to put you at ease.

Flirting has become something of a lost art these days, but it's great fun when done well. And you can flirt almost anywhere, even with people you know well. Flirting can happen online, over the phone, by e-mail, or face to face. Flirting is a way to "offer bait," to let the other person catch glimpses of attractive things about you—your eyes, your sense of humor, your quick wit. It is a great way to move a relationship from friendship toward a more emotional connection. Flirting with a person you have cultivated as a friend sends the message that you want to change the nature of the relationship.

Flirting basics

To begin flirting, you have to single out one person to focus on. After all, flirting is an invitation, an expression of interest, and to be effective you need to focus it on one person at a time. If you are new at this, you might want to practice your flirting skills on someone you know—someone you're not interested in as a date. This will let you get some practice in without feeling intimidated. Once you've got the skills down pat, you'll be ready to take them out into the dating scene with confidence.

What's your flirting style?

Flirting can be either lively and animated, or quiet and intense. While flirting always has sexual energy, tension, and excitement, your personality and that of the other person will determine whether your flirting takes on a giddy, animated quality, or an intense, sotto voce (lowered voice) feel.

Either one is fine, as long as you don't let anxiety get out of hand, and become too loud or boisterous. If you feel the energy rising too fast, simply quiet down and look the other person in the eyes for a moment. You'll feel your own energy re-focus and settle down, and so will your partner's.

The power of your gaze

The best flirting tool you have is your eyes. In fact, the word "flirt" originally meant a brief glance. If you're in physical proximity, keep glancing at your chosen person, then back to what you are doing, or around the room, then back to the person again. When you catch his or her eye, smile. After a few times, that person will know he or she is your target, and hopefully will be flattered and interested.

The approach

If your interest is returned in the form of smiles and glances but you're flirting partner is a stranger, and you're too far apart to talk, try mouthing something such as "Hello" or "Nice night." The other person probably won't understand what you've said, but he or she will respond in some manner. Generally speaking, if the person is male, he will move closer to you. A woman is more likely to stay put but to smile or otherwise signal that she has noticed your effort to communicate. Her smile is your signal to move in her direction. If you're getting an invitation to move closer, and you want to, go ahead. If the other person comes over, smile and nod your welcome. Once one of you moves closer, you can begin to talk a bit. This is where your verbal skills will be key—but keep those eye-to-eye gazes going, too.

The conversation

When you're face to face with a flirting partner, even the simplest conversational gambits can take on a whole new dimension. You don't need to be a Shakespeare to flirt successfully, but if you're good at putting extra meaning on words (subtly, of course) now's the time to begin. You can say indirectly flattering things like "suddenly, this party is a lot more fun" or, "I'm really glad I came here tonight."

If you're meeting this person at a place with some content, such as a class, a volunteer group, or a church group, you'll already have something neutral to talk about, which helps relax both of you. Your focus then should be on moving the conversation toward the personal. A question, like "What did you think about what the teacher said tonight?" focuses the conversation on your friend's opinion,

Watch Out!
An inviting gaze, as if you're drinking in the other person with your eyes, is attractive. A staring contest is not. If you lock gazes, and both of you seem stuck, just move your eyes around the other person's face, or look at your drink or your hand to break the stare, and give the other person a little space. After a few beats, give him or her your full attention again.

yet still relates to the content of the event.

If you're flirting over the phone, you don't have the opportunity to use the eye contact to reinforce the personal content of your words, but by making little noises of assent—"uh-huh," "yes," "OK," "I agree," or "I understand"—you can let the person on the other end of the line know you're following with rapt interest.

If you're carrying on a flirtation via the Internet, you've got a truly difficult task—you can't use eye contact, nor can you use your voice to express your interest. What you say (that is, what you type) becomes even more important.

No matter what venue you're communicating in, keep in mind that a sense of humor, wittiness, and clever conversation are the essence of flirting. It's a subtle way of letting the other person know that you're interested without saying it out loud. Flirting is an adult form of play—and a way to make a connection. Have fun with it.

Unspoken communication

At the same time you're carrying on your verbal conversation, especially if you're face to face, another conversation is going on behind the scenes. Your body language, the tone of your voice, the expression on your face, and, most importantly, your gaze, are all conveying messages of their own.

Even if you're only talking about the weather, but holding each others' gaze, giving a lot of non-verbal encouragement with nods, smiles, and little "uh-huh" or "um-hmm" responses (verbal "nods"), the excitement level of the conversation will gradually increase.

Over the phone, this happens simply with the tone of your voice and your voice cues. Those little encouraging verbal nods make a big difference in how understood your partner feels. If, on the phone, your partner ever says "are you there?"—either you aren't responding enough or you are not giving frequent enough verbal nods.

Being understood, desired, and admired are the keys here. If you communicate interest and understanding to your partner, and you get a similar response, your flirting is going well.

How to speak silently

Sometimes silence is the most effective conversational tool you can use. If you allow a silence to be there for a couple of beats, while holding your partner's gaze with a pleasant, interested, smiling expression, the energy level in your flirting will usually rachet up a notch or two. Silence also allows both of you to feel comfortable with not having to have something to say every second, and produces a sense of restful familiarity.

Too much silence, however, if you are shy or get tongue-tied, can feel awkward and jarring. Don't worry about a silent moment, but if you feel inhibited or "stuck" for something to say, just smile and say "I've just gotten a little shy." It's charming, and very attractive, and it doesn't force your partner to guess what's happening.

Suggesting without suggesting

Flirting is a meta-conversation. That is, there's an underlying meaning to everything that's said. The surface meaning is, "I'm interested in what you're saying," and the underlying meaning is "I'm interested in you—perhaps sexually." Your exchange of meaningful glances is the medium for this underlying, more personal communication.

Bright Idea
If you aren't enjoying a conversation, and have decided you want to squelch the flirting and just resume normal contact, simply remove your gaze (look vaguely over the other person's shoulder, or down at your own hands) and let your energy subside. If, in addition, you give brief answers that don't invite a response, you'll soon be back to a normal conversation from which you can easily excuse yourself.

If you like what is going on between you (especially if you know this person is safe, through the ways recommended in the last few chapters), now is the time to heat up the conversation a bit. If you know how to play on words, and use double meanings, you can move the conversation more toward the personal, and away from your general topic.

For example, your partner says: "I can get really enthusiastic about things I like to do." "Oh really?" you respond with a raised eyebrow and a grin, "I'll have to find some things you like to do." If this produces a blush, a return grin, or a smile with eye-contact from your partner, you're on target.

Volleying the conversation

Perhaps the most difficult skill to learn when flirting is how, in addition to all this underlying and unspoken communication, you still keep the surface conversation going. Since flirting is ultimately about showing interest, understanding, and attraction, demonstrating that you are interested in what your partner is saying, and want to hear more, is essential. This means that you must make certain that the conversation flows smoothly, back and forth, between you and your partner, much along the lines of a volley in tennis. Here's how it works:

- **Concentrate:** Listen carefully to what your partner is saying—don't wander off mentally into what you want to say next.

- **Volley (respond):** After your partner says something, respond directly to it, letting him or her know that you heard and understood what was said, and, if possible that you have similar thoughts or experience. But don't argue: There is definitely a place for spirited discussion in good conversation, but be careful not to get too oppositional in this flirting phase. Your objective is to establish understanding.

- **Return the serve:** At the end of whatever you say, invite a response by adding "don't you think?" or "What do you think?" or make your response a question.

- **Serve again:** If your partner drops the ball, or you run out of things to say on the first topic, offer a new topic—ask a question about something that was said before, comment on an accessory your partner is wearing and ask about it, or comment on something that's going on around you, and ask your partner's opinion.

If your tennis match goes on long enough, you'll learn a lot about your new friend, and you'll both feel you have "so much to talk about." If the tennis match is a struggle, and the other person isn't returning your interest, what you're learning is that you should focus on someone else.

Stealth interviewing

Learning while you converse about miscellaneous topics is what I call "stealth interviewing." Interviewing is just encouraging a person to talk about certain topics by asking questions. Professional interviewers do it with a microphone, and perhaps a TV camera, and it's very one-sided.

Stealth interviewers disguise the interview in a conversation by answering the interviewee's questions, responding to his or her answers, and using the tennis match approach. Interviewing techniques were explained in detail in chapter 3. Practice the techniques enough that you can interview someone just by being interested in who he or she is, at the same time that you're flirting. Just pay attention to the answers, and take the time later to think about what they mean.

If you're successfully flirting with your "squirrel," you'll find that the conversation will take on a much more intimate tone, and you'll get even more information about your friend's past relationships, etc.

I know all this—flirting, eye contact, double meanings, the tennis match, and stealth interviewing—sounds like a lot to do at once, but you probably do most of them instinctively when you're interested in someone. The purpose of this detailed explanation is to make you aware of everything you're doing, and to let you know if you're missing any useful techniques.

Unofficially...
While talking to friends about a column I was writing on cyber-relationships, and asking if anyone had reliable research, one friend e-mailed back. "Tell them to be very careful, there are many sleazebags on line, like the one who raped my daughter."

The versatility of flirting

If you've been doing all your flirting on the phone or the Internet with someone you've never met, you'll eventually get to a point in your relationship where meeting is the next step. Then, much to both of your surprise, you'll probably begin this flirting phase all over again on a new level, face to face.

Be careful not to just accept that a stranger from the Internet is someone you know, just because it feels great. Anyone can tell you almost anything about themselves on the net, and it's difficult to check.

A case in point is the story of "Joan," who presented herself as a disabled older woman on Compuserve's "Between the Sexes" converence. Over several years, "Joan" developed online relationships with many other women, who were ultimately shocked to discover that "Joan" was, in reality, a male psychiatrist. This type of "online crossdressing" and other types of personality manipultion are very common, and for this reason many computer users are wary of interactions on the Internet.

If you're going to meet people on the Internet, or anywhere you're meeting strangers you don't know anything about, be extremely careful. As the case of "Joan" makes clear, flirting online can be misleading, making you think you know someone well, when you actually don't know if anything you've learned is true. The flirt can go on for an extended period, and cause you to forget that the other person is a stranger. Other venues where you are meeting total strangers are equally dangerous.

If someone toys with your emotions by impersonating the wrong gender, or lying about age, weight, or financial condition, you're simply going to be disappointed and hurt. But, if someone conceals a prison record, fraud, or a history of sexual offenses, spousal abuse, or worse, you could be in danger.

Wherever you're meeting new people, follow all the precautions in this book, and never trust anyone you haven't checked out. This is the main reason to meet people at places where you can get to know them and see them in relationship to other people.

Taking the next step: Circulating

Flirting can push a relationship into the next level, but it might also fall flat. Once you have chosen someone and tried out your flirting technique, if you still want to look around, try circulating.

If you're in a group situation, at a party, a bar, a singles gathering, or a church picnic, you need to find a way to connect with several of the people there—meeting as many people as possible gives you more chances to find the people you want to know.

Don't go to a group event and then stay in a corner with friends you already know. Get out and circulate! Here are some good ways to do it.

Hooray for the host(ess)!

If you're in a setting with a host or hostess, you have a natural ally and helper. A knowledgeable host intentionally moves through a party, helping people to connect and enjoy each other. If you're looking for eligible people, and you let your host or hostess know, you'll be introduced to whoever's there and appropriate. This way, a lot of the effort is made easy for you. If you ask your host(ess) (before the party) to introduce you to single friends, you'll be introduced around the entire party. Your host or hostess may even invite some people specially to meet you.

Being circulated by the central person of the gathering is not only easy, but enhances your status, and makes it easier for others to remember you.

Being in the center

Being in the center of things makes it easier to meet more people and catch someone's eye. If you're at a party or a singles event, volunteer to help with the drinks or the food table, or to greet people at the door.

If you're in a bar setting, sit in the center of the room, near whatever the action is—the dance floor, the pool table, the music. If you position yourself well, you'll be in the center of a stream of people, and able to scan the crowd, smile, and catch the eye of anyone you want.

But you don't have to pick one spot and stay there. Another way to see who's at a party or gathering is to circulate through the room. This is especially effective if you know some of the people there and can say "Hi" to several people as you go by. Stop and chat here and there, and smile at everyone you pass.

Survey the room as you walk through, noticing where the people are that you might want to single out later. As you pass, give that person or those people a bit longer glance, smile, and nod. When you come back to chat with that person later, you'll have established a pleasant expectation, which will make flirting easier.

Making a connection

Getting to know someone to the point where you want to date each other begins with making a connection. If you've been getting to know people in this group over a period of time, then connecting with someone on this particular occasion will be easy.

When you circulate through a group or party, or you position yourself in the center so the people move past you, or even if your host introduces you, you need to be able to keep your new friend's interest until you get a chance to establish a connection. And to do that, a conversation is necessary.

The conversation

While circulating, the kind of conversations you will have will be a bit disjointed because of the atmosphere you are in. People will be passing by, you have no privacy, and your surroundings are distracting. Keep the conversation light, teasing, humorous. Show your interest in the other person, but focus on simply making a good impression, and intriguing the other person enough to make him or her want to see you again.

With your attention and demeanor, you need to non-verbally give this impression: "To me, you are the most interesting person here, and I wish we had an opportunity to talk more than we can now." That means, your attention should not wander away from your quarry unless it's truly unavoidable (someone bumps into you, or speaks directly to you); and it should be obvious that you are listening intently and enjoying every moment of the conversation.

Your eyes and your smile are your main conversational tools here. You will probably be standing, so attempt to stand as close as you can without crowding your partner, look into his or her face, and, if possible, turn your back to the rest of the room. Stopping to talk to one person in the midst of circulating, or intentionally coming back after greeting everyone, is a way to let someone know they are getting special attention from you.

The tennis match: Volleying the conversation

The tennis match in the context of a large gathering only really happens when you settle down from circulating and decide to focus on one person for a while. Again, the chaotic nature of the environment is going to make a smooth conversation difficult. Relax and have as good a time as you can.

A few comments about how difficult it is to talk here, how much you're enjoying the conversation, and how much you'd like to talk more, should result in some agreement from your quarry. If you get that agreement a couple of times, you can move to overt suggestion. If you're at a private party, invite your partner out onto the patio, or into another room, if one is available (such as the library or den), that has fewer people in it. If you're in a more public venue, suggest that the two of you go out for a cup of coffee either right after the event or at another time.

To move your connection a little further along, moving to another room or going out for coffee is a great way to get to know this person better. If this is a new person, move into making friends, get together with friends, and follow the suggestions for getting to know someone in all the previous chapters.

Keeping your goals in mind

Meeting someone while circulating at a party doesn't give you much of a chance to find out what you want to do with this person. To figure out what you want, you need to gather more information. You may be fantasizing about what you'd like to do, but the only way you'll know what you want is to get to know more about who this is.

If you should be tempted to walk away from this party or gathering with someone you just met and wind up in bed, remember you're leaving an impression that you'll go to bed with any stranger you meet. This is not a very favorable impression, so don't be surprised if you don't get asked on a second date. Being cautious, on the other hand, leaves an impression your partner can respect and admire. It's your choice.

Phone savvy

Ah, telephone flirtation. It has all the comfort of being online (it doesn't matter what you look like; it's safe as long as you're only talking on the phone), and there's that wonderful feeling of being caressed by a voice. Why do you think billions are spent on phone sex and date lines yearly? The phone is a very sexy medium.

Who calls who?

Keep the tennis match rules in mind when flirting by phone. Whoever calls first should then wait for the other to make the return call. If you've been given a phone number, it's natural to assume that means the other person wants you to call, but, unfortunately,

Moneysaver
Be careful on the phone—bills can mount up quickly. If you get a phone connection established with someone who's a toll call, keep a stopwatch or timer by the phone, so you know how much time you're talking. Check with your phone company about getting the best possible rate for the other person's area, or call on a phone card, so the call is prepaid, and you can look for bargains in advance.

that's not always the case. To get a phone flirtation started, you have to take a risk of rejection, even if your desire is simply to increase the level of an established friendship to a flirtation on the phone. So, alert your support system in case you need some sympathy—then take a deep breath, and call.

If you receive a call from someone you're interested in, great! The tennis match rules still apply. Be gracious, responsive, and remember to toss the conversation back into the other person's court each time. Be careful to find out why the person is calling you, before you get too excited. You don't want to jump into animated, flattered, excited chatter only to find out he or she wants to know if you remember what s/he did with a credit card, or if you saw anyone steal a coat. Be glad to hear who it is, but a bit reserved until you find out if the other person wants to chat, to invite you to something, or to collect for a charity.

After hello—then what?

Before you call, have something to say. It can be a continuation of a conversation from a party, or an amusing story you found that relates to your friend's interests. (For example, as I was writing this book, several friends called up to read me cartoons or tell me jokes about dating.)

You can call to let him or her know that something of interest is happening, such as a local art opening, jazz concert, or lecture (this can lead to an outing or date, also). If this call is the result of meeting via e-mail, a dating service, or a newspaper ad, the reason is clear, and the call will be expected. If you're calling a friend you already know a little, the welcome will be warm, and the call will be easier.

The first thing you need to do before risking a

phone flirtation is to find out if the timing is convenient for your friend. For example, it's very awkward if you begin teasing and flirting and your friend's mother is visiting at that moment, or the other person doesn't really have time to talk.

If, once you state the reason for your call, the other person responds by chatting a bit, you can use tennis match rules to encourage a longer conversation.

Telephone topics

Once past the opening exchanges, if you have established that there is time to talk, you can relax into a more free-wheeling conversation, and introduce some flirting. Laughter, humor, teasing, and joking will set the right mood.

If you have had conversations with this person before, and you found you have some subjects in common, return to those topics. If this is a call to someone you know from a class or group, finding a topic should be quite easy.

At this stage, it is best to talk about impersonal things, such as hobbies, career, activities with friends, and interests such as movies, books, TV, the arts, politics, national affairs, the stock market, sports, and other general topics. More personal topics, deep feelings, spirituality, the nature of your relationship, and sexual topics should be saved until the intimacy between you has grown.

You can use stealth interviewing techniques to find out what your friend enjoys and what is interesting to him or her. On the phone, a conversation will often turn more intimate, more quickly than in person, because it feels safer and less intimidating when you can't see each other.

Silence, of course, doesn't communicate much in

> **"**
> If you really look, it's not long before you really listen, if you really listen, it's not long before you really touch, and if you really touch, orders come from hindquarters and you have to make a decision.
> —Rev. Denton Roberts, MFCT, M. Div.
> **"**

the absence of any visual cues, and that, by forcing you to ask what it means, can also further the intimacy. Without visual information to go on, you are both forced to explain more of what you mean, which can work to further understanding and intimacy.

If you want to go further

If your flirting goes well, especially if it's with someone you already know, you'll find you both want to take your relationship to the next step.

If you know the person you've been flirting with, going to the next step is wonderful. It you've been flirting with a stranger, it could be dangerous. Here's what you need to know.

Establishing your priorities

Now that you've got your own and the other person's attention, it's time to make sure that this squirrel is the kind you want. Review what you learned in Chapter four about how to choose the ideal mate, beginning with who you are and who you'll need to complement that.

This is a great time to do this, because the excitement and thrill of successful flirting probably has you dangerously close to not thinking. Remember, you must choose your new partner from the neck up as well as from the neck down—intellectual thought as well as physical/romantic/sexual excitement.

This is the very moment your old, dysfunctional patterns can take over, so take the time to think about this relationship, and don't get lost in fantasy. A little fantasy is fun, too much can spell disaster.

After you have checked out the other person, gotten to be friends, and then raised the level of your relationship to a new emotional peak (and just enjoyed that for a while), your new relationships will begin to take shape. If your relationship lasts, whatever habits you develop in this time will quickly become ingrained. If you avoid talking about problems when they arise, it will become more and more difficult to talk about difficult subjects.

If you begin here with power struggles, arguing, jealousy, and criticism, your relationship can easily become locked in those patterns. However, if you strive to work together and build teamwork and goodwill right from the beginning, you can begin a pattern that will lead to a solid bond, and a love based on lifelong friendship.

But flirting is only the beginning of making significant connections to potential dating partners. Sooner or later you're going to move on to an actual date. The next chapter will deal with what happens when you move on to that next stage.

Just the facts

- Flirting is a wonderful way of expressing interest in another without committing to a real date.

- Communication is the essence of flirting—from body language to tennis match conversation.

- One key to successful flirting is to keep it light.

- Flirting allows you to "test the waters" of a potential relationship without the risk of major rejection.

- Successful flirting can be taken in stages, from lighthearted first contact to an actual date.

Timesaver
If your relationship begins to be serious and looks as if it might lead to marriage, you can save a lot of time, trouble, pain, and struggle by having *pre-commitment counseling*. An experienced counselor or pastoral counselor can help you take a more objective look at your relationship and any problem patterns that might be developing, and fix them before they become ingrained.

GET THE SCOOP ON...
First impressions ▪ Dater's survival kit ▪
Control issues ▪ Rules for dating

Oh My Gosh!
It's a Date!

Chapter 9

When you actually have invited someone or been invited on a "real date"—which implies some interest in developing a relationship and intimacy—it's natural to be nervous about looking good. Taking the time to figure out appropriate clothing will give you the security of knowing you will make a good impression, at least visually.

There is such freedom of dress today that it's easy to get the impression that no one cares how you look, but don't get lured into that trap. The freedom we all have to dress as we like means the way you look is much more of an expression of your self than it used to be. How you dress sends several clear messages to the people who see you.

To get an idea of what messages clothing sends, just look through the ads of a few popular magazines. (I suggest magazines rather than other media, because they have still color photos you can look at long enough to evaluate the clothing.) Look at the way the models are dressed, what the ads are selling, and who they are selling to, and you'll see quickly how much information is conveyed by the style of dress. Clothing can suggest intelligence, youth, creativity, fun, a sense of self, and many other things.

Appearances count

Depending on your age range and lifestyle, what seems appropriate for you could be drastically different for what is appropriate for someone else. There are a few things to keep in mind when trying to decide what is appropriate clothing for this date:

- **Ask!** If you don't know what you'll be doing, or what is considered appropriate where you're going, ask your date or someone else who knows. If you've been asked to go to a wedding reception or a cocktail party, you'll dress very differently (one would hope) than for a picnic or a ball game. Don't be embarrassed by showing up for what turns out to be a roller skating date in a formal suit or dress.

- **Think attractive:** Go for what your date would find suitable and attractive —rather than what you'd like to wear. Don't be too flamboyant, too overdressed, or too underdressed. If you're going to make a mistake, err on the conservative side.

- **Think neat and clean:** The media have been showing unshaven male leads and tousseled, tight-sweatered, cleavaged female stars a lot lately, not to mention the "trainspotting" or "heroin chic" look, but if you show up looking unkempt or like Morticia Addams or Gabby Hayes, you might not get the same adulation. Until you know what your date likes, stick to the middle of the road. Be tidy, showered, shaven, and ironed.

■ **Think activity:** If you're going dancing, find out what kind of dancing. Country Western line dancing requires far different clothing than hip-hop, swing, or salsa. If the dancing is going to be very active, choose clothing that can take it. Don't have such cleavage that you'll be worried of falling out of it, or such tight jeans or boots that you get chafed when you begin to perspire from the activity. If you're going to dinner and a movie, are you going to a fast-food restaurant or a fancy eatery? If your date says you're going "for a walk," what kind of person is talking? Will a walk be a gentle stroll in the city, or a real hike in the desert? If you're not sure, just ask what to wear.

■ **Use caution:** If you have expensive jewelry, don't wear lots of it on your first dates, for three reasons:

1. You don't know if you'll be going somewhere where an expensive watch, ring, or other jewelry will make you a target for robbery.

2. You don't know your date that well yet, and you don't want to give the impression you're very wealthy (even if the jewelry is inherited, and you're poor).

3. You don't want your date to think you're flashing wealthy and privilege around.

■ **Have fun:** Wear colors you like, and something that looks and feels good on you. No matter what your age, weight, body size, proportions, or ethnicity, certain clothes will enhance what you have, others will detract. Learn how to make the best of your appearance, and you'll have more

Timesaver
If your date is after work and you've no time to go home and change, wear something basic for the day and bring some accessories to "dress" it up for the date. If you're wearing a suit, use a convertible shirt or blouse, replace the jacket with a sweater, change shoes, and you're a lot more casual. For evening, wear a dark suit or a plain dress, add jewelry or a nicer watch, a pocket handkerchief, and a bow tie. Voila! You're more formal.

fun because you feel good.

First impressions—visual messages

If you've made an obvious effort to prepare for this date, your clothes look good, your car (if you're using it) has been washed and vacuumed, and (if you suggested the evening) you have a plan and whatever is needed, your date will get the impression that this is important to you. This is exactly the image you want to create. Whether it's coffee out or dinner at your house, you can make an effort to show this is an important moment.

Following the suggestions presented so far will ensure your clothes give your date the impression that this date (and therefore your friend) is important to you. Once you get to know each other, you'll both pay less attention to the outside and more to the inside, but for now, remember that your partner is still gathering sensory information about you. Look your best.

Your fashion sense (for men, too)

In the media, fashion is a matter of the latest fads and designer names, but *your* fashion sense is the style of your clothes, how well they match, and what they say about who you are.

If you're beyond your early twenties, wearing the latest fad does not usually give a good impression. If a style (big chains, narrow ties, short skirts, the baggy look) looks silly on you, it doesn't matter how fashionable it is. On the other hand, if a current style suits you, adapt it a bit and make it your own. Walking around covered with designer logos does not make you look stylish, just slavish.

One way to adapt current styles to your own personality and needs is to look at the clothing depicted in magazines and advertisements. See which of the models have styles you like (for example, you like the way a scarf or hat is worn, you like the more casual or more preppy looking models), then adapt these looks to your own style.

As we explored in chapter four, learn how to dress in a style all your own, with the help of a stylish friend, if necessary. Selecting colors that look good on you and blend well, adding just the right accessories, and putting together a "look" that suits you will help you make a great impression, which you can adapt to various environments.

Putting together your survival kit

Because you're going out with someone you don't know well, and because the situation is new to you, be prepared for a variety of possibilities. If you put together a "kit," a collection of the things you might need, and make sure you have it with you, you'll find it comes in handy, and boosts your confidence. Put a kit like this together once, and you'll always have it, not just for your first date, but for all dates and travel.

Money/credit cards-ID/phone card

Hopefully, you've screened your date well enough that you can be sure he or she is reliable, but, just in case he or she becomes argumentative, hysterical, too aggressive sexually or otherwise, drinks too much, or is otherwise unpleasant, you need to be prepared to act independently.

This part of your kit consists of some extra "emergency" money beyond what you think you'll need for the evening. A fifty dollar bill tucked away in a side pocket of your purse or wallet is handy, as is a credit card, your identification, and a prepaid phone card.

Carry your driver's license and AAA card, if you have them. With these items you can always find a way to get home from where you are if your date drove or the car breaks down, or take care of yourself in any emergency.

Condoms and the "OSB" Kit

Even if you're determined not to have sex on this first date (which is a good idea), it's better to be safe than sorry. Men and women should both make it a habit to carry condoms. I recommend placing what I call an OSB (overnight shack bag) kit in your car. This kit contains your contraceptives, toothbrush, deodorant, shampoo, perhaps a change of underwear, and maybe even something casual to wear in the morning. This may seem as if you're working against yourself, but if you have this kit with you, you're prepared to stay in a hotel if you get stranded somewhere, and it gives you more flexibility and freedom. Such a kit can double as a travel bag to throw in your suitcase for instant packing.

Emergency stuff: Makeup, sewing kit, etc.

Have a few necessities with you just in case. Women will probably have what they need for makeup touch-ups and feminine hygiene, but even men should carry a little matchbox-sized sewing kit (the kind they give away in hotel rooms—these can also be bought at the drugstore), a couple of Band-aids, some individually wrapped towelettes, a nail file and clippers, a pocket knife, and a comb. These items fit easily in the glove box of a car, but if you're traveling by public transportation, you can make a small enough package to fit in an inside coat pocket, evening purse, or men's pocketbook.

These items come in handy in myriad ways, and

make it unnecessary for you to endure an evening with a missing button or a stain on your tie or blouse. Also, you'll look very resourceful should your date cut his or her finger, break a nail, or catch a sleeve on something and tear it. They also double as instant packing for travel.

Getting clear on who has control

Before you go on this date, make sure you have worked out who will be in control at what times, and in what situations. You don't want to be caught fighting with yourself over a decision when you need to make one.

Decide in advance what behaviors and situations will be acceptable to you and what won't. As long as you are comfortable and feel these boundaries have not been breached, you can relax and let your date be in charge, if that's what's happening. But, once a line is crossed, you must be willing to take control of yourself and not just go along with something you find uncomfortable, unacceptable, or dangerous.

First date—or later dates

Boundaries will be different on the first date than on later dates. The more you know your date, the more relaxed you can be. In the beginning, however, set the line pretty high. If your new date shows signs of rage, drunkenness, hysteria, rudeness, disrespect (such as leaving you alone and flirting with others), recklessness, or other embarrassing or dangerous behavior, do not be polite or tolerant. Remember, your date is supposed to be on his or her best behavior, and if you tolerate this, it will only get worse.

Don't hesitate to leave if you find yourself in a situation that makes you uncomfortable. If you're driving for both of you, tell your date you will take him or her home immediately. If you're not the one driving, tell your date you want to be driven home (unless the driver's been drinking too much), and if that doesn't work, get yourself home by taxi or public transportation.

Leave your date, male or female, at the restaurant, in a bar, at a party, or at a movie, if his or her behavior is seriously out of line. This is precisely the reason you prepared your emergency kit. If the date is your treat, leave enough money to pay the check, or see the waiter before you leave.

If you stick to your limits on the first date, you'll find that your date will get the message, and either move on to someone else (good riddance!), or apologize and correct the unacceptable behavior.

To avoid the possibility of finding yourself confused by unexpected problem situations, it's a good idea to think through the kinds of things that might occur on your date, and have a clear idea of where your limits are on each issue. Here are some areas where limit setting is important before you set out on your date:

- Your drink limit (driving and not driving)

- Your date's drink limit (driving and not driving)

- Behavior limits (rudeness, social acceptability)

- Sexual limits (don't allow yourself to be pressured)

- Territory limits (not going to dangerous places)

- Distance limits (not getting too far from home)

Who is this you're dating?
By now you should recognize the importance of get-

ting to know your partner as a friend before dating, but we can all be fooled at times, no matter how careful we try to be in selecting our dates. Should you find out that the person you thought you knew is too dangerous or bizarre or insensitive, be willing to change your mind. If you have been seeing this person in groups, as advised, you may, in rare cases, find that in private, or around alcohol, his or her behavior changes. No matter how well you think you know this person, be prepared to take care of yourself if necessary.

On the other hand, if your date turns out to be exactly who you hoped he or she would be, you can relax and have a wonderful time. If you've gotten to know your date as a friend first, the odds are excellent that you'll have a wonderful evening.

Modern dating etiquette

In today's world, the customs about who pays, who extends the invitation, and what it all means are all changing. If the old rules were just completely gone it would be easier, but they remain in the background, especially for those of us over forty, who were adults when the current changes began to take hold.

If you have gotten to know your date before this first official dating occasion, you will probably have an idea of how traditional or modern your date is, which will make figuring out who asks and who pays much easier. However, if you don't know, the best solution is to ask. If your date has asked you out, offer to pay your share when the bill comes, just in case. If you are the one making the offer, and you want to share the costs, make that clear at the point of asking.

If you want to keep your relationship on an equal

basis, and your date pays for an evening, make sure you make the invitation and pay the next time.

If you allow your date to pay for most of your dates you'll find there are resulting expectations. Be careful that you know what it means when the other person buys expensive dinners or orchestra row tickets, and sends flowers. Accepting such lavish attentions doesn't mean you have to go along with what is expected in return, but it can set up a very uncomfortable situation when you have to say "no."

What is safe?

The more you know your date, the better your chances of being safe. If you've never been alone together, however, use some caution until you know how safe things are. One of the safest ways to get to know a potential partner socially is by dating in groups. But make sure that you know some members of the group well. There is safety in numbers.

Of course, if the entire group is known only to your date, you need to be cautious. Until you know how much the group is likely to drink, and whether there is a designated driver, you should probably drive your own car and meet them. This way you maintain your independence from the group, should the situation get too boisterous.

Your physical safety is clearly important. If you've gotten to know your date, and you keep your ability to think clearly, you're unlikely to encounter too many problems. But if you're still in the "finding out" stage of dating, there are some real danger areas to be careful about.

Alcohol abuse. Alcohol is a major cause of violence, death, and relationship difficulties. Overindulging in drink is a sure recipe for disaster. Know what your limit is, and keep an eye on your date. If

Moneysaver
If your incomes or financial status differ, you don't have to invite your date to as expensive an evening as you were treated to. You can be creative in coming up with inexpensive dating plans. A picnic, homemade dessert after a little theater production, a college ball game, or a free gallery opening can all be lovely, cheap dates.

you drive, don't drink. If your date drinks, don't let him or her drive. If you want to live for another date, and if you want your relationship to succeed, you'll do whatever is necessary to control your own drinking, and you won't accept a date's excessive drinking.

Safe-driving issues. As an author on tour, I arrive in a city and usually am picked up at my hotel by an escort, who takes me from appointment to appointment and drops me off at the airport at the end of the day. Most of these escorts are wonderful, knowledgeable, and have very nice cars. One very young man, however, showed up in an old VW sedan that looked like it was held together by chewing gum and which he drove like the Starship USS Enterprise. I spent the entire day holding my breath, praying that we'd make the next appointment in one piece. As soon as he left me at the airport, I dissolved in tears of relief. Driving with a complete stranger, in an unreliable car, can be terrifying.

But it's not just the condition of the car that you need to concern yourself with. Your date can be very reliable in every area, yet reckless behind the wheel. Don't agree to a date that requires a long drive until you know what a short drive with your new friend is like.

Lonely or dangerous spots. If your date has the poor judgment to suggest you go into a lonely or dangerous spot on your first date, there's only one sensible thing to do: refuse. There is no crying need to spend a date in a scary part of town, or miles away from nowhere.

If, on a later date, you do find some reason to go far away, be sure you trust the person you're going with. It certainly wouldn't hurt to have a cell phone with you. If your date is somewhat of a daredevil, pay close attention, and don't be led into doing things that are too dangerous. There's a big difference between being a good sport and being foolhardy. In short, take good care of yourself.

Your place or mine? Inviting a virtual stranger into your home, or going to his or her home, is not a good idea. You could be setting yourself up for robbery, date rape, or just a difficult time extricating yourself from an uncomfortable situation. If you know your date well, have made friends first, and spent time in group situations, you may have already been in each others' homes, and the decision to go there is a much easier one.

Watch Out!
It is very common for people to ask you out in order to "case" your home for a possible later theft. If you are wearing expensive clothes and jewelry or watch when you meet your new date, he or she may romance you to get close to your assets, not your heart. Be careful.

Whose place you decide to go to, and when, will depend on many circumstances. The easiest way to do it is for one of you to invite the other over for dinner, or to watch a video or special televised event such as the Academy Awards or Monday Night Football. Keep in mind that being in a date's home, unless there are roommates, children, or other people present, is usually interpreted by at least one of you to be an opportunity to have sex. If you have any doubts, talk about expectations beforehand.

Of course, if you have children at home, it is especially essential that you be completely certain of the safety and reliability of your dating partner before you invite him or her to your place. And it is equally important that you prepare your children for the prospect of meeting your new interest beforehand.

Children and dating. If you have children, the necessity for caution is especially strong. As you'll learn in greater detail in Chapter 13, your personal relationships—and especially your sexual relationships—should not be obvious to your children, and you must behave very conservatively in front of them with your date. Remember, when you bring a date home, your children are vulnerable. They will be exposed to your date's behavior and attitudes. Their safety depends on your judgment and caution.

Sexual safety. Sexual safety is a critical issue in modern times. In Chapter 2, we discussed sexually transmitted diseases, and what to do to prevent them. On the first date, even though you don't expect to have sex, you should be prepared with condoms. It is far too easy to get carried away in the moment to take the chance of finding yourself without protection.

Whatever your attitudes or expectations about sex, before you get to the point where you're doing it, you should talk with your date about it. This needn't come up on the first date, unless you're feeling that there are expectations you want to confront, or fully intend to become physically involved very quickly.

While many people shy away from this kind of conversation with somebody they've only recently begun dating, there's no reason to feel awkward. After all, if you are intimate enough to have sex, you should also be intimate enough to talk openly about your expectations, your wants, and your fears about sex.

If you have rules about not having sex on the first date, and your date seems to be signalling that a sexual encounter is expected, for example, by asking you in for a drink, your best option is to talk about it.

You can minimize you awkwardness by making sure that you know your own thoughts about when it's OK to have sex, and what it means. If you can be casual about sex, and not get emotionally bonded to your partner prematurely, deciding how soon you have sex will be a lot easier decision than if it means you expect monogamy and bonding.

But do understand that having sex on the first date makes it much more likely that there will not be a second date. Although some people do follow through after a "one-night stand," the phrase exists because most people don't take a relationship seriously if sex happens too soon.

So, before you go out with somebody with whom a sexual relation is likely, make certain that you are clear on your own sexual expectations. To help you find that sense of clarity, here are some questions to ask yourself about your expectations of your partner:

- Do you expect that you and your partner should be sexually monogamous?

- Do you expect that both of you will use safe sex techniques?

- Do you feel it important for both of you to be tested for STD's before becoming sexual?

- Do you have rules about sexual conduct or demonstrations of physical intimacy in front of your children?

- How do you feel about such demonstrations in front of friends—whether they're your friends or his?

- What do you feel about steamy phone calls at work?

Before you have sex with your date, whether on the first date or later, make sure both of you understand each other's sexual expectations.

Another ground rule you may need to establish about sex is where it is likely to happen, although this concern may be premature for the first date. If

> **❝**
> [Miss Manners] would have to spell out what the term "one-night-stand" meant and explain that no, dear, she could not chastise a participant for not calling and sending flowers the next day, because these gestures had to do with another, unrelated social form called courtship.
> — Judith Martin, in *Miss Manners Guide to the New Millennium*
> **❞**

you or your date have roommates, live with parents or children, or live in a close-knit neighborhood where your neighbors will notice an overnight guest, you may have some trouble finding a place to go. If you are uncomfortable having sex in your date's home, or in your own, this is definitely something to talk about in advance.

Setting your standards

We all have minimim standards of behavior that we expect from the people with whom we associate. But sometimes, in the first flush of romance, you can lose track of the standards you would otherwise set. In addition to the obvious things like whether your date can smoke around you, or drink before driving, or how much you yourself can safely drink, there are certain rules you should set for *yourself* in order to make this first date a success.

Keeping your cool

Getting to the point of a first date is exciting and energizing. Of course you should have fun and enjoy the moment, but if you get too excited, anxious, and giddy, you might come on too strong. It's important that your anxiety not mask the real you.

Keep your thoughts on the reality that this is just a first date, and you don't know what is going to happen to the relationship. Pay attention to what you are learning about your date, and allow the relationship to develop slowly over many dates like this.

Charming is as charming does

Remember how powerful your smile can be, and use your eye contact and tennis match techniques to keep the conversation flowing. Think about what interests you about your date, and show interest in his or her opinions, experiences, and activities. Be complimentary whenever possible, and respond intelligently to whatever is said to you.

In spite of what I have said about all these cautions and safety factors, the best thing you can do is keep your date light and easy, and have a good time. If you keep the focus of your attention on being pleasant, having fun, and not getting too far ahead of the relationship, you will be great company.

You can talk about anything, including your personal lives, past relationships, and love in general, but don't be the one who brings up the intimate topics first. Be careful not to pry too deeply into your date's private life and secrets, unless the information is voluntarily offered.

Keep your focus on learning about your date and don't get into talking too much about yourself. Dole out some information about you, especially if it relates to what your date is saying, but don't let yourself talk endlessly about your own life, opinions, experiences, or activities.

Pay attention! You have things to learn here!

The most important aspect of this date, in addition to having a good time, is to get to know each other better. No matter how excited, turned on, or thrilled you may be about this date, listening to what your date says, watching what your date does, and understanding how your date feels are still your primary objectives.

One of the easiest ways to lose your objectivity and balance in this is to let yourself worry about what your date thinks about you. I call this "getting into your date's head." If you spend your time essentially trying to look at yourself through your date's eyes, guessing what he or she is seeing when looking at you, or hearing when listening to you, you'll miss what's really happening. It's a very self-involved thing to do, and it makes it impossible for you to relate intelligently to your date.

What your date thinks of you is not really your business. You have a responsibility to pay attention so you know what YOU think of your date. Hopefully, in all these considerations, because you've thought about the serious issues in advance, you'll still be able to relax and have a good time—so good that you decide to keep dating each other.

And if *that* happens, you'll have a whole new world of dating experiences to learn about and enjoy. In the next chapter you'll find everything you need to know to handle a deepening personal relationship with style.

Just the facts

- Dressing appropriately for your first date will help give you confidence.

- Keep an emergency kit with you on your date— with everything from contraceptives to transportation money—so you can handle any eventuality that arises.

- Be clear on your own personal safety rules before you go out on a date, and feel confident about enforcing them if the need arises.

- Maintain your standards for behavior—don't accept unacceptable behavior simply to seem like a good sport.

- Remember that a first date is a time to learn more about your partner—pay attention.

Chapter 10

GET THE SCOOP ON...
Emotional and sexual intimacy ▪ Sex
and commitment ▪ Performance
anxieties ▪ Saying no

Becoming Intimate

If you've been on several dates with this new person, you'll soon be creating intimacy in a number of ways. You have begun to know each other a bit, and if your dates have been going well, you probably feel very good about each other. The next hurdle to get over is intimacy.

- **Mental intimacy** is what you feel when you know a lot about each other, you've shared ideas, and you are excited by getting to know each other.

- **Emotional intimacy.** When you've spent positive time in each other's company, enjoyed it, experienced give-and- take, and created mutual understanding, you begin to bond, to feel emotionally connected and linked to each other.

- **Spiritual intimacy** is a little more elusive, but occurs when your beliefs and values closely match those of your partner, and you can talk deeply about the meaning and purpose of life.

- **Physical intimacy** begins when you first are face

237

to face, and your sensory system begins to take in the sight, smell, sound, warmth, and touch of each other. From sitting close in a restaurant, to hugging, touching, kissing, and caressing, physical intimacy is built slowly to the climax of sexual contact.

Of all these kinds of intimacy, emotional and physical intimacy are the ones which cause the most anxiety and problems.

Emotional intimacy

Emotional intimacy can be simultaneously the source of great joy and pleasure *and* the cause of great pain and disappointment. It is what we long for and seek out, yet, when something goes wrong, we are deeply hurt.

Emotional intimacy grows over time, and is formed in layers, as we get to know each other. After just a few dates, you can feel very close to someone, but, if everything goes well, in the months and years to come your intimacy will deepen. But bonding too quickly to someone you don't really know can be a painful process if, when the truth comes out, you are bonded to someone who isn't capable of really caring about you, or who just doesn't feel the same.

If you hold back a little, remembering to be cautious, until you have a chance to find out who you're dealing with, you are more likely to reach true intimacy with someone worthy of your love.

Sexual intimacy

If the chemistry is there, sexual intimacy is pretty easy to create. When you get together with someone who "turns you on," the issue is more about whether you should resist it, and how to say no. The problem that comes up with sexual intimacy, in addition to

Unofficially...
Trust is an emotional form of credit. Just as you would not give all your money to a stranger just because you liked him, don't give complete trust to a likeable stranger. Rather, let your trust build over time. If a friend proves to be fair and good with money, you get more and more willing to trust her with it. Dole out your emotional trust the same way.

the ever-present health issues, is will you bond more to the person after sex, and do you know it's emotionally safe for you to do that?

Are you ready?

Have you worked through the leftovers from your last relationship? Can you be open to whatever kinds of intimacy are appropriate with this date? Readiness for a new relationship doesn't mean that every problem you've ever had has been solved, but new intimacy will tend to bring up old fears.

If you've worked through the leftover hurt, grief, fear, and abandonment of your previous relationships, you will at least be familiar with the causes of these fears when they arise. Readiness means that when old hurts come up you can recognize them, explain them to your partner, and not blame this partner for problems you bring into the relationship. If your current date does something (such as show up late) that is different from, but reminds you of, your previous partner (who stayed late after work to cheat on you), you need to be able to know the difference, and let this new partner know what bothers you so much, and why.

If you're comfortable and familiar with your fears, hurts, and grief, you'll be able to talk about them when they come up, and they won't get in the way of developing intimacy. In fact, a good, open discussion about your mutual fears and past hurts can considerably deepen your intimacy.

Addiction and abuse problems also indicate that you (or your date) have work to do before you'll be ready for intimacy.

Do you know the rules and regs?

Before moving into the deeper stages of dating and

Watch Out!
If you have problems with sexual activity stemming from childhood abuse, rape, incest, or other serious issues, physical intimacy can be a real problem. Do yourself (and your partner) a favor and get professional help to work out those issues before getting seriously involved. Don't get involved with someone who has such problems and has not gotten counseling.

relationship, make sure you have a clear idea of your rules and regulations for intimacy. Here are a few suggestions:

- Don't try to develop intimacy with someone still in or fresh out of a previous relationship.

- Do discuss hopes and dreams.

- Do discuss your mutual hurts and fears.

- Do talk about what each of you wants in a relationship.

- Don't assume having sex means a commitment.

- Do discuss sexual rules. (see below)

- Do talk about what troubles you in your new relationship.

- Do talk about what you like about this relationship.

- Do discuss prior relationships as a learning exercise.

- Don't expect your partner (or yourself) to be perfect.

- Do discuss problems that come up between you.

- Do discuss what you like and don't like.

- Don't rush things—allow them to develop.

- Don't accept or excuse bad behavior or rudeness—confront it.

Your personal rules for developing intimacy may be different from these, but take the time to write them down and know what they are.

Have the two of you talked?

If you and your partner are going to have a successful relationship, you need to be able to discuss intimacy, sex, and feelings. Bringing up your "rules," and asking your partner to come up with some also, so you can work out a mutual list, is a good way to begin talking about the relationship itself—what you want and how it's going.

The safer sex discussion. Unfortunately, the nature of the times has made a difficult, awkward discussion one of the first you need to have. Because couples tend to be sexual relatively quickly in this liberated age, and because of the danger of sexually transmitted diseases, it is imperative to have a safer sex discussion before you have sexual contact, which will probably mean having it early in your dating.

Because it is awkward, bring it up as soon as the conversation and your connection seem to be leading toward a sexual relationship. You can begin by bringing it up in the abstract ("This whole idea of safer sex seems important, but difficult to talk about"), which makes it a little less embarrassing, or you can bring it up indirectly ("One of the things I miss about being in a relationship is not having to think about issues like safer sex").

To have the discussion, you need to be prepared with a definition of what safer sex is, and what you are and are not willing to do. Alternatively, you may want to talk about not having sex before marriage. Either way, it's essential that you talk about it, when the whole idea of a sexual relationship first arises.

The "you want/I want" discussion. Any couple is bound to have some differences in what they want in a relationship. Such issues as whether you want to date exclusively, and exactly what that means, or how often you want to see each other, how many phone calls is too many, what you do with friends, how to

Bright Idea
Initiate "state of the union" meetings between you and your partner, in which you talk about your relationship and how it's going. You don't have to formally schedule it, as you would family meeting. You can just ask "how do you feel about the way we get along?" and (perhaps with a little more prompting) the discussion will take off from there.

handle dating expenses, and what time you have available for each other are all important issues to discuss, and you can differ on any or all of them.

The "it means what?" discussion. What does love mean? Some use it to mean obligation: "If you love me you'll..." Some use it for dependency: "I love you, I can't live without you." Some use it for ownership: "We're in love, we belong to each other." Some use it for charity: " I do this for you because I love you."

What does dating every weekend mean? Are you "going steady"? What does that mean? Are you in a relationship? What does relationship mean? How much commitment does it entail? Is it an exclusive, monogamous relationship?

What does having sex mean? If you have sex, are you in a committed relationship? Does it mean your partner will now be faithful and monogamous?

What does it mean if you're introduced to your date's friends and/or family? Does it mean you're getting serious? What does that mean?

In order to know what is meant by such ambiguous words and actions, you need to have specific conversations about what your individual definitions, without being side-tracked into who's right or wrong. The more open and mutually understanding your discussion of these concepts is, the better chance you'll have of reaching an agreement about what each term means.

The "I'm afraid of..." discussion. One of the most valuable talks you and your date can have is about what scares you about commitment and relationships. If you're getting serious about your relationship, you need to know what the sensitive places are.

Talking about the problems in your past relationships, the ways you've been hurt before, and what your concerns are for the future will help you to know where problems can arise, so you can either avoid them or deal with them early.

Avoiding discussion at all. In my relationship counseling practice, most of the couples I see who are having severe relationship problems have not been able to talk to each other about difficult issues, so they remained silent, piling up resentment, until it began to eat away at their love.

The most tempting thing is to avoid talking about topics that can be uncomfortable, embarrassing, and awkward. It seems easier to avoid them. This is a big mistake, because one of the essential skills you'll need to make your relationship work is the ability to talk about uncomfortable topics. Avoiding discussion of uncomfortable topics—and avoid taking responsibility for your actions—is accomplished in a variety of ways. The two most common excuses are:

1. **"Gosh, was I drunk!"** A very common way to avoid talking or having to confront sexual rules directly is to have too much to drink, and wind up having sex without any forethought or safety precautions whatsoever. This ploy is known as "Gosh, was I drunk" because that's what people say the next day. However, if you avoid talking about sexual issues this way, you not only endanger your health, you also avoid creating true intimacy, and any chance at a real relationship is doomed.

2. **"I didn't practice safe sex because it was a surprise."** Another popular way to avoid taking responsibility for having sex is to not be prepared because you "aren't planning to do anything." Almost every pregnant teen uses this excuse, but adults who should know better have

often used it, too. Take the time and trouble to be prepared, and you'll gain the respect of your partner, and protect your own health.

Taking responsibility for intimacy

I highly recommend not having your first sexual intimacy if you have been drinking. If you have to get drunk to have sex, what does that say about your intimacy?

When you have make love for the first time, respect yourself enough to wait until you feel prepared, and you've discussed all the important rules and agreements. In our society, we have made sex such a significant act that it's easy to feel pressured. You should know what sexual intimacy means before you get there.

Often the pressure you feel actually comes from yourself. You can pressure yourself in a lot of ways: "If I don't have sex, he won't like me." "If I don't make a move, she'll think I don't care about her." This kind of mental harassment makes it difficult for you to think clearly and make a sound decision.

Even if you don't pressure yourself, you may get pressure from your date. If your date uses guilt, pleading, or threatening, or pressures you in any way, that should be reason enough to say no, not only to sex, but also to future dating.

Are you equipped?

Once you've made the decision to be sexually intimate, it is your responsibility to make certain that you are properly prepared and equipped. Here are the key areas to consider once you've decided to be sexually active with your new partner.

- **The OSB**. Every date, every time (until you're at that point where you can leave a few things at your date's house), your OSB kit should come with you. Your kit should contain contraceptives (women may want to investigate a diaphragm and contraceptive gel, which helps protect against disease as well as pregnancy—your local Planned Parenthood Clinic is a great place to go for information), toothbrush, change of underwear, and anything else you think you might need should you decide to have sex, along with credit card, ID, extra money, sewing kit, Band-aids, and aspirin.

The importance of being equipped cannot be overemphasized. Your kit means you can be independent and leave if anything goes wrong (even if you didn't drive), and you are prepared for whatever happens.

■ **Where and when**. Make sure you feel good about where and when you decide to be sexually intimate. If you're serious about creating a relationship, mutual respect is essential, and where and when you have sex makes a big difference in how you feel about each other.

For couples whose trust is fully established, I often recommend a little "sleazy" sex, experimentation, and acting out fantasies. It can be a lot of fun and recharge things. But sexuality is a delicate thing, and in a new relationship, too much adventure or spontaneity can leave the wrong impression. By all means have a good time, and enjoy what you're doing, but pay attention to how your partner is reacting, and be careful that the heat of the moment doesn't create a negative image of who you are.

- **Dealing with children**. In Chapter 13, I emphasize over and over that children should not have any awareness of your sexual relationship until your status as a couple is secure. If you are becoming serious, by all means introduce your date to your children (as a friend only), and get to know your date's children. But **do not** make your children your confidantes, and **do not** make your sexual or romantic relationship obvious to them.

Modern sex and old-fashioned commitment

Social mores have certainly changed in the last couple of generations. Divorce, living together, single parenthood, and a vastly freer sexuality have become the norm. However, when it comes to serious relationships, people are still looking for reliability, trustworthiness, and commitment, and they tend to make these judgments by observing behavior. So, if you're very free and easy with your favors (whether you're male or female), you're sending a message that you are not reliable enough for a long-term relationship. You need to know what you want and behave accordingly.

Are you looking for commitment, or just fun?

If all you want out of this dating experience is a good time, affection, and sex, that's your right and your decision. All you need to do is be honest and clear about that, so your partner doesn't develop other expectations.

However, if you want to build something more serious, "walk your talk." That means, your actions should be consistent with your words. If you want to attract a solid, reliable, loving partner, be exactly that, and don't waste too much time on a partner who isn't like that. Don't fall into the trap of thinking your partner will change. Dating is a "best behavior" time. Your date won't get more affectionate, reliable, sincere, or honest as he or she gets more committed. Rather, as the two of you get more comfortable and relax, your behavior will get more casual and relaxed also.

If relaxing your behavior will be an improvement, then making a commitment will be great. If it will make things intolerable, you may want to reconsider this person.

What about your partner?

Do you know whether your date is just having fun, or looking for something more? Fun without commitment is fine, if you both know that's what you want. If one of you wants commitment and the other is just having fun, someone is going to get hurt.

To prevent needless hurt feelings, be sure you both attach the same meaning to dating and especially to sexual intimacy. Having sex with someone who thinks it means commitment when you aren't interested in a serious relationship is just asking for a disaster.

The only way out of the problem is communication. If you are clear about whether you're trying to build something lasting, or you are just having a good time, and your partner is equally clear, then you will probably be able to work out what you are doing together. By communicating, you'll eliminate most problems, unless your partner is willing to lie to you to get what he or she wants. To find out if your partner is "walking the talk," and telling the truth, pay close attention to all his or her actions. Before long, the actions will tell you more than the words.

Don't be another notch in the bedpost—unless you want to

If you're really enjoying someone's company, but you want a commitment and he or she doesn't, it's tempting to go along hoping that your partner will change his or her mind. This is almost guaranteed to wind up hurting a lot. You'll feel very used if you allow yourself to get attached, and then find out your partner doesn't want to get serious. If someone tells you he or she is not interested in commitment, pay close attention, and believe what you hear.

No assumptions, please

If you don't talk clearly about what you want, you'll be making assumptions about what your partner is doing and thinking. While it can be helpful to "read" your date's behavior to make sure the actions bear out the talk, don't assume you're always getting it right. Assumptions always lead to confusion. If you are not sure what your partner means, or you are getting mixed messages, ASK.

Don't assume that your partner means what you would mean if you did or said the same thing. Again, successfully discussing the difference between your assumptions and your date's intent sets a pattern for communication throughout your relationship.

Sexual performance

When you decide to be sexually intimate with a new partner, especially if you have high hopes for the relationship, sexual performance can be a big issue. Everyone wonders whether they are going to be good enough to make a partner happy. To add to that anxiety, we all have seen lots of sex in movies, TV, books and plays, where sex is either glamorized or demonized, depending upon the particular show. Don't fall into the trap of expecting your real-life sex to be like this movie simulation.

Keep in mind that sex is just another form of communication, and must be worked out again with each new partner. Whatever you did with your last partner may not work with this one. Approach sexual intimacy as an opportunity to learn about yourself and your partner, and you'll avoid a lot of anxiety.

What's your experience?

Have you had lots of sexual experience, or just a little? Is your attitude toward sex positive, or are there some problems? If you have serious sexual problems in your history—abuse, rape or incest—you will need get some counseling to resolve those issues and be ready for an intimate relationship.

If you have only a little experience, even though it was positive, you may feel intimidated by the possibility of having sex with a more experienced partner. If you regard every sexual encounter as a learning opportunity, a lack of prior experience becomes less of a problem, because in terms of *this* relationship, both you and your date are equally inexperienced.

Your partner's?

Your partner may also have some problems with sexual history, and issues to deal with. You can become partners in your healing process as well as lovers, if you remember to pay close attention to each other, rather than reaching for some sexual performance ideal that is not realistic. This is one place where learning to talk comfortably about sex in the early part of your dating experience lays the groundwork for communication as your relationship progresses. If you begin by talking about sex in a matter-of-fact manner, by the time you get to discussing a commitment, open, honest, and loving sexual discussions should be routine.

Are you teaching or learning?

If you have less experience than your partner, you may feel a little less secure, and more passive, seeking to learn from your more experienced date. If you are the one with more experience, you may take a teaching role. What works best is for both of you to learn from each other. No matter how little experience you have, you still have your own senses and sexual responses, and your partner has never experienced you before. So, you have a lot to teach. No matter how much experience you have, this partner is a brand-new deal, and you have lots to learn.

Sexual sharing is a matter of teaching and learning simultaneously, being open to your partner's ideas and feelings, and discovering and growing together.

Sex is a laughing matter

We in America tend to overdramatize and overemphasize the importance of sexuality, because we have been taught to be ashamed, embarrassed, guilty, and generally uncomfortable about it. It's hard to be relaxed about something so taboo we can't talk about it in public, yet so tantalizing we even sell cars, politicians and shampoo with it. No wonder our sexual behavior and attitudes are fraught with unnecessary drama.

Rarely is any of us taught that sex is natural, fun, simple, and a blessing. We cannot freely say no, and we cannot freely say yes. It is possible to have sex in a healthy, responsible manner and still be lighthearted about it. You'll be a lot more successful if you add laughter and humor, hope and happiness into your sexual life.

Your most memorable sexual experiences will turn out to be the ones with laughter, even with tears—the ones that felt as though it didn't matter what you were doing, because you cared, you were close and in harmony.

TV and movies rarely show the delightful humorous side of lovemaking: laughing because the doorbell rang just at the "big moment", or because the cat picked that very time to jump on the bed and throw up, or because we got tangled in the fancy new bedspread.

Sharing a sad, intimate moment and gently moving from tears to lovemaking—somehow these moments become more memorable than having orgasms all night long. When you remember your lovemaking, it's not the sex that counts, it's the love. Sex is a fine and glorious way to communicate love, and to share all dimensions of your selves: physical, mental, emotional and spiritual. Sex is an adult form of play.

Our bodies are no less than miracles. We come fully equipped, no batteries needed, to share our joy and our humanness: mentally, emotionally and physically. The only restrictions we have are inherent in the equipment: keep it healthy, don't abuse it, play nice and respect each others' toys.

You can relax and enjoy your sexual selves. Often the only obstacle is your own resistance to the ease and pleasure of it all. Sex could become more fun, with more laughter than you have ever known: giggles, guffaws, and smiles.

Potential problems

Like any other form of communication, sex will present some problems at some time. If you approach sexual problems by blaming, criticizing or calling each other wrong, you will create a true relationship disaster. If you approach it by working together to

> 66
> It's sad to think of all the people who have been convinced that their preferences, sex drives, or intimate sounds are weird or wrong. In response, they learn to hide or to be self-conscious about who they really are sexually. What a painful decision with lifelong consequences.
> —Sex therapist Marty Klein in the *New Age Journal.*
> 99

work it out, you'll find lots of possible solutions that will work for both of you. Here are some common problems areas in sex, and ways to overcome them:

- **Anxiety**. If you find that your sexual performance, or that of your partner, is hampered by anxiety, pay attention to your (or your partner's) feelings they are trying to tell you something. Does either of you feel pressured or uncomfortable about the sexual situation? If so, you need to talk about it. If the anxiety comes from something in your past, discuss it with your partner. Anxiety that is truly debilitating, and brings on shortness of breath, panic attacks, or other physical symptoms, is a clear indicator that therapy would be a good idea.

- **Different wants**. The most common sexual problem couples have is a difference in the frequency of sexual contact that each person wants. The person who wants sex less often will constantly feel pressured, and the one who wants it more often will feel deprived.

  Treat this like any other differences that you work together to solve as a team, both of you caring about each other's satisfaction and happiness. There's such a huge variety of sexual acts, you will most likely be able to work out an amicable solution. If you find that you're unable to discuss your sexual differences without a struggle, and you want the relationship to continue, the most effective thing you can do is to seek counseling.

- **Taboos**. Often couples run into problems when what one person wants is "taboo" to the other.

Some people love giving or receiving oral sex, others find it objectionable. These personal objections are very deeply rooted, and often not easily changed. If your desires and taboos are too drastically different, your sexual connection may just be unworkable. Again, if the relationship has developed into something significant, and these taboos get in the way, the only means of working out the problem may be couples counseling.

- **Performance problems.** Difficulty in sexual performance problems can be caused by emotional or physical problems. Men who have diabetes, prostate surgery or take blood pressure medications are often unable to get erections. There are several mechanical devices, such as penile implants, and also the new drug, Viagra, were developed to handle these problems, and none of them were perfect.

Men can also be unable to have erections for emotional reasons. Stress, anxiety, sexual abuse and insecurity can have the same result. Premature ejaculation is usually an easily solvable problem which is a hangover from adolescence.

Women can be unable to accept vaginal intercourse, or not able to have orgasms, or have severe, painful dryness problems due to menopause or hysterectomy, and the same problems can be due to anxiety, stress, rape and sexual abuse, and also insecurity.

If any of these problems occur, consult a medical doctor (Internist, General Practitioner, Urologist or Gynecologist) first, to make sure

Timesaver
If uncomfortable sexual issues arise, see a sex counselor right away, even if you're not sure where this relationship is going. You'll save a lot of time and heartache if you get a professional evaluation early. Knowing what you can expect, and what's changeable and what's not, can save you a long, fruitless struggle.

the cause is not organic, and if everything is OK medically, a sex therapist can help you either solve the problem or work around it to create mutual sexual satisfaction.

- **Sexual communication and problem solving**. If your relationship is growing, sooner or later you will get to a point where you want (or need) to open up your sexual communication. The following exercise will help.

    1. Begin by asking your partner to risk telling you one small truth. The truth can be about anything: something he or she likes or doesn't like about sex; a fear about your friendship with someone; concerns about body image. Then take whatever time is necessary to be able to respond calmly. Take a few deep breaths if you get anxious or if your feelings are hurt. Respond by repeating in your own words what was said, or ask for more explanation if you need it. Once you both agree that you understand, then share your feelings about the truth your partner has expressed. Put as much gentleness and understanding into this process as you can.

    2. Then share a truth yourself, and give your partner time to hear and react to it. Ask for a guarantee of gentleness; don't share your truth until your partner can guarantee this. After you have shared, listen calmly and openly to your partner's feelings about what you have just said.

    3. Repeating this process a few times in one session will give you a sense of what sexual honesty feels like. If you and your partner

practice this exercise over several months, you'll find that your trust will grow. Once the two of you have developed a loving atmosphere free of fear, being honest and trusting about sexual matters will come more naturally.

4. An important side benefit of this exercise is that your sexual encounters will improve. Trust between partners provides a sense of security and an environment conducive to relaxed, open, and free sexual expression. When you both know that you can say whatever comes to mind without fear of a negative response, you open mental doors that can lead to very close connections.

5. As you build this trust, you will be more and more able to solve whatever sex-related problems and issues come up between you. The key to sexual problem solving is open communication. Once you have that, then, even if the problem is medically related, or related to an abusive past, you can work together to get the expert help you need.

■ **Kinkiness, outright weirdness, severe problems**. Be aware that some of the problems resulting from rape, incest and abuse are so severe that your partner may not be capable of having a healthy sexual relationship until that work is done in therapy. If your partner's sexual behavior seems too weird or scary for you, do not allow yourself to be drawn into things you won't feel good about later.

A little kinkiness, such as playing fantasy games, can be fun if you are both enjoying it. But, if the games get too intense or scary for you, stop

> 66
> There are sexual behaviors that are destructive, of course, and others that are unpleasant, unhealthy, unusual, boring and even offensive. But note that our feelings accrue not to the act but to the way it affects the people involved. Oral sex isn't abnormal, but doing it when you don't want to is unhealthy
> —Dr. Klein
> 99

immediately. Ask for a time out, and discuss what's happening. If your partner is too intensely involved in some kind of sex that's not comfortable for you (bondage, discipline, cross-dressing, fetishism, and so on), you may want to reconsider whether you want the relationship to go any further.

What to expect after

When you have your first sexual intimacy in a new relationship, what happens after depends largely on the preparation beforehand. If you have been following your "tennis match" conversational guidelines, and therefore created a relationship of mutual energy, most likely you will know who is to call whom.

Good communication beforehand will let both of you know what the other's expectations are, and create a feeling of mutual respect and responsibility that should prevent any big disappointments. A friendship built before any intimacy began means that both of you will be concerned about each other, and both will want to make sure that intimacy doesn't end the friendship.

If, on the other hand, you have leapt into intimate contact without looking, you can expect that your partner will not feel responsible for calling you the next day.

Beware of obsessing

Sexual intimacy often tempts people to obsess on the partner and the relationship. If things go well, being all starry-eyed afterwards is fun, and you should enjoy it. However, if thinking about the relationship begins to interfere with your life, or your work, if you can't get your regular chores done, or if you begin to cut off contact with all your friends and focus solely on the relationship, you're getting into unhealthy territory.

If you find the relationship is taking over your life to an unhealthy degree, a few counseling sessions can be very helpful in getting you back in balance. This is especially true if the relationship *doesn't* work out, and you obsess on why the partner didn't call, what happened, etc. If you had a connection, it's natural to be disappointed and grieve, but if you're seeing the above signs of obsession, contact a therapist right away.

Handling euphoria

If things are going well, keeping your feet on the ground while your head is in the clouds will be your biggest problem. Euphoria, giddiness, silliness and irresponsibility can easily result when the first impact of successful intimacy hits you.

Walking around with silly smile on your face, telling your friends how wonderful it all is, and fantasizing about the future are all symptoms of what has been called "limerance" the giddiness that you feel when you enter a state of new love and lust. It is harmless, unless it impairs your judgement and you begin making bad decisions based on fantasy.

Keep in mind that all relationships have problems, and if you can't see what your problems could be, you are probably not being very realistic. Remember that a new love is not going to solve every thing in your life, either, and your job, your car, your family and friends still require your attention.

Co-dependency, that unhealthy love that leads to disaster, comes from loving your partner, or even the idea of a relationship, more than you love yourself. Check yourself out in the mirror every day, and remind yourself that you are the person who is responsible for your happiness, not this new addition to your life. This is great for now, but in the long run, whether the relationship succeeds or fails, you will still be here with you.

Taking care of yourself

Whether your relationship has been successful or is having problems, you need to focus on your own life, and taking care of yourself. When you're not with your date, you have a lot of responsibilities. Your friends, family, children, work, whatever is important to you should remain important.

If someone new begins to take up some of your time, of course you'll have to re-evaluate your schedule, and a new relationship will use up some of the time you have for friends but if you find yourself dropping all your friends and activities, it's a warning sign. Look at it this way. If your date falls in love with you, he or she is loving the person you are right now. If you abandon who you are, and make too many changes, you are no longer the person you were when your date fell in love.

Just saying no

There are many reasons why you may want to say no to further intimacy with this date. Some are temporary, some permanent. Knowing how to say no in a way that can be heard and understood will make this difficult task much easier.

Whether you've decided that you are not really compatible, or you find out things about your date that you don't approve of, or your sexual relationship is not working, you have a right and a responsibility to yourself to say no directly, and not let things drag on.

Moneysaver
More money has been squandered on new love than on anything else in the history of the world. When you're in the early stages of euphoric new love, do not make any big financial decisions, such as buying a house together, moving in, or even getting married. Talk about possibilities, but make sure you're thinking clearly, and you have someone you can trust before making any financial commitments here.

It's OK to wait

You have the right to not want to have sex, for any personal reason whatsoever. Your body and your sexual favors are yours, and you don't have to feel bad about saying "no." However, it is important to be clear and kind about it. If you thought you wanted to be physically intimate, and now that the time has come, you don't, you'll have to say it. Don't just act disinterested or turned off and expect your partner to understand.

Saying no will often make or break a relationship in this early stage, because it will let you see how your date handles frustration and disappointment. If the response is ugly, you may want to reconsider being in a relationship with this person. If the response is caring and thoughtful, you may feel more secure and more enthused about being intimate.

Often, saying no is an unconscious test. If you feel unsure about whether you're being respected, valued, or cared about, you may feel like saying "no." After you say it, if it is handled with respect, caring and consideration, your questions may disappear, and you may change your mind about the intimacy.

You have as much right to change your mind as you do to say "no." Your partner has these same rights, too, so be prepared to take "no" for an answer yourself.

If it's not mutual, don't do it.

If you don't feel that the desire for intimacy is mutual, you have a good reason not to do it. Sex is not going to be enjoyable if both of you aren't fully involved and willing. If something doesn't feel right to you, even if you feel it's your partner and not yourself who is reluctant, stop what you're doing and ask what is happening.

Use what you've learned about sexual conversations to begin right now finding out what your partner thinks and feels, and doing your best to be reassuring and supportive. Where sex and intimacy are involved, sweetness succeeds far more often than bitterness.

If you tried sex, and it didn't work

If you had a sexual encounter that didn't work—you weren't excited, your partner wasn't excited, someone got upset or angry—you have yet another occasion to talk. What is happening may be the result of a misunderstanding between you, or someone's childhood issues, or a past relationship. Until you know what it is, you can't fix it.

Therefore, the most important thing to do is to listen to your partner, and try to understand. Once you understand your partner's problem or reaction, ask your partner to listen, in turn, to your feelings. Only by talking it out can you find out how serious the problem is. It may be something small, some confusion, or just first-time jitters. Give yourself a chance to be effective by finding out exactly what's going on.

No call, no flowers now what?

What if sexual intimacy doesn't go as well as you thought? What if your date doesn't call the next day, there are no flowers or sweet notes, and things turn decidedly chilly?

If your intimacy was of the one-night-stand variety, there's nothing you can do. You just need to cut your losses and go away, taking a look at what you can learn from the situation. If you did know each other, and this is a complete surprise, by all means ask what happened. You may get a response that reassures you and clears up the whole misunderstanding, or you may get a response that's indifferent, and indicates the other person didn't care as much as you thought.

Sometimes emotional or sexual intimacy is a test of feelings, and the feelings flunk. Getting sexually intimate is a confrontation if the right chemistry isn't there, or if someone is not ready, the intimacy will point that out in unmistakable terms, and the relationship will end abruptly. If that happens, all you can do is attempt to save the friendship, if there is one, and deal with your disappointment.

Handling disappointment

Most of this chapter has been about what to do if the relationship develops further intimacy. But, if the intimacy doesn't work, you may find out, upon getting closer, that one or both of you doesn't like what you see, or isn't sufficiently turned on, or just gets scared and goes away.

Part of successful dating is anticipating that some things are not going to work out, and being prepared to let them go. Depending on how attached you have gotten, you will probably have to grieve, to feel bad, to talk about your disappointment with understanding friends.

Keep in mind that hanging on to something that's not working so early in the game will delay finding another person who is more ready for a relationship and who cares for you as you are. It is as easy to obsess on a failed relationship as a successful one, so if you see the signs of obsession or feel overwhelmed with unbearable grief, see a counselor.

If this relationship doesn't work out, use it as a learning experience see if there were warning signs you ignored, or dating guidelines you could have followed more closely to either correct the problems or

Unofficially...
I have a dear friend with whom I wrote two successful books, and who has been there for me every time I needed him. We met 25 years ago, and dated for a few of weeks, had a great mental and heart connection, but not too much else. It took some effort on both parts to learn to be "just friends" but all the years of solid friendship have been worth it.

to find out more quickly that things weren't going to work out. Anything you can learn is a bonus.

Finally, to feel better, keep in mind that it's your date's loss. You know how special you are, and your date never got to find out.

Let's just be friends

If the romance doesn't work, but you have already built a friendship, the issue is more complicated, but also may not be as big a loss. It's difficult to go "backwards" (as most people view it) from a potential romance to a friendship, but it can be done, and it's worth it.

In order to resume being friends, you may need to have a long, difficult talk, to take a break for a little while, or to renegotiate how the friendship will be from now on. This can be uncomfortable, but if you both valued your friendship before becoming more intimate, it can easily be worth the effort.

One of you has to begin with a "let's be friends" conversation. You can say "Dating doesn't seem to be working out for us, and I miss the friendship we used to have." and see what your friend's response is. If you dated for a while, or if only one of you wants to let the romance go, it may take some time before you are both comfortable again.

If you want to resume being friends, invite the other person to do one of your favorite things you used to as friends, and see what happens. If you keep the new friendship boundaries clear, and don't lapse into romantic behavior, after a few times, you'll both relax and become comfortable again. If, on the other hand, your dating does go well, sooner or later you'll want to make it official. In the next chapter, we'll explore how.

Just the facts

- The decision to have sex with your dating partner is yours, and yours alone to make.

- As a responsible adult, you must be honest with yourself about your sexuality—and be prepared for safer sex.

- If you are close enough to your partner to consider having sex, you should be able to have open, frank discussions about sexual safety and about your own needs and desires.

- You have the right to say no at any stage in your relationship with your partner.

GET THE SCOOP ON...
Dating's focus ▪ Evaluating your date ▪
Making the grade ▪ Setting up future dates

Chapter 11

If It Goes on from Here

Dating is one of those things that people want to fantasize about, but not think about. But, dating actually has a function, and if you know what it is, you'll have a much better chance of succeeding at what you want.

A primary function of dating, of course, is having fun. However, if fun was your only reason for going out, you'd have a better chance of really relaxing and having a good time with some old friends. The fun associated with dating can obscure the other functions, which is to get to know each other, to, in effect, "try each other on" to see if the relationship can work. It's a discovery process. Dating is, therefore, serious business, so even while you're having fun, you should be paying attention to what you're discovering.

The reasons for dating

Dating is a way to get out, to do something different, to break out of your rut. But you don't go out on dates alone—you're with somebody new, doing things together. Getting to know this new person is also introducing new ideas into your life. And that's one of the real pluses of dating: Even if the relationship doesn't succeed, you can still benefit from the new ideas and insights you've picked up along the way.

Once you've determined you're safe, be open to new ideas and experiences—allow your date to show you some of the favorite things he or she likes to do.

Timesaver
Be prepared to suggest some fun things to do. Keep a "fun list" somewhere handy, and whenever you hear of something you'd like to do on a date—a good restaurant, a free concert series, an inexpensive play, a new place to hike, an art gallery opening, a roller skating rink, or a great beach— write it down, so that when you want to suggest something, you can just look it up on your list.

Relationship practice

Dating is a chance to practice relating to a number of different people, *before* committing to the intense intimacy and the responsibility of a true relationship. The whole point of dating is to experience your new friend without making a commitment. No matter how intense your feelings might be, don't assume that your date is interested in a commitment until the subject is discussed.

If your dating experience with this person lasts awhile, you will hopefully have an opportunity to disagree with one another, to solve some problems together, and to spend enough time in each other's company in enough different situations to figure out whether your relationship will work.

Information gathering

Your dates are opportunities for you to gather information about this new person on an intimate, one-on-one level. Keeping your balance and thinking clearly can be difficult in this context. If things go well, your temptation will be to go all starry-eyed and romantic, and you may find that you have stopped thinking about what kind of permanent partner your date will make. If you encounter problems, the temptation is to panic and struggle, when you could be using the problem as an opportunity to find out whether you can be a team.

The best approach is to keep in mind that you are here to have fun, to learn, to grow, to find out about each other, and to build the foundation of a relationship. If you can keep this perspective, you'll have a better chance of a good dating outcome.

Keeping perspective

But it's easy to get confused in the first flush of a relationship, and to forget what the point of dating is all about. We love to fantasize about romance and "love at first sight." But it's important to keep in mind that there are no guarantees when you're dating.

For example, even if your dating goes really well, it's essential that you keep in mind that you have not made a commitment, and neither has your date, until you've talked about it conclusively. It's easy to assume that affection, statements of emotional closeness, and even sexual contact mean love, but unless you *discuss* making a commitment, and what it means, you can't assume you have one.

And even if you progress to steady dating, or go further, to some kind of formal commitment, you must not lapse into thinking that you have (or should have) control over your new partner. A healthy dating relationship is marked by mutual respect and caring, not mutual restriction and pressure. On the other hand, the one person you do have total control of is yourself. Make sure you're behaving according to your own values and objectives, and not letting your standards lapse just because you want to keep this new person interested in you.

Keep your antennae up

Even if you feel very close after dating for a while,

you have no guarantee that you're learning all there is to know about the other person, or that he or she is telling you the truth. Continue to interview and pay attention. If your date is concealing some truth (such as a marriage, financial problems, a problematic past, other relationships), paying attention to the conversation over time will begin to expose the conflicts and flaws in the story.

Continue to follow the suggestions earlier in the book for meeting your date's friends and family, and learning more about him or her. The closer you get, the more important it is that you find out who your date really is. After all, your objective while dating someone is to figure out if there is a basis for a relationship—dating, by itself, is not enough evidence to assume that you have a relationship.

During dating you can, indeed, lay the foundation for a relationship, and practice developing relationship skills, but you have many things to learn about each other before you'll know. You're having a good time dating, but is this the person you want to spend your life with?

Until you have established what both of you want in a relationship and agreed that you have it, and made a clear, *mutual* commitment, you don't have anything but a dating connection.

Dating and sex

Whether you are paying for the date or being taken out, don't assume there's any obligation to have sex if either of you doesn't want to. Although this may seem obvious, when someone has expectations of sexual "favors" just because they paid the bill during the date, sorting your difference of opinion on this matter can be very awkward and even lead to problems. If you're getting signals that the other person doesn't understand the sexual "rules" the same way you do, you may need to talk about it before the end of the evening.

Signs on the road to a relationship

If you've progressed to a second date (or more) with someone new, hopefully that means his or her behavior on your early dates was fine. You're compatible enough, and had a good enough time, that you both wanted to see each other again. So far, so good.

Seeing your date more often means you'll get a good chance to evaluate his or her personality, and find out what's beneath the surface. Is it really as good as your first impression?

There are some warning signs to look for. If you find them, be careful and try discussing them with your date. No one is perfect, and the best of dates may exhibit a warning sign or two. Most of them are not fatal, taken singly, and they may not mean that you have severe problems, but you should talk them over and work them out, when they crop up. If you do, you'll have the additional benefit of an opportunity to find out how you deal with problems together.

Your date's just *too* charming or practiced

If your date is not at all nervous or awkward and never at a loss for words, you may be very impressed. Such a polished approach is very attractive and pleasant to be around. However, there could be a down side to this smoothness. It can mean that you're dating a "professional dater"—someone, unlike you, who's been single (or only in brief relationships) for a long time. This sort of person has dated a lot, and is therefore very practiced and comfortable.

This is fine if you just want to have a good time

Watch Out!
If your date is able to drink a lot without showing it, that's a sign of alcohol tolerance—such a person is used to drinking. It might be a warning that you're dating an alcoholic whose drinking doesn't show readily, but who still has serious problems. If your date drinks more than one or two drinks in an evening, or two glasses of wine with dinner, pay attention.

dating. But, if you're going to get attached, if you want a more meaningful relationship, or if you want a commitment from someone, this is probably not the person for you.

Highly polished dates really like dating, and don't want more. Sometimes, they're not really available because they're married, or for various reasons they don't want to commit to one person. If your date seems very slick, is enthusiastic about dating but doesn't seem to want to open up beyond a certain point, has had many short relationships, or shies away from discussing personal details, be careful, and don't be too trusting.

Out of control behavior

Out of control behaviors, such as rage (perhaps at the waitress, or while driving the car), too much drinking, talking about drinking too much, missing work, or being depressed, can be clues about serious problems that can make a healthy relationship impossible. If you get such clues, be very careful, and go slowly until you have a chance to see if they really do indicate problems.

A number of years ago, a friend of mine called me up and said "I've met this wonderful girl—I want you to meet her." So, the three of us got tickets for a play. During the 30 minute drive, at dinner, during the play, and while we were having coffee afterwards, his date must have mentioned drinking ("we got together for a couple of beers" or "we sat on the porch and had a couple of beers" or "we were pretty loose, we'd had a couple of beers") twenty times. Although she only had one glass of wine with dinner, her conversation stood out for me. My friend never asked for anything but comments on how wonderful she was, so I never said anything—but he went through a year of agony with this young woman and her alcohol-related problems. The clues were there from the beginning, but he was too charmed to see them.

And conversational or behavioral clues can indicate more than just problems with drinking. Short-tempered outbursts, aggressive reactions to minor irritations, impatience with everyday annoyances—all these are signs that your friend has trouble keeping control of his or her temper. Evaluate these behaviors carefully if they come up during your date—and don't succumb to the temptation to make excuses for unacceptable outbursts.

Beware the possessive control freak

When your date has it all together—makes all the arrangements, can't wait to see you again, phones frequently, is intense and persuasive in discussions, always knows what he or she wants to do, sends cards or flowers, arranges things to perfection—it often feels very good, at first. It's so nice (especially when you've been alone) to have all this attention, you may not notice how important it is to your date to have everything go his or her way. There's a big difference between attentiveness and an attempt at asserting control. Be careful not to confuse the two.

Similarly, jealousy can also be flattering. If your date gets upset when he or she thinks someone else in the restaurant is looking at you, or wants you to be exclusive right away, it *might* simply mean that he or she is smitten with you. But it can also be a sign of emotional instability. That flattering interest in your attentions can turn in to a chronic lack of trust and suspicion.

Controlling people are usually very smooth when you're only dating, while they're still unsure of the degree of possession over you they have. But, after they charm you into committing and bonding to them, the control can turn very unpleasant, and even lead to stalking or abuse. Be careful of the "too perfect" lover. What feels good on an occasional basis can be very oppressive when it's every day behavior.

Signals of an abuser or user

Anger, control, and possessiveness are all warning signs that your date may have a control issue, which can lead to abuse, but there are other signs to watch for as well. This is one of the reasons I so emphasize the "tennis match" approach to conversations, phone calls, and other aspects of dating. Strict adherence to that policy early in your dating will help you avoid getting attached to a user.

Users are often charming, sometimes childlike, and usually appear to be somewhat helpless. Because they are so personable, it is easy to get sucked into doing a lot more than your share of the relationship work. We all want to help, to be caring and useful, to feel needed—but helping should go both ways. Until you know who you're dealing with, be careful you're not just being used.

Users may con you out of money, but more often they just lay back and let you give more of the love, time, and attention, until you feel unappreciated, drained, and hurt. Users are often *narcissistic*, a Freudian term which means they are so focused on themselves and their wants and needs that they aren't even aware that other people *have* wants and needs. For various reasons, a truly narcissistic person has not developed emotionally past two years old, and is really incapable of empathizing with you or recognizing your rights, needs, and wants.

Money Issues

Most of the difficulties that occur in long-term relationships are about sex, control, or money. Pay careful attention to your date's relationship to money.

Everyone has a unique relationship to money, or what I call a "money style." Money styles vary widely, from ultra careful to completely reckless, and every variation in between. You and your date don't have to be similar in money style to make a relationship work, but you do have to be able to work out your differences. If you believe your date is wildly irresponsible or obnoxiously controlling, you'll probably have a tough time working out a smooth financial partnership.

If you go on a few dates with this person, you'll have plenty of opportunities to observe his or her money style. Here are a few to keep an eye out for during your dates:

- **Careful with $?** Does your date always count change, keep bills all facing the same way and divided by denomination, or carefully keep credit card or ATM receipts? If you divide a check, does he or she figure it to the penny?

- **Careless with $?** Does your date shove change in a pocket? Crumple bills into a wad, and drop it on the floor when taking it out of pocket or purse? Laugh about mistakes made in the checkbook that result in bouncing a check now and then? Just split the bill in half, without worrying who had what?

- **Thrifty?** Does your date enjoy telling you about bargains, from a great deal on a new car to a thrift store find? Invite you to restaurants that are tiny, inexpensive places with good food

Bright Idea
Sticking to the "tennis match" approach will expose narcissistic problems and users very quickly, and save you a lot of hurt and disappointment.

(another bargain)? Does he or she have savings and investments? Own a home? Worry about retirement? Know about interest rates and mutual funds?

- **Spendthrift?** Does your date say things like "money's no object"? Buy drinks for everyone? Order expensive wine, and generally show off about money? Seem to come up short just before payday?

- **Neurotic?** Does your date fret over every nickel spent? Get upset if a bill is split four ways, and you had less than the other couple? Tell you how you should spend (or save) your money? Complain in shocked tones about other people's spending habits?

- **Compulsive spender?** Does your date frequently have bounced checks, rejected credit cards, or financial problems? Ask you (or a relative) for money? Talk about shopping a lot (spending a lot on clothes, computer accessories, car parts, hobby supplies, or drugs)?

- **Rescuing?** Does your date always seem to be giving money to a sibling, child, parent, or ex? Or "lending" money that never comes back? Bailing someone out of jail? Does he or she make excuses for that person, and seem to feel responsible beyond normal limits?

There's a wide range of money styles that are within normal limits, from very careful and thrifty to more relaxed and generous. Within this range, if you were in a relationship, the two of you would simply need to be able to respect each other's differences and work out your problems—sometimes difficult, but usually workable. However, if your date seems to fall into the last three categories given above, you could be inviting big financial problems into your life if you get any closer.

Remember, a serious, committed relationship is also a financial partnership. Even if you just divide expenses evenly, rather than pooling your funds, you may still get stuck with your partner's share of the rent, if he or she can't manage money well. And if you commit to someone who is neurotically controlling, you may find that, even if you earn your own money, you're asked to account for every cent, and struggle to spend it (or save it) the way you want.

Dating a flake

When your phone calls are not returned, your date is late a few times, or doesn't show up at all, watch out. It's an indication that you, your time, and your value are not being respected.

Keep in mind that you and your date are both doing your best to make a good impression right now. Things will not get better later—they are likely to get more relaxed. If your date is *not* making a good impression, keep in mind that it may still be the best he or she can do, and make your decision accordingly.

Heed your instincts

You may not realize it, but you have the ability to "feel" another person emotionally. This ability is called "empathy" and we are all born with it—it is how we relate to parents and others before we begin to use words and thoughts. If your feelings are at odds with what you think you know about the person you are with, pay close attention. If you're feeling tense, stressed, or physically uncomfortable, your body may be giving you clues that all is not right in

Moneysaver
The best way to save your money is to know that your prospective partner is a good "money style" match for you. Staying out of relationships with people who can't control their own money can save you huge financial disasters, such as divorce costs, huge credit card debts, bankruptcy, and foreclosure.

your relationship. Your body's reactions could be wiser than your brain's.

If the "hairs on the back of your neck" are raised, if you feel intimidated, frightened, uneasy, inexplicably angry, or any other feeling that seems out of synch with an otherwise pleasant dating experience, your subconscious might know more than your rational mind. Honor these feelings by being more cautious and going even more slowly, until you have a chance to find out what is going on.

Dishonesty

If, after you've gotten to know each other a bit, your partner is more reluctant than necessary to give a home phone number, or to have you meet friends, or has very little time for you, he or she might have something to hide, such as a spouse. Check out the left fourth finger of your date's hand for a "pale" spot or an indentation that indicates a wedding ring usually sits there. Similarly, if your date is reluctant to talk about past relationships, or if everything seems too positive and rosy to be real, you may be dealing with someone who has had a number of relationship disasters. For your own protection, go slowly with such a person until you've had a chance to make certain the possibility that his or her past (or present) commitments won't make trouble in *your* relationship.

Even if your date tells you openly about past relationships, that's not enough to guarantee that all will go smoothly now. Some people have trouble owning up to their own responsibility—somehow, whatever goes wrong is always the other person's fault. If your new dating interest claims every past relationship partner "didn't understand," was unreasonable, addicted, selfish, crazy, or just plain mean, and takes

> **"**
> The [person] who was late almost every time when you were courting will be very late coming home when [you're] married... Happiness is what you're willing to settle for, so be careful that you don't settle for the minimum.
> —Sonya Friedman, *Men Are Just Desserts* (Warner, 1983)
> **"**

no personal responsibility, be cautious. You could be the next one on that list of terrible people.

Every relationship disaster takes two. If nothing else, your date should be taking responsibility for getting into, and staying in, a bad relationship. A healthy person *does* make mistakes—and admits to them. And people in relationships can grow apart, but your date should know—and be willing to acknowledge—what he or she could have done better.

The trouble with loners

Beware the date who has no one in his or her life but you. Unless you've just met a person who's brand new to your city (or to this country), your date should have an active social life. Even someone who just came here should have had an active social life back home to talk about, and should certainly be working to create another network here.

No social life, no friends, and not enough to do are all indications that your date has some problems relating effectively to people. While that can mean that he or she is at your beck and call in the beginning, it also can mean you will be expected to fill up your date's life, and that can become a lot of pressure for you.

Rude awakenings

Rudeness, no matter what the excuse, is an indication that your date doesn't really respect and value you as an individual who deserves undivided attention. The most modern excuse for rudeness is the cell phone and pager. In an extreme situation, such as if your date is a medical doctor on call and must be available at a moment's notice, you at least deserve an explanation that this is the case, and you should have the option to accept this as a fact of your dating life or decline to get involved.

If your date ignores you to use a cell phone at the dinner table, or has to leave repeatedly to answer a pager, you are being treated rudely, and you need to discuss it before another date takes place.

Certain cell phone interruptions might be OK, for example if your date is a single parent, and hears from a child or a baby-sitter; or if your date is caring for an elderly parent and checks in with the person on duty. Even for such a good reason, the possibility of a call should be explained to you in advance.

Watch Out!
Pay attention if you find yourself with a knot in the stomach, tight muscles, a clenched jaw, headaches, or chronic fatigue. Your body may be sending you warning signals that all is not well in your relationship. If you feel physical distress when with your friend, or even when thinking about him or her, it's time to re-evaluate the relationship.

Sexuality issues

Ah, sex: to be or not to be sexual, when, and how often—that is the question.

Sooner or later in your dating, you will get sexual to some degree, even if you've decided to wait until marriage to have full intercourse. Cuddling, kissing, and petting are all stages of sexual contact, and will tell you a lot about your current dating partner.

If your partner wants to have sex when you don't, it's natural for him or her to be disappointed—but if that disappointment turns into hostility or pressure, that's a warning sign that you should never ignore.

On the other hand, if there's not much warmth or sexual energy at all, it makes sense to wonder why. Sex is a vital part of a lasting relationship. While it takes effort to keep a sexual relationship satisfying over the long haul, a solid sexual connection at the outset is a big help. So if you don't seem to be compatible sexually, or your ideas about appropriate sexuality and frequency are at odds, it could turn out to be a big problem in forming a long-term relationship.

Signsposts to successful dating experiences

You'd think the positive signs in a date would be obvious, but with all the excitement, the most important clues can be overlooked. What makes for a great date may not be all you need for a great relationship. This list of positive signs will help you evaluate your date in a realistic manner.

- ■ *Sense of humor:* Of all the characteristics that are essential for getting through life successfully, a sense of humor has to be in the top ten. But, what kind of a sense of humor should you look for? Joking at someone else's expense or at inappropriate times can be counter-productive. Using jokes to avoid taking responsibility for one's behavior can prevent you from solving problems. The sense of humor you're looking for is the generous, positive kind that makes life more fun and the tough times easier. If your date can make your laugh, and lift your spirits, that talent may help you through some future difficulties.

- ■ *Considerateness:* A date who asks for and listens to your opinions and feelings, and better yet, who remembers what you say and builds on it later, and who responds with empathy, sincerity, and caring, is someone you can communicate with and therefore, more likely to be able to form a partnership with you. If you pay attention, you can quickly notice the difference between the appearance of caring and real caring.

- ■ *Communicative:* If your relationship is successful, you'll have years of talking to each other, so find someone who is interesting to talk to and also interested in talking with you. Your date should be able to carry on an interesting discussion on a variety of topics, and at least show interest, even if the topic is not something he or she is familiar with.

■ *Independence of Mind:* A truly good conversationalist not only listens to your words and responds, but also has ideas and opinions. Your date should not hesitate to disagree with you or to bring up new topics.

■ *Cooperativeness:* Recent research shows that the single most important quality for determining that a relationship can succeed is how well the couple solves problems. If you have a disagreement while dating, welcome it as an opportunity to see how well the two of work it out together. If you can discuss your differences without becoming defensive or sarcastic, and you can listen to each other and work together toward a solution, your relationship has an excellent chance.

■ *Accepting:* A popular book asserts that *Men Are from Mars, Women Are from Venus,* but I think it's more that we're *all* from different planets. You and your date are unique, special, and individual, and need to be able to understand each other, and accept that you'll perceive things very differently. But even when you and your date see things differently, you should be able to agree to disagree.

Disagreements need not be problematic in your relationship. Remember, the security and comfort in your relationship will come from where you and your partner are similar, and the excitement and growth in the relationship are generated from your differences. Different interests, opinions, attitudes, and ideas will keep things fresh and alive between you. If your date does not become defensive or threatened by your differences, you can be interesting to each other for a long time.

- *Openness:* The whole point of dating, as we said before, is to get to know each other. While you both may want to take a little time before disclosing too much, your date should be comfortable talking about him or herself, and it should not be like tooth pulling to find out what you need to know.

- *Well-adjusted:* A date who has a full, interesting life you would want to be a part of is more likely to be a healthy, balanced person. While it's important to have some relaxation time, and time to meditate or think, a life that includes a good career, hobbies or sports, community service and friends and/or family is reassurance that your date is motivated, focused and able to relate.

- *Intelligent:* Your date doesn't need to be a member of Mensa or a mathematical genius, but look for enough intelligence that you can respect and admire each other. There are several kinds of intelligence, from school learning to independent education by reading, working, traveling, and life experiences. An "airhead" who looks good and may be fun to play with, will not keep you interested for long. A date who is not interested in learning and growing intellectually may not be able to keep up over the long haul.

- *A balanced sense of self:* As you learn about this new person you're dating, observe his or her character and personality for signs of a balanced sense of self. If your date can keep success and failure in perspective, admit personal shortcomings, and rise above disappointments and losses, he or she does have a balanced personality, and the kind of resilience that can travel through life's highs and lows and keep it all in perspective.

- *Emotional maturity:* While it's fun and charming to be able to be childlike when in a playful mood, it's essential to be an adult whenever necessary. A date who is responsible, self-regulating, emotionally responsive, motivated, and in control of his or her impulses, is capable of being a supportive, fully participating partner, no matter what joys and sorrows, successes and failures you may face in the course of a lifetime.

- *Healthy relationship history:* Of course, if both of you are dating again, your relationship history will probably not be perfect. What counts is whether your date has learned from the problems, confronted his or her own weaknesses and shortcomings, and grown as a result of the setbacks. If your date is willing to talk openly about his or her past relationships, and can explain what went wrong and how he or she is learning to correct the problems, the difficulties in past relationships can be an asset rather than a liability. If your date expresses a willingness to seek counseling in the event that problems should occur, score that in his or her favor.

Now that we've been through all the positive and negative personality traits you should be observing, remember that a smart date will be watching for the same characteristics in you. To do well in a relationship, learn to be the partner you would like someone to be for *you*.

Looking toward the next date

Based on how things have gone so far, and how much you're enjoying each other, you may be considering another date. Whether you make an invitation, or accept one, will depend on how you feel about your success so far. Now's the time to do some honest evaluating of the experience.

Taking stock of your dating success

Have you been having a good time, and do you feel that there are possibilities you want to explore further? Has your date exhibited enough positive qualities and good character to make a relationship seem possible? If your date still looks like a good possibility, and still seems interested, then another date is probably a great idea.

There's an old expression. "If you'd like to see someone again, leave a glove." This means, you can guarantee that you'll get a call by leaving something of yours in your date's car or apartment. Leaving a lipstick, a cufflink, or a notebook gives your date a reason to call, and if that doesn't happen, you've got a great excuse to call.

Keep your insecurities at bay

If you're worrying that your date might not be interested in another date, do a reality check. Is there any real reason why your date would be turned off? Review the warning signs above, and see if any apply to yourself. If you find any that do, examine your own behavior and try to correct it, getting help from friends or a therapist if necessary.

If there is really no good reason, stop worrying needlessly. Just relax and give it a little time. If it's your turn to call, go ahead and take the risk. If you get nowhere, at least you'll have given it your best shot. What you don't want to do is indulge any unfounded sense of insecurity—it serves no constructive purpose.

Besides, if your date actually doesn't call, it may have nothing to do with your behavior. In fact, it could even be a kind of complement. If you had a great time, and the next one doesn't happen, the reason might be that your date was afraid of commitment, and you actually were *too* successful. If a partner is afraid of commitment, a relationship that seems as if it actually has a chance of succeeding could scare him or her away.

If that happens, the only thing you can do is keep looking for more people to date. If this date gets over the fear, you'll get a call eventually, if not, there's not much you can do. It helps to remember that you cannot force someone to want to be with you.

Your relationship reservoir

Every relationship (including family, friends, and parent/child relationships) has what I call the "relationship reservoir." Over the course of your relationship, the interaction between you—every kind or unkind word, every gesture of support or criticism, every honest or dishonest interaction between you, every gesture of affection or coldness, add up over the time you spend together.

If you fill your reservoir with good feelings, forgiveness, support, honesty, appreciation, caring, affection, sexual and emotional intimacy, you build up a backlog of good will and affection—your memories will be warm and mutually admiring. If you fill it with coldness, criticism, ingratitude, dishonesty, demands, and dissatisfaction, you'll have a reservoir of resentment and disdain.

Each time your relationship makes demands on you as a result of major problems, separations, disagreements, illnesses, and stress, you will draw on your relationship reservoir. If you have built up a supply of good feelings and goodwill with your daily interaction, you'll cheerfully give what's asked of you. If not, whatever's asked will seem like too much to give.

The next chapter will discuss what you can create as your relationship builds.

Just the facts

- One of dating's primary purposes is to open yourself up to new experiences, new people, and new ways of looking at your world.

- Make sure you learn as much as you can about your dating partners—and for your own safety, and for the chance to get to know them better.

- Maintain your standards and priorities when you date—don't let yourself be pressured into doing things you don't want to do.

- Develop a clear sense of the positive attributes you'd like to see in a dating partner.

- Your experiences with people fill your "relationship reservoir"—do what you can to make certain that it is a positive one.

GET THE SCOOP ON...
Bringing your date into your
life ■ Emotional growth ■ Intimacy ■
Long-term relationship skills

Chapter 12

Officially Dating

Here you are, where you always wanted to be —officially dating! Your search has been a success, and you and your date have really hit it off. Everything has gone well so far, and you've weathered all the tests. Now, you both want to make it official—but officially what? And how do you do that? Will calling your relationship "official" change anything?

Each time you achieve a new level in your relationship, with its wonderful feelings and future fantasies, your old feelings from the past, along with your fears of what might happen in the future, will come up again.

You are not a teenager in first love, you know what all the possibilities are, positive and negative. Handling your feelings, and providing for the potential problems, is part of making this new relationship official.

Merging your relationship with your real life
Ah, love! When it works, it wipes out everything for

a while, and, if we're lucky enough to find it, we want to wallow in the throes of it, ignoring everything else in our lives. But, before long, the realities of an already-established life intrude. You have work, families, friends, and stuff to deal with.

John Donne, the sixteenth-century poet, knew what it was to be older and in love—a mixed bag of feelings, indeed. But, no matter how much you may want to ignore life and live on love, you know it's not possible, and you need to rearrange things to integrate this new love into your existing life.

In order to give your relationship official status and have it recognized by those close to you, you need to let others know and face their approval or disapproval. How you present this relationship to your world will, to a very large degree, determine how the people who care about you respond to it. Setting things up properly now will gain support for your love, leaving the wrong impression will put pressure on your relationship later.

No matter how much you think you have the right to love how, whom, and when you want (which is technically correct), if you have a life with supportive, active friends and family, and a career that is important to you, and especially if one or both of you has children (young or adult), presenting your relationship to everyone in your life is a big deal. What you want is for your support systems to support both of you in your new relationship, and for that you need to give them the proper information in a way they can accept. If you startle, shock, or upset your friends in presenting your news, their reaction is likely to be negative.

There are other kinds of precedents you're setting now, as well. As I said before, what you do in the early stages of a relationship sets patterns, good and bad. As you mutually decide you have an official relationship, you define it and set your intentions for it. Whatever intentions you set, you'll tend to fall into certain patterns repeatedly as the years go on. These patterns can be changed, but it's so much easier to set them properly in the beginning. For example, if you develop a pattern of not wanting to talk about problems, they will get harder and harder to bring up. If you set an intention of open communication, your connection will get better and better, and talking out your problems get easier and easier.

Emotional growth and intimacy

To be successful all the way through life, it is essential that you have room to grow—mentally, emotionally, psychologically, and spiritually. Such adaptation allows us to stretch and accommodate all the changes and problems life hands us. Our relationships, therefore, must have enough room in them to allow both partners to change. We cannot wait until we're perfect to begin our relationships, so we have to build room for our rough edges into the relationship.

Intimacy tests us—it's a human fact that we're all emotionally clumsy, and it's too easy to hurt each other unintentionally—the closer we get, the more vulnerable to hurt we become. So it's essential that we learn to forgive, to accept responsibility, and to work together to heal the hurts. By beginning now with a attitude of willingness to change and grow, you give your relationship the best possible start.

Sharing your life stories

One way to begin open communication is the natural process most lovers follow of telling each other

Bright Idea
Before you decide to officially call it a relationship, sit down and discuss what you want the next ten years to be about. Allow yourselves to fantasize and to also discuss the real possibilities. Then, write your ideas down. You'll set some ideas in motion that will help you shape your reality. Whenever you get off-track, you can pull out your written mission statement, and it will help you refocus.

their life stories. When you and your partner spend time talking about childhood, grade school, high school and college, your past relationships, and other details about your history, you are establishing a pattern of sharing. Don't hesitate to open up and talk about your past. By encouraging each other to talk, showing interest, and treating the sharing as a gift, you create an atmosphere of safety.

Most of us have parts of our history we're uncomfortable about, whether it's a tale of childhood abuse, sexual impropriety, an embarrassing incident, a health problem, a family "black sheep," or some other thing that we find talking about uncomfortable. Encouraging your partner to open up about such things, and sharing your own secrets, will deepen your intimacy and (if there is support instead of criticism) will build trust between you.

Drawing your partner out

In addition to sharing history, you can encourage your partner to talk about feelings and thoughts if you decide to learn from what you hear. If you ask interested questions, and use the conversational techniques you used to learn about him or her when you first met, you will learn even more about this person you're getting bonded to, and you can also learn what warning signs to look for.

Pay attention, for example, to what went wrong in your date's previous relationships, and also what was good—from those stories, you'll learn a lot you can use in your own future.

Making note of these recipes for disaster helps you to be alert to signs that they might be occurring in your relationship. For example, if your date says he and his ex "just grew apart," and later he stops talking to you, don't let it pass, bring it up that you're worried that what went wrong before is happening again, and ask him how he feels about it.

For example, if your date mentions that her ex was very critical, and you find yourself feeling unhappy about her appearance or her messiness, instead of criticizing (which you know is fatal) find a more gentle and positive way to bring up the problem in a family meeting.

Also, a thoughtful conversation about your own past relationships can help you understand more clearly, with the help of your current partner's perspective, what happened.

Establishing safety (and commitment)

Trust, safety, and commitment are the three dynamics that create security in relationships. You begin building them from the moment you meet, and how well you succeed in creating these three dynamics determines whether your relationship will last, and whether you will feel secure with your partner.

1. **Trust** is built through ongoing open communication, your ability to make and keep your agreements, and not creating unpleasant surprises for each other. If you keep each other informed, and do what you say you'll do, your trust will grow. If your partner keeps being surprised by things he or she didn't know, the trust will be destroyed.

2. **Safety** is created when you feel sure your partner won't attack you or undermine you, even if you disagree or struggle about differences. In short, you'll work as a team to solve problems to your mutual satisfaction.

3. **Commitment** is not something you can do—it's a measure of something you experience. You are

> **"** The good news is that the experts say we can make love last. Love is not something that just happens to us... Couples who hang in there, fighting through problems by talking about them.... are much more likely to find that comfort and happiness a long relationship can give." John Stossel, on the televised show Love, Lust, and Marriage: Why We Stay and Why We Stray (transcript) **"**

committed to your partner and your relationship because of the level of importance it has for you—not because you intend to be committed, but because you have an emotional investment in being committed. Most people cannot sustain a commitment that does not express what they feel is true.

Building security is a main task of this early stage. If you build enough security, your first response when you face a difficult situation will be to turn to each other for help, and to work together to solve the problem. Research shows that successful problem-solving is the single most important factor in the success and survival of couple relationships.

Think of it this way: If you and your partner feel secure, and trust each other to work together to solve problems, why would you want to take the risk of trying someone else? It's the best guarantee I know of fidelity in any relationship.

Your relationship reservoir, and how to fill it

Christopher Reeve, the former "Superman" who had a riding accident and wound up paralyzed, is fortunate to have a loving wife standing by him without reservation, now that he needs her. The strength, love, and security in their marriage is obvious. No matter what the emotional and physical cost, her commitment to him is clearly visible whenever they appear on camera together. Each of them draws on the reservoir of their shared history to gain the strength to keep going today.

They are an example for us all. They have the three primary ingredients to a strong relationship, which is why they have been able to weather the hard times. They have a full, deep relationship reservoir.

As I said in chapter 10, every couple, through the nature of their interaction, creates a relationship reservoir, or a backlog of good or bad feelings, As your relationship progresses, you'll have more and more opportunities to fill that reservoir with positive feelings you can draw on in times of stress. It's difficult to adequately describe the value of this reservoir, or to fully express its potential destructiveness of it if it is negative in nature. But there are definite things you can do to create a positive reservoir through your relationships.

Discussing problems

Research conducted for 25 years by John Gottman at the University of Washington shows conclusively that the ability to discuss problems amicably and cooperatively is the major thing that makes or breaks a relationship. In other words, learning to discuss problems without shutting down, blaming, accusing or defending is an essential skill for building a lasting relationship.

If you find yourselves fighting instead of problem-solving, take steps to change the situation. Enroll in a class or get counseling to learn the communications skills you need. If your partner won't go with you, go by yourself. You can learn enough in a class or in therapy as an individual to make great improvements in your couple communication.

Celebrating success

One of the most effective patterns you can develop as your relationship grows is to celebrate and appreciate your accomplishments, your love, your relationship milestones, and each other. Motivation and commitment grow out of celebration and appreciation.

By appreciating what you've already accomplished, and celebrating your previous successes,

Watch Out!
Couples who fight a lot quickly begin to generate resentment, which I call "the great destroyer," because, in my experience, it's the only thing that can kill the couples feeling for each other. If you feel resentful, or see signs in your partner, regard it as a serious warning, and do something about it immediately.

you'll add a lot to your relationship reservoir. Treat each other with kindness and understanding, be very generous with praise and gentle with expressing problems, and you'll create a sense of pride and achievement, and a great deal of pleasure. You will feel loved, loving, and very motivated to make the relationship better.

All of this can be accomplished through the two "magic motivators": celebration and appreciation. Don't be embarrassed and uncomfortable; you can't be too generous with praise. There is no such thing as too much praise or celebration. Is there too much motivation? Of course not—the more the merrier. Fresh flowers on the table just to say how much you appreciate your partner can do a lot toward creating happiness. The important point is that celebration of what you have accomplished already will create motivation to accomplish more.

Get creative with your celebrations, have fun. Celebrate a solved problem with an impromptu lunchtime picnic and a balloon. Above all, have fun. That's the objective! And whenever you find your relationship motivation flagging, look at your appreciation style. Are you expressing your love and caring? Is there some appreciation you need? Take a few minutes with yourself every day just for appreciation. It's easy, fun, and very effective. Imagine living and loving every day, energized and motivated!

Building teamwork and a partnership

Partnership and teamwork are the strong foundation of any healthy relationships. Couples who talk openly, who look to each other for help, who work together to build a future, and who discuss plans for the future, stay connected and in love. After all, isn't that partnership the main reason you want a relationship in the first place?

Author John Gottman has discovered four kinds of behavior that predict divorce. He calls these behaviors the "four horsemen of the apocalypse." They are criticism, defensiveness, contempt, and withdrawal. Here's how to unhorse the Four Horsemen and build a more positive connection:

- **Criticism**: When you talk about a problem, learn to be positive and supportive rather than critical. If you find yourself criticizing, find a way to rephrase what you're saying more positively, in terms of what you feel, and what you want, rather than in terms of what your partner is doing wrong. Use the formula "When you _____ I feel _____" For example "When you make a mess, I feel uncared for and taken for granted." This makes it much easier for your partner to hear and to empathize with you.

- **Defensiveness**: Whenever you talk, even if your partner makes a mistake and gets critical, try not to be defensive. Don't make excuses, deny that you did something, or accuse your partner in return. Instead, say "tell me more," " I'm sorry that upset you," and "What can I do to help?" Finding out what the problem is, and understanding what your partner is saying, is not the same as agreeing that you're wrong or at fault. Often, the source of a disagreement is a difference in perception, and when you understand what your partner really means, the problem is easy to solve.

- **Contempt**: Any thing you do to give each other the impression you don't value each other— sneering, poking fun, calling each other names,

> **"**
> Marriages end with a whimper. People grow apart. They're no longer friends, they get lonely and eventually there's no connection.... We've found that the real basis for romance and passion are these very small moments when people either can turn toward one another or turn away from one another.... in marriages where romance continues, people are connecting in this everyday small way.
> —John Gottman
> **"**

refusing to listen, or laughing at each other is terribly destructive to the trust in your relationship. How are you to believe that someone who has contempt for you and doesn't respect you could possibly love you? To be successful in your relationship, treat each other with respect and caring, and spend a lot more time talking about what you love, not what you don't like, about each other.

■ **Withdrawal**: Shutting down emotionally, refusing to talk, physically turning away, avoiding spending time together, and cutting off affection or sex are all evidence that you're withdrawing from each other. This differs from just taking a break or getting a little space from each other. If you don't stay in active contact, your reasons for wanting to be together disappear. If you feel you or your partner is withdrawing, talk about it, even if you have to force the issue.

These behaviors are learned in childhood, or result from hurt feelings or fear of losing each other. Most of us engage in one or another of them from time to time. A little bit of damage inflicted by occasional lapses is easily fixed, but if you find yourself behaving in any of these ways frequently, it's worth your time and effort to change. If you need counseling to correct these problems, it will be worth the expense.

Coping with the "waffle"

If it seems that your partner is giving you mixed messages, or is running hot and cold and you feel very confused about what is going on, you may be feeling the results of what therapists call approach/avoidance conflict (the "waffle"). When someone fears the results of intimacy, is afraid of getting attached and then experiencing loss, or of getting hurt, or fears being trapped in a relationship, he or she may invite you to come close and then suddenly seem to push you away or withdraw.

This kind of behavior is often called "waffling", or wavering. Even people who have a strong urge to commit can waffle now and then. Here's what to do if your partner seems to suddenly get undecided:

- **Don't panic.** Your partner is probably going through some "intimacy jitters," and worried that the growth in your intimacy will lead to getting hurt. These feelings can be a result of childhood problems or past relationship hurts, and normally subside in time.

- **Don't push.** Patience works best with the waffle, but it's hard to do if you're anxious. If you're tempted to coerce or persuade your partner, reconsider. Back up and remember your tennis-match skills, and reassure your partner by giving him or her some space.

- **Offer to listen.** Waffling is best handled by calm, supportive listening. If your partner can tell you about his or her fears, they will subside and be less of a problem. You can use the waffling as an opportunity to grow in your mutual understanding.

- **Back off quietly.** If you feel you're being pushed away, go quietly—no drama, no scenes, no accusations. Give your partner whatever space he or she seems to need to handle whatever feelings come up. Backing off takes a great deal of patience (and support from a

Bright Idea
If either you or your partner is nervous going into the relationship, take it slow. Give yourselves time to get comfortable with one another.

good friend), but it can be incredibly effective.
When you give your partner room, he or she is
more likely to realize that commitment doesn't
mean being trapped, and that the pressure is
coming from internal sources—not from you.
Back off as far as you're asked to, as easily and
calmly as you can. Then stay at that distance
until you're invited back in.

On the other hand, you could find yourself feeling scared and undecided, with your *partner* com-
plaining about mixed messages. Are you waffling? If
you suspect you are, here's what to do.

- **Listen to your inner self.** If you are feeling
  indecisive, respect your own inner wisdom. Ask
  yourself what you're feeling, and what the problem is. Get some help understanding your feelings if possible.

- **Keep reevaluating your position.** Just because
  you have initial hesitation, don't despair and
  decide it's all over. Give yourself a few days or
  weeks, and then reconsider how you feel.

- **Talk to someone who is objective.** To help sort
  through your feelings, find a friend you can
  trust, who is supportive, and ask him or her to
  listen. Or, see a counselor or minister. If you're
  confused, telling someone who will listen
  sympathetically and objectively will help you
  figure out what you need.

- **Keep your partner informed.** Let your partner
  know if you're feeling unsure about your commitment, and also what you're doing to figure
  things out. Keep the lines of communication as
  open as possible.

Keep in mind that occasional waffling is normal,

everyone has doubts in the early stages of a relationship. The above steps should help you get past the waffling, but if it doesn't, couples counseling will help.

What is happily ever after?

We have all heard many fables and stories that end "...and they lived happily ever after." We have also heard true tales of misery and breakup, and even probably have experienced them. Is happiness really possible? Can you have a relationship for life?

What will happen when you spend many years together? As intimacy grows over time, love matures and becomes more realistic. As the newness and magic of your initial romance fade, both of you begin to relax, revealing your innermost, imperfect selves. This can make you feel vulnerable and even awkward with each other. You may argue, struggle for power, and become irritable and distant. As a result, you need lots of reassurance and attention, but you may have trouble giving it.

Unless you've been through it and recognize this stage, it can be frightening, but if you hang in there, you can establish a new level of intimacy, one that is more mature and honest.

The settled-partnership phase presents more new issues. In this phase, you learn to handle long-term intimacy, sexuality and personal growth. Once you have resolved these issues, you are able to experience the pleasures of lasting love, and to love each other for who you really are. In this way, you acquire the experience, cooperation and mutual understanding necessary to keep your commitment alive.

Long Term Skills

You have probably heard that love fades over a lifetime relationship, and you may have experienced it or watched friends become bored with each other. While it's true that, for many couples, sexual and emotional intimacy recede into the background of daily pragmatic issues—housework, children, career, social obligations—this shift is by no means inevitable. To maintain healthy and satisfying intimacy in a long-term relationship, a couple must develop skills in four basic areas.

1. **Maintaining sexual attraction and generating romance**. Following the guidelines above about keeping communication open and avoiding the "four horsemen" will help keep your connection and your intimacy alive. Don't hesitate to seek help if you find your sexual relationship is fading. A certified sex counselor can help you keep your love alive for the life of your relationship.

2. **Dealing positively with life changes**. Life presents many changes we can't foresee, including health problems, financial ups and downs, the loss of people who are close to you, career changes and problems, and aging. Working together to acknowledge the changes, to see the positive aspects of change, to accommodate whatever happens, and to celebrate your successes will allow you to recognize all your mixed feelings—sadness and excitement, frustration and elation, anger and joy, loss and gain. Looking back and celebrating all you've been through and survived together is a great joy of being in a long-term relationship.

3. **Resolving disappointment**. No matter how blessed you are, life is not always going to give you what you want. Learning to resolve your disappointment about things that happen and loss-

es you have to face will strengthen your bond. When life is difficult, do your best to be even nicer to each other than you usually are, and to be supportive and caring. When you come through difficulties by helping each other, you'll find that you feel closer than ever.

4. **Avoiding boredom by learning how to play, to celebrate and to laugh.** If boredom begins to descend on your relationship, it's usually the result of avoidance—of each other, of acknowledging change, of responsibility, or of life. It's a signal that you have begun to take each other for granted; you're stuck in a rut. Life is serious business, but it doesn't have to be grim. Laughing and playing together will liven up the atmosphere and chase the boredom away. After the initial excitement of a new relationship wears off, if all goes well, a sense of humor will set in.

Partners in long-term relationships generally have the self-esteem and confidence to laugh at their quirks. It's a wonderful way to relieve pressure and remind ourselves that we're human. You and your partner need to continue celebrating throughout your lives to keep your energy high and maintain your motivation. Celebrate your love often, with a quiet dinner for two, a secret smile or touch and an occasional party.

Sex for the long haul

Most people don't realize it, but the sexual skills needed to make long-term sex work are different from those that you use when you first meet. To keep romance and sexuality flourishing, give it a special place in your life. Don't bring up problems, chores, bills, or other potentially distressing or distracting

Watch Out!
Don't confuse
sexual attraction
for emotional
bonding. They
are two very
different things.

issues when you have a chance to be close. Allow yourselves time and space to "get away from it all."

Perhaps the most important thing you can do to keep attraction and romance alive over a long period of time is to remember who you were when your lover originally fell in love with you. Nothing is more boring than being bored, and nothing is more interesting than being interested. The secret to long-lasting sexual satisfaction and ongoing romance is as simple as that.

Sex is one of the most reassuring, soothing, and energizing elements of a lasting relationship. By eliminating pressure, keeping sexual communication open, maintaining attractiveness, setting aside special time, and introducing some change from time to time to keep things fresh, you can eliminate the sexual stagnation that can poison long-term romance.

Real life issues to work out

When you decide it's an official relationship, you are creating (or accepting) a significant change in your life. This means you'll have a lot of practical things to work out. Among the first of these issues is deciding who to tell about your new, couple status, and how to tell them. Who you tell and how you present it helps determine how well your relationship is received and supported, so choose carefully.

Breaking the news to your ex

If your ex is still in your life, perhaps because of children or financial connections, or if you are friends, how you tell him/her depends on your current relationship. If you have not been broken up long, telling is delicate, and should be done with some thought for your ex's feelings. Just tell your ex that you're dating someone. You don't need to say more unless you've become really close friends.

If you have children, and they know, your ex will probably find out, so tell your ex as soon as you know the relationship is significant to you. Reassure your ex that you'll let him or her know in advance if there are any changes that will affect your children or your ex.

Letting your other dates down gently

Of course, if you've been dating other people, and you decide one other relationship is going to be serious, telling these dates you're no longer available is the caring and respectful thing to do. Don't just disappear out of their lives—tell them that someone you've been dating has become a serious relationship. Remember to mention that you've enjoyed dating them, and what you like about them. If you like a particular person, and you think he or she is mature enough to handle it appropriately, you may want to invite him or her to remain friends.

Telling your friends

Hopefully, your new relationship will not be a total shock to your friends. In fact, it's probable that they've already met your date, and they know you've been dating. Telling them that it's getting serious should be fun, if they know and like your date.

However, if your friends don't know your date, or if for some reason they don't like the person you've been involved with, announcing that it's getting serious may not go over too well. Also, if you have dropped all contact with your friends and obsessed on this new relationship, you'll get worried or angry responses from them. If you're in this situation, tell each friend individually, and allow time to talk. Explain what's been happening, and then arrange for a time for your friend to meet your date. The support of friends is crucial to the long-term success of a relationship, so mend your bridges now.

If you have kept in touch with your friends, and they know both of you, introducing your individual friends to each other will be a fun adventure. Once everyone is comfortable with your relationship, announcing that it's official will be a cause for celebration.

Telling the children

In Chapter 13 you will learn in detail how to introduce your relationship to your children. The basic rule of thumb is that you need to let your children get to know your date gradually as a friend. Consult them on their feelings about this new person, and refrain from telling them that this person is more than just a friend until you're sure your relationship is mutual and solid. If you've done all that, telling them you're getting serious should be easy. In fact, if you give it enough time, your children will help you break the ice by asking questions as things progress, such as "Why is _____ (your date) here so much?" "Do you like _____?" and even, "Are you going to marry _____?"

If your children like your date (which, if they're young, is an essential prerequisite to living together—don't move in if your children are not comfortable), they'll be fine with the relationship. If you haven't taken time to blend the family, you're going to have endless trouble.

If your date doesn't want to be around your children, or doesn't get along well with them, it's OK to let the relationship continue to be outside your family circle, even though it will be inconvenient—but don't try to force the blending. Trying to force everyone to get along will create a disaster.

If your children are grown, whether they like your date is less important, but, as with your friends, if you've chosen a good person to date, and they're given a chance to get to know him or her, they will usually be happy for you.

Informing the family

Your parents, siblings, and other relatives also will do better if you don't shock them with a sudden announcement. How close you and your family are will determine how you introduce your date to them. Bringing your date to a family gathering, picnic, barbecue, or even to church on Sunday is a good way to have everyone meet, letting them all know this is just a "friend."

After this has happened a few times, you and your date can invite family over to your house for dessert and coffee, or to watch a game or movie on TV, or play cards—whatever activities your family does together, if any. By this time, your family will be asking questions, and you can gradually let them know the relationship is more than just friends, and eventually, that it's officially a relationship.

Then, if you're considering taking the next step—getting engaged or marrying—each new phase can be introduced to everyone, and your family will be there to support and help you.

Making new living arrangements

As excited as you must be to have such a wonderful thing happening in your life, don't be so excited that you rush into living together too soon. Many relationship disasters I have seen in my counseling practice have happened because someone had to move, and they decided to move in together before the

Timesaver
If everyone knows the relationship is getting serious, a general announcement that's not really a surprise will be better received than one that's a shock. But, at this early stage, you may find that it's easier to make your announcement on a person-by-person basis. If you give friends a chance to ask questions, and to get comfortable with the idea, you'll save a lot of time and hassle.

relationship was solid enough to support living together. What they didn't recognize was that living together adds a lot of pressure to any relationship. Don't be too eager to do it.

Coping with the kids

When you decide to make your relationship official, in addition to telling your children, you must work out together how you're going to deal with them. This is especially true if you decide to share a single household.

Moneysaver
"Two can live as cheaply as one" is a time-honored saying that may or may not be true. Yes, moving in can probably save you some rent and utilities, but if it puts too much pressure on the relationship, the costs (not to mention the pain) of moving out again if things don't go well can be very high.

If the children are young, it's essential to work out your child-rearing philosophies, to learn family traditions, and in general to work together to make adding a new person (or people) to the family group as smooth and easy as possible. Whenever children are involved your relationship cannot be just about the two of you. The children's needs must be considered first, and carefully planned. Creating a blended family is an art—there are a lot of feelings and dynamics to deal with.

Don't make the mistake of thinking that children will see this the same way you do. Use your family meetings to find out how your children feel about the issues involved, and work together, as a team, to solve your family problems.

Establishing relationships

Your children must each be encouraged to form their own relationships with your new partner (and you with your partner's children, also). If both of you have children, they will also need time and opportunity to form their own relationships. This is a delicate process, and trying too hard to encourage or force it will create problems. If, in the beginning, you introduced your new companion as just a friend, and if you have the patience to allow the relationship to grow gradually, you will have a lot less trouble than if you insist that everyone "just get along."

Whatever you do, don't get in the middle between your partner and your children, or between your partner and his or her children. Make your communications direct, and not through third parties. If one of your children says "Mom, I don't like it that John calls me nicknames," use that as an opportunity to suggest the child talk to John directly. If a child says "Dad, I don't want Mary to ruffle my hair." again, use that as an opportunity to create direct communication.

This is where it's essential that you and your partner have discussed discipline styles, who is in charge, and so on, so that when you talk to children directly, you know what to say.

Family communication

Family meetings, with everyone involved, are essential. Children need to know that their wants and feelings are important to you, even if you have to say "no" about some of them. In the beginning, invite your partner to occasional family meetings, and encourage everyone to talk.

When you are alone with your children, let them tell you what they think about your partner, without being too sensitive about it. If they can tell you they think your date is a "dork," and you laugh, and acknowledge how they might think that, but also point out some positive qualities, you'll create a freer atmosphere, and get a chance to influence your child's opinion.

But it's not just the children who need a chance to communicate about how to handle situations that arise within a blended family situation. When you get serious enough to consider blending your families, you'll need to discuss sharing discipline, teaching and working together with the children.

This is where your differing philosophies of child-rearing may come into conflict, especially if you're both parents. Take plenty of time to work this out. If one of you thinks the other is too harsh, or too lax, you're going to have problems unless you can make agreements that satisfy both of you. While a new partner can bring a fresh, more objective view to the child-parent relationship that already exists, you don't want to make drastic changes, which will throw things into chaos, and make your children resistant to the relationship.

Of course, the actual parent, who has been the authority so far, should continue to have the final say, but you'll find it's necessary for the new partner to have some authority, as an adult who will also be responsible. If you have created teamwork as a couple, this should just be a further application of your ability to work together. Stretch the team to include the children in every way you can.

Step-parent families

If your relationship has progressed to the point where you're all going to live together, you have even more dynamics to work through. If you decide to live together and/or get married, you not only have your immediate family relationship to work out, but other people now get involved, such as ex-spouses, who are also parents of the children, in-laws, grandparents, and other relatives. And the reactions of neighbors, old friends, school teachers, and parents of your children's friends can potentially add more stress.

The difficulties step-parent families face are well documented, and there are many fine books and even classes on the subject.

Step-parents are under a lot of pressure, from the "You're not my Mom (or Dad)" rebellion of children, to suspicion from the children's other parent and grandparents, to the issues of re-creating a family that's already established its dynamics. Add this to the stresses and problems any new couple relationship faces, and you can see how tough it could get. No matter how much you love each other, you're going to have problems dealing with all this.

I highly recommend counseling for any couple attempting to blend families, and create a healthy step-parent relationship. This is a complex, pressurized and vitally important process, and should only be done with expert help and advice.

Divorced parent issues

If you're dating again with children, then most likely you have an ex, the other parent, also in the picture, who will have his or her own reaction to your new relationship. Issues such as how well resolved your problems with your ex are, the terms of custody and visitation, the ages of your children, and the agreement you have worked out will help determine how supportive or resistant your ex is to this new relationship.

It is natural for your children's other parent to be concerned about who your new relationship is, and how well he or she will treat your children. For the sake of your children, don't resent this kind of questioning. Give your ex as much reassuring information as you can. In fact, if your relationship with your ex is amicable, he or she should meet your date (as a friend) just as your friends and family would.

If your children have met your date, your ex will know about it anyway, so provide an opportunity for your ex and your date to meet and get to know each other a bit. Hopefully, everyone will be capable of being an adult about it, and actually meeting each other will reduce the worry factor.

Even though you and your ex have divorced, he or she is still part of your family as parent to your children, and working out a comfortable arrangement now, if possible, will reduce a lot of problems later.

Grandparents and others

If you have arranged for your family to meet your date, and things went well, your own parents should be happy for you and supportive. If not, you'll have to have some discussions with them, also.

Your ex's parents are the grandparents most likely to see your date as a threat to their connection with their grandchildren. Depending on how close this connection is, you should make the same effort (again for the children's sake) as you are making with your ex to reassure and inform them so they have no need to worry.

Financial matters

Don't be in a rush to actually pool your resources, but begin at this stage to discuss how you will do it later. Now that the relationship is official, you should be disclosing private financial matters to each other, and learning where each of you stands in this regard, including responsibilities to ex's for child support, investments, debts, income and so forth.

View working out your finances as a test of how well the two of you can work together on major life issues. Since finances are a major source of problems for couples, if you can create a plan that suits both of you *before* you actually pool resources or move in, you'll have nipped a lot of problems in the bud.

If you are contemplating moving in or marriage, consider a pre-nuptial agreement. This protects your children, each other and takes into account the current laws of your state. Working out the agreement, which you can do yourself with a kit if you like, will give you a crystal clear picture of your financial status and arrangement.

While it seems unromantic to many people, working out this agreement is such a great exercise in the reality of your relationship, I suggest you view it as a very healthy step in creating true commitment rather than romantic fantasy.

Marriage—or not?

Eventually, if things go well, the question of whether you should marry will arise. If marriage is important to you, for religious or family reasons, the answer will be obvious—if the relationship is right, you'll want to marry. But, if marriage is not something you value in itself, if you (or even your parents) have been through a disastrous divorce, or if you fear marriage will change the nature of your relationship, you may not be so sure it's a good idea.

This, of course, is a very personal decision between the two of you, and no one else can decide if it's right. What I *can* recommend is that you regard the discussion of whether or not to marry as one more exercise in developing teamwork, trust and caring for each other. If only one of you wants to marry, what does that person want it for? Why is it important to the other person not to marry? Make lists of the pros and cons, legal, financial, personal, emotional, and spiritual, for marrying and remaining unmarried.

For example, many couples today are finding that they fare far better income tax wise unmarried than married. If you are entitled to social security income from a deceased spouse, you may lose that if you marry. Other people have personal or family reasons for not remarrying. For example, a woman may not want to have a different last name than her children.

There are many options you can choose. Did you know, for example, that you can be married in the eyes of your church, and not in the eyes of the law? If you have a clergy person perform a ceremony, you are married in the church, but if you don't have a license, and you don't register the marriage, it's not a legal marriage for tax and other purposes. You are also free to have any ceremony you wish, with or without religious sanction, and not make it legal with a marriage license.

If issues such as these concern you, consult a lawyer, your minister, rabbi or priest, and/or a marriage counselor to get sound advice and help in reaching an agreement.

As wonderful as it is to think of successful dating that leads to marriage, there are also many potential problems in the process. In the final chapters, we'll discuss those problems and what to do about them.

Just the facts

- Moving from casual dating to bringing your date into your regular life should be done with caution.

- Open communication is a way to speed the process of getting to know your date well enough to move to deeper levels of intimacy.

- Partnership and teamwork are the foundation of

any healthy relationship.

■ Keep your relationship vital by celebrating your life together.

■ Don't let life issues fester untended—work together to resolve problems and your relationship will grow ever closer.

Dating's Dilemmas

GET THE SCOOP ON...
Single parent dating ▪ Managing family
and dates ▪ Scheduling issues ▪
Setting groundrules

PART V

And Baby Makes Three

I f you're a single parent, you probably have so little free time that dating seems an impossible task. Yes, single parents do date, in unprecedented numbers, so if you're looking for a counterpart—another single parent to date—you'll have little trouble finding one.

Single parents who try to juggle families and dating are forced to be efficient, however, just because they don't have endless time to waste hanging around waiting. As a responsible single parent, you'll also want to be very cautious about whom you date and eventually bring home—for the safety and well-being of your child(ren). In this chapter you'll learn many tips for making the whole dating process more compatible with fulfilling your parenting responsibilities, and you'll get the answers to some of the most frequently asked questions about dating that single parents ask.

When you are a dating parent

If you are the person in the relationship who has children, you may feel guilty or unsure about

317

whether dating is OK. Of course it is, as long as you do it responsibly. Your children, however, should not be disrupted by your dating. The age of your children will influence your dating opportunities and choices, as will whatever custody arrangements you may have worked out with your children's other parent.

If you share custody with the other parent of your child, and the children are gone some or most of the time, especially on weekends, that is of course the most obvious time for you to date. Since your free time with your children is somewhat limited, you'll want to be with them when you can, which means you won't want to use "their" time for dating.

If the other parent only takes the children occasionally, or not at all, then you need to arrange for the children's care when you're dating, or meeting new people. There are some ways to meet new people with your children along, and we'll cover those later in the chapter. In any case, dating, until you know the new person well, should *not* be something your children share.

When your date is a parent

If you are dating a single parent, you face circumstances that are different than if you're dating a single non-parent. Depending on the children's ages and on how much of the time your date has them at home, their presence can have a major impact on your dating, primarily because a single parent is not as free to do whatever he or she wants as a non-parent can be, and must always consider the needs of his or her children first.

If you do not have children of your own, you may not understand some of your date's concerns and issues. This chapter will help you learn what to expect, and what is appropriate, when dating a single parent.

You both are single parents

If you are a single parent, there are several advantages to dating someone else who has children.

- You understand each others' issues, needs, and pressures.

- Once you have established a good connection, both of you and your children can do things together (but see the cautions about bonding that appear later in this chapter).

- You can share parenting information and issues.

- Sudden problems, like a sick child, will be taken in stride.

- Your partner probably likes and understands children.

- Budget constraints are probably mutual, and will be understood.

The basics of the dating parent

Parents who date are a relatively new phenomenon. Until divorce became widespread, not many educated, affluent parents were free to date except for the occasional widow or widower. So, the basic information you need to know is relatively new also.

The first thing you need to understand is that dating as a parent requires not only finding someone you like and who likes you, but also someone who is comfortable with your children. The children add extra dynamics to the situation, which can be frustrating, but should not be ignored or overlooked.

If your children do not like someone, or if your

date is uncomfortable with them, you can continue to date, but it is advisable to keep your dating separate from your children. This may severely limit your involvement with your date if the children are young. Most importantly, your children should not know you are dating until the relationship is serious—you don't want them to become attached to a string of boy- or girlfriends who don't stay around very long. If you keep their relationship with your date light and casual during the early days of dating, they'll have time to become comfortable enough with your new friend, so that when you get serious they will be able to handle the situation with few problems.

If you pressure your children to like your date, or go too fast for them to get comfortable with the situation, you are asking for a lot of trouble. By following the rules here, you will make sure your children have the time they need to get comfortable with your new date, and that will help make things go smoothly.

Safety and sensibility issues

Your first priority, for yourself and your children, needs to be your safety and theirs. Following the guidelines in this book will maximize the safety of dating and meeting new people, but today's society is very mobile, and it's easy for unsavory people to hide their backgrounds. That is the major reason that I suggest getting to know people as friends before dating.

Group activities, daytime activities with the children along, being in public places, and establishing someone's character before being alone together (and especially before leaving your child alone with them) is the safest way to go.

By now you've already learned several techniques for keeping yourself safe. When you're a parent, the issue of your safety becomes even more critical—there are people depending upon you. Don't be too quick to get into a car with a person you don't know, or to be in a stranger's home, or have a new acquaintance in your home, especially when your children are present—for their safety as well as your own.

Meeting other single parents at PTA, church, and school or sports events is a great, non-threatening way to begin dating as a single parent. The public setting provides safety and a chance to get to know the other person, to find out what others think of him or her, and to meet his or her children. This last is important—you'll have a chance to learn some things about the kind of parenting they have received. In addition, in parent-oriented settings, your children will meet your new friend as the parent of other children, not as your date, so the situation is likely to be much less threatening and ominous to them. There is less pressure on everyone.

Who's minding the kids?

When you do get to know someone well enough that you'd like to move to the next step and begin individual dating, rather than group activities, what do you do with the kids? This will depend largely on how old the children are, what arrangements you've made for their care while you work, and your custody and child care arrangements.

It's easiest to date on nights when your kids are with their other parent, but that's not always possible. If your children are very young (infants to early school age) you'll need a baby-sitter—unless grandparents, relatives, or their other parent will take them for the evening. It is not a good idea to try to

Moneysaver
Baby-sitters can be really expensive. To minimize the expense, create a "village"—a network of other single parents, and parents of your child's schoolmates, who will trade off letting your child stay overnight, if you invite theirs to stay with you at another time. This way, you can share child care for free.

entertain a date at home with the children there—especially early in the relationship. Even if the kids are supposed to be asleep, you're likely to be distracted—and in the early stages of dating your kids simply shouldn't be that involved.

Being clear about priorities

As a parent, you have rights—but so do your children and the person you're dating. Respecting everyone's rights requires establishing a firm set of priorities, making sure everyone understands them, and sticking to them.

Children's rights

If your children are small, they have a right to be primary in your life. They should not have to feel that the attention they deserve has been taken from them and given to your new relationship. They should not have to compete for your time, attention, and affection. Maintaining a balance here will not be easy, because as a single parent your time is probably already at a premium. The older your children are, the less time they need from you, and the more freedom you should have to date as you want to.

As soon as your children are old enough to understand the concepts, you should explain to them that you have some rights to spend time with your friends and that there is a certain amount of time you need to call your own. You do not need to explain about being lonely, or needing a new partner. This should not be their problem.

Once you have arranged for appropriate care for them, you can do what you want with your own time, including dating. However, your dating arrangement should not bleed over into the time that you spend with your family, at least not at the start of a dating relationship. Keep your family and your dating separate until you are sure you are ready to blend them responsibly.

Giving your date his (or her) due

Your date has a right to understand the importance of your family, and to make the choice to explore what can develop with you. But no one has the right to disrupt your family life. To ensure that this doesn't happen, you need to make clear *from the very first moment you realize you're interested in dating someone* that you are a parent first, and a dating companion second.

The person you are dating should also be told your rules about parenting, and how much say he or she has over your children's behavior. As a friend, your date has no child-rearing authority or rights to discipline your children, but he or she should not have to tolerate impolite treatment,. And *you* have authority to make sure your children treat your friend politely—you should exercise that authority if the occasion to do so arises.

If the relationship goes well, and your date's friendship with your children grows, these priorities may change a bit. They will also change as your children get older. But such changes should happen slowly. If your relationship with your dating partner deepens to the point that you begin to form a new family, then your partner should gradually begin to have some say over your children's behavior. Again, however, such changes require a lot of discussion and problem-solving among all of you.

Who meets who, and when

When you introduce your date to your children, (unless you meet as parents of children of similar

Unofficially...
Years ago, I
stayed overnight
with a new date,
and got up very
early in the morn-
ing to use the
bathroom. I
encountered my
friend's 3-year-old
son in the hall.
He said to me
"Are you going to
leave like every-
one else?" It
broke my heart,
but I stayed
around (as a
friend to his dad)
and watched him
grow up into a
fine young man.

ages) let the first contact happen naturally—do your best to avoid making a big deal out of the introductions. There's a fine line to tread here, because if your relationships gets serious it's vital that your date and your children get along, but you don't want your children to get bonded to someone who's not going to be around for long. They've already lost one intact family when you split up with their other parent, so more people coming and going in their lives is not a particularly good thing for them to have to cope with. It's less traumatic for them to handle the "disappearance" of a casual acquaintance, but they'll be hurt and confused if someone with whom they've closely bonded suddenly drops out of their lives.

Both the parent and the person dating a parent have the responsibility not to put the children through difficulties they have not asked for. You must be sure you are both adult enough to maintain at least a friendship even if you break up if you decide to allow your date to get close to your children.

Your children, especially when they're small, shouldn't be subjected to a "revolving door" of people coming and going in their lives. It's fine to have them meet acquaintances and say "hello," but not to get close to person after person who soon leaves. There is enough loss in life that we can't control—it isn't necessary to add unnecessary losses to the mix.

Kids shouldn't have to compete

As a single parent, you have your hands full, but your children should never feel they have to compete with your adult relationships for your time and attention. It is fine to ask a child to play for a while so you can talk to other adults, but you should never neglect your children in the process.

Too many single parents drag young children around to adult functions where they don't belong, feel out of place, and have nothing to do, because the adult feels guilty about leaving them with a sitter. But this really accomplishes nothing positive. The child doesn't get any *real* time with the parent, and is really being disrespected and disregarded. While it's appropriate to teach children of school age how to behave in adult settings, it is not appropriate to drag them everywhere you go.

If you cannot keep an appropriate balance between the attention you give your children and the attention you give to your friends or dates, you may need to consult a family therapist and learn some skills.

No big decisions without kids say-so

Among your child's rights is to have his or her opinions respected. You don't have to agree or go along with what your child wants, but you should at least know what it is, and your child should know why you're overriding his or her preferences. Regular family meetings, where everyone including the children expresses feelings, negative and positive, and all of you work together to solve problems, can help a lot.

Begin family meetings as soon as possible, before any of these dating issues even come up. Choose a time when everyone can get together weekly, and suggest to your children that you order pizza, or cook something they like. At the meeting, everyone (including yourself) begins by stating three good things about others in the family, Then, each person gets to mention one thing they want to improve, and what they want to do to make it better. Small children will need help until they understand, but they will catch on quickly. Even you and one child can do this.

If it looks as if your dating partner is going to become a long-term relationship, the family may decide to invite him or her to participate in some of these meetings. It's a great way for everyone to begin to work out blending someone new into the family.

Rules for everyone

Rules may sound like a drag, but, if they're sensible and reasonable, they can help a lot. When the rules are clear, everyone knows what is expected of them, and what the consequences are of breaking the rules. If you set rules early, and are consistent, everyone is more likely to feel respected and secure.

Rules apply to everything, including dating. And children aren't the only ones who need rules to follow. If the adults involved (you, your date, your ex, grandparents, friends) do the right thing automatically, they are following their own internal rules, but if the rules you, date follows don't work for you and your children, you'll have to inform him/her of yours.

Ages and stages

The rules vary a lot according to the ages of your children. When children are infants, they are too young to know what rules are, but as they grow, more and more rules are needed, until they get old enough to make decisions rather than obey rules. Understanding and living according to rules of behavior early in life gives a child the foundation he or she needs to self-regulate behavior as a teenager and young adult.

Infants/toddlers. Babies cannot understand and

Watch Out!
Con artists and sexual predators often see single parents as "easy prey." Before you allow a new person too close to your home and family, be very sure you have checked the new person out.

follow rules, but they catch on quickly if their feed-ing, sleeping, and playing schedules are regular. When you're dating, the rules about your infant child will be for safety and good care. You'll want to arrange your dating and outings, baby-sitting, staying with Grandma, etc., so your child's schedule is not disrupted.

Toddlers begin to understand simple rules as soon as they understand language. They are learning from you, so keep in mind that your behavior is teaching them. In terms of your dating, your tod-dlers only need to know they're going to be taken care of while you are gone, and perhaps, after you are certain your date is of good enough character, to learn how to say "hello" to your adult friend, and the very beginning rules of politeness, when you all spend time together.

As the relationship grows, your toddler and your date will have to form their own connection, and you should give them enough space to do that, once you're sure your relationship is reliable enough to be worth it.

Grade-school age children. Should children of this age group happen to meet your date (which is not at all necessary at first) all they need to know is that you are going out with a friend. In addition, they should be required to be polite and sociable when they meet your friend (after you feel sure it's a worthwhile enough person to make introductions). As the relationship grows, if you begin to think it will last, you will want to go on outings with the children and your date. A ball game, a trip to the zoo or the circus, a picnic in the park, will give everyone a chance to get acquainted. These are all opportuni-ties for your children to learn the socially acceptable forms of politeness and good behavior. You are responsible for discipline and organization, and your date should not be involved in these issues yet.

Teenagers. The dating issues get more complicated when your children are pre-teens or teenagers. They will understand the significance, or the potential meaning, of your spending time with your new friend, and what it means to them. They will be much more likely to project into the future, and may feel threatened by the possibilities that your dating represents.

This is an age group for which it is most important that your date begins by making friends and takes the relationship slowly. As long as it is evident to your teenagers that you are just friends, they'll be a lot more open to getting to know this new person. As soon as you're sure this new person will be safe around your kids (and don't be too quick decide), you can begin doing relaxed, casual things together, such as going to appropriate movies, attending the kids' sporting events, having barbecues, and going to the beach or the lake swimming.

If the relationship gets more serious, if everyone is getting along comfortably and you're certain your new partner is reliable, you can begin to talk to your children (without the partner around) about your feelings. This is a great topic for family meetings, and once you've broken the ice on the topic privately, your date can be invited to join in on occasion, if everyone agrees.

Be very careful about making the decision to try to live together, and never pressure your kids to like your new love. As much as you would like everyone to get along and to be as happy as you are, your children have a right to choose who they want to live with, and they should definitely have a say on this subject. If you make a unilateral decision, force the issue, or insist, you will make yourself and everyone else miserable.

Adult children. If your children are grown, hopefully they'll be generous enough to care about your happiness, and support your dating process from the beginning. But that is not always the case. Adult children sometimes have a problem with the idea of a parent dating. This is especially true if your former spouse, their other parent, has died, because it's difficult to think of replacing a parent who has passed on.

If you value the judgment of your adult children, and they are worried about you, pay attention if they are negative about someone, just as you would pay attention to the concerns of any dear friend. Find out what their reasons are for their distrust or dislike—your own judgment may be impaired by your emotional involvement. But, if you think they're just being possessive of you, you may need to ignore their objections. As with your teenagers, this will be easier if your adult children originally meet any new person you date as "just a friend."

Whatever they feel about your dating partner, you have a right to expect that they will be polite and pleasant to your dates when they meet, and if you decide to deepen the relationship, they should make an effort to get along with your new partner.

But one major thing you need to consider about your adult children, especially if you remarry, is their financial rights. Keep in mind that, if you remarry and then die without making proper provisions, you may put control of their inheritance in the hands of someone who doesn't honor their claims. This is very unpleasant to consider, but as a counselor, I've seen a lot of terrible problems created by just this scenario. Before remarrying, get good, solid financial advice about protecting your children's inheritance.

Rules for the kids

In addition to the considerations you need to make for your children, there are expectations and rules you should set for them. When it comes to your dating, the expectations for your children are just extensions of the everyday behavior standards you set for them.

Politeness. When you bring someone home, your children should know the basic rules of politeness, how to behave around adult company, and how to treat an adult friend of yours when they meet for the first time. Your children should be able to meet a new friend of yours with the same social graces they use to meet your business associates, their new teachers, and other adults they encounter.

They should be able to respond properly when introduced, to call an adult "Mr. or Ms.," to use all the polite forms such as "please," "thank you," and "may I be excused."

Children don't need special rules beyond these for meeting a date of yours. Ordinary politeness is sufficient, because your date should be treated as any adult friend of yours.

If a new date begins to get to know your children in a more relaxed setting, he or she may invite them to use first names. If all goes well, and everyone gets along, the more formal courtesy will relax naturally.

Who counts more? If you are careful about going slowly and getting to know someone as a friend, your children will not feel pushed into the background by your dating, and they will not compete with your adult friends for your attention. Even when time is at a premium, your children should have enough alone time with you, so they can also enjoy being with your adult friends.

As teens get older, if they don't feel threatened by your relationships, they will be more and more absorbed with their own lives and activities, and you will have more free time. Your adult friends, especially someone you're dating or going to date, are important to you, and if your children like them, they'll gradually become equally important to the children.

Taking the time to let everyone become comfortable may be difficult when you're excited about a new relationship, but it will make a huge difference in whether everyone learns to get along.

Rules for your date

From the first, your new friend should understand how important being a parent is to you, and that dating has to take a back seat. If your date is also a parent, he or she should understand, and should feel the same about his or her own children. If you're dating a single person, this may be more difficult to get across.

Face the fact that being a parent, while your kids are still underage, can cost you a few relationships. If a person you find attractive doesn't want to have to face the responsibilities children present, then you will not get very far until your children are old enough to be on their own, off to school, or at least in high school and very involved in their own activities and friendships.

Your new friend should understand what behavior and language is off limits in front of the kids. If you're telling the children you are friends, you should act like friends—no physical affection or terms of endearment.

This stranger should also understand and accept your need to make sure he or she is safe before introducing your children. Not only that the children are physically safe, but also that there will be no drunkenness or heavy drinking, emotional outbursts, inappropriate behavior, etc. This is where being with your new friend around others can save you trouble, because you can observe behavior for signs of addiction, immaturity, bad temper, harsh criticism or sarcasm, and so on.

Once you determine your new friend is safe, and introduce him or her to your children, times spent with the children should focus largely on them, not on you two adults. Having fun as a group is what's most important—not how excited you are about your new relationship.

As everyone gets to know each other better, and if things go well, your date should be gradually introduced to your household rules, family meetings, holiday celebrations, and so on, with the intention of blending in to your family times as they are, and not changing them substantially.

All these rules will also apply to *you* if you are in the presence of your date's children.

***Don't* bond with kids**. Bonding with the children should be done with extreme caution. If you met as single parents at a school function, and some bonding with each other's children has already occurred, then you must be careful that if your dating does not work into anything more you can remain friendly around the children

Don't be overanxious about your children and

your new date getting along. Take your time, be very low key about it, and bonding will happen naturally. If you all bond successfully, everyone will gain from creating a blended family.

Be wary of bonding with your date's children, also, for the same reasons. If you are too quick to let yourself get close to your date's children, or let your date get close to yours, and the relationship doesn't work out, everyone will be devastated.

Don't surprise anyone. Do your best to communicate what your intentions are all along the way. If you want to make friends first, be clear about it as soon as you know, or from the beginning. If that goes well, and you want to deepen the relationship, make that clear, also.

Don't make sudden big announcements to your children or your date. If you are doing this according to our plan, each new stage of your relationship, and the relationship with your children, will happen gradually, and you can talk about it slowly as it happens. You and your children can have talks about your new friend, and how much you all like him or her, as things develop. Your date and you can talk about how things are going between you, and also with your children.

Life offers enough surprises on its own—you and your kids may have to deal with illnesses, bad weather, tough situations at work or school. If you have to surprise them with a relationship development, either you're going too fast, or you haven't been communicating regularly enough.

Rules for yourself

The buck stops with you, and that's where the toughest rules are. Because you're a parent, you must be responsible, even if a new date makes you feel like

Timesaver
Speed up the time it takes to know someone is safe by getting to know his or her friends. When doing things in a group, invite your new friend to bring friends along, and take the time to interview them. You'll be surprised what they'll tell you about past relationships, family history, and job history. Compare what they say to what your date's told you. If it matches, and sounds OK, great. If you're not allowed to meet friends, be suspicious.

kicking the traces and letting your hair down. You are the only one who can make sure that your dating process is good for both you and your family.

Careful, careful...

Remember that your children are more vulnerable to hurt and disappointment than you are, so be very careful not to set them up for painful situations. If you're dating again, it's likely that your children's family life has already been disrupted once—when you and their other parent broke up. You don't want to force them to go through that kind of trauma again.

Being careful means not only keeping your children, your home, yourself, and your possessions safe, it also means making sure your children witness only healthy interactions. Being very sure about who you bring home will make sure you don't expose your children to hysterics, arguments, violence, drunkenness, rudeness, and abuse.

Sex is a secret

Your children who are not adult should know nothing about your sexual experiences. Part of your responsibility is to make sure that you keep this aspect of your dating life private. Don't take risks, even if it feels exciting. And if your date values your responsibilities as a parent, he or she will help make sure you have sex at appropriate times and places.

If your relationship has developed to the sexual stage, you will already know quite a bit about your date. Make arrangements to be sexual at your date's home (if there are no children there) rather than in your own. If you both have children, once they get to know and like each other, you can have them all stay at one of your homes with a baby-sitter, and go to the other home to be intimate. If this is not an option, rent an inexpensive motel room from time to time, or even get permission to borrow a friend's house while they're gone.

Keep in mind that you're demonstrating your behavior to your children. If you wouldn't want them to do what you're doing, make sure they don't witness it. When a relationship becomes a real commitment or marriage you can sleep together.

You are a parent first

You deserve to have a good time, to meet new people and make new friends, and you can do that with no problem for your family, if you plan carefully. But parenting is your first concern, and taking care of your children your first responsibility. Still, you don't have to be discouraged. Meeting new friends can be a fun experience for you, your date, and your family. All it takes is that you understand—and follow—a few basic rules:

- Make sure you know a lot about any new person before inviting him/her into your home.

- Make friends before considering a romantic relationship.

- Always introduce new adults to your children as friends, nothing more.

- If your children are old enough to have opinions of your new friends, listen to what they have to say.

- Do not pressure your children to like your new friend, or to spend time with him or her.

- Insist that your children behave appropriately and politely to your adult friends.

- Have regular family meetings with your children.

- If you want to get serious with a date, find out his or her feelings about children, especially your children, first.

- Gradually introduce a new date to your children by doing family oriented activities together. Give your children and your date a chance to develop their own relationships.

- Don't sacrifice your children's alone time with you to your dating. Don't miss sports or school events in order to date.

- Don't share inappropriately with your children. Do not use them as "confidantes" for your relationship confusion or problems. Don't allow them to find out about your sexual relationship.

If you have the self-discipline to follow these rules, you will maximize your chances of successfully dating and keeping your family life going well.

Just the facts

- Single parent dating requires that you pay special attention to safety issues—for your sake and for the sake of your children.

- No matter *who* you're dating, the children come first.

- Keep your dating life separate from your family life until you're certain that your relationship is serious.

- Children should never have to compete with your date for your time or your affection.

- How you tell your children about a relationship should take into account their ages and their ability to cope.

GET THE SCOOP ON...
Safety first ▪ Suspicious situations ▪ Couple
problems ▪ Breakups ▪ Handling mistakes

Chapter 14

The Potential Downside of Dating

It will come as no surprise to you who are dating again, that dating has its downside. In this book, I have shared every method I know of protecting yourself, taking it slow, and holding back to give yourself time to know who you are getting close to. If you follow these recommendations carefully, your odds of being successful and of *not* getting hurt, emotionally and physically, are pretty good.

In this chapter, however, you'll learn in greater detail about the pitfalls you might encounter while dating. But never fear—I'll give you information and advice that will make your odds of being safe, from both physical and emotional hurt, even better.

Maximizing your safety

The media today tend to overemphasize problems and dangers in all aspects of modern life—not just dating. But regardless of what you read or see on TV, most of your dating experiences will not be risky. In fact, more people are physically injured by people they *know* will hurt them than by strangers who surprise them. So, if you take care of yourself when you see the signs outlined below, you will most likely be fine.

Still, we live in a very anonymous society, quite different from the protected little world provided for most of us by our parents and schools. In this environmt, it is wise to be cautious, even over-cautious.

If you must err, it's advisable that you do so on the side of caution. The worst that will happen is you'll have to apologize to someone for being too suspicious, or you'll miss out on a possible connection with someone you falsely suspected. If you totally miss a connection due to false suspicion, you will probably never know, so don't worry about it. If you find out later that someone you avoided is OK, you can reconnect, or, if necessary, apologize.

If you get any internal warnings or uncomfortable feelings, use them as an early warning system. Pay very close attention and find out what is causing your negative reaction.

> **"**
> If only one
> could tell true
> love from false
> love as one can
> tell mushrooms
> from toadstools.
> —Katherine
> Mansfield
> [Quotable Woman]
> **"**

Routine precautions

There are certain precautions you should take in the early stages of any new relationship, relaxing them one by one, as you learn your date is trustworthy. Here's a list of the basic security precautions that you should make a part of your dating routine. Some of these precautions will look familiar—they've cropped up throughout this book. They are recapped here for your convenience.

- Make friends first. By keeping the relationship in the "friends" category, you will know more about the person before taking risks.

- Begin in groups. By meeting people in safe

venues and groups, you automatically begin as friends, and know more about your date before you begin dating. You also get the benefit of your other friends reactions to your potential date.

■ **Minimize or eliminate alcohol on dates.** Alcohol severely limits your capability to take care of yourself, your ability to judge what is safe, and your capacity to observe your partner objectively.

■ Don't be alone in a stranger's car, apartment, or other isolated places. The risks are obvious.

■ Don't bring a stranger to your house, especially if you have children. Get to know someone first away from your home, which is a very vulnerable place.

■ Learn to recognize over-controlling or out of control behavior. If you are with someone you barely know who wants to know everything you do, or someone who is "over the top" emotionally or who drinks too much, or flies into hysterics or a rage, be aware that those are danger signs, and get out fast.

■ Pay close attention to your partner's financial integrity, and don't get financially involved unless you've checked him or her out thoroughly, and you're sure he or she is trustworthy. Until you know, regard any money (or possessions, such as loaning your car) you give to be a gift you'll never get back.

■ Don't let attraction overrule your common sense. Sexual and romantic attraction is very powerful, and makes it difficult to think clearly. If you feel overwhelmingly attracted to

> **“**
> When a woman first meets someone and gets a good or bad feeling, there's usually something to it.
> —Ron Ruggio, psychology professor at Claremont McKenna College.
> **”**

someone, regard that as a warning sign, and deliberately slow down until you have time to know what kind of person you are responding to. Your libido can't tell an ax murderer from a saint; but your rational mind can.

■ Make sure your date walks his or her talk. Anyone can make themselves sound good; make sure sweet talk or impressive achievements are real. As a matter of fact, some real gems *don't* present themselves well—don't overlook someone who is not gorgeous, charming, and glib, but has all the qualities you really need in a partner.

■ Practice sexual safety as if it were your religion. That is, be very consistent and careful about your sexual safety until the relationship progresses to the point that you become monogamous, and both have been tested for STD's. The nicest people can be infected with a disease and not even know they have it. If you have had unprotected sex, have your doctor do a screening for STD's. Don't assume your partner is monogamous—especially if you haven't discussed it in detail.

If you follow these precautions *every time*, your personal safety odds will be nearly 100%. If you read sensational stories about people who were victimized, you'll see that most of them were not following these guidelines. Usually, there is alcohol or poor judgment involved. You can protect yourself, physically and emotionally, and still date successfully, if you're willing to take responsibility for your own safety.

What to do if the worst happens

If something terrible does happen, know what to do

about it. I hope you never need any of the following information, but knowing what to do will make you safer, and may come in handy to help a friend or a relative someday.

Date rape

Date rape is what happens if your date drugs your drink, physically overpowers you, threatens you, or otherwise forces or coerces you into having sex against your will. It often happens between people who know each other, but not always.

Following the basic precautions listed above will protect you against most people who would commit date rape, because such a person hasn't the patience or character to get to know you well. Furthermore, a date rapist is a controlling individual—one who tends to try to force others to do as he or she wishes while personally lacking in self-control. Such traits generally become obvious if you get to know each other—which is one very strong argument for avoiding being alone with a new person during the early stages of dating.

If, in spite of precautions, you should encounter date rape, do what you can to keep yourself safe, call the police at your first opportunity, press charges, and get a restraining order against the rapist. Needless to say, never allow yourself to be alone with this person again.

If it happens to be someone you know, like an ex-spouse, report it anyway. This person had no respect for you, so you needn't worry about turning him or her in.

Financial rip-offs

One of the reasons to be so cautious about inviting people home before you know them well, even if they seem like very nice people on the surface, is that it is possible for someone to "case" your house, and return later to rob you. This is more likely, of course, if you have a very nice home with expensive furnishings and jewelry. People who do this are most likely to have a drug habit or some other reason for taking such a risk; and they're pretty easy to figure out if you get to know them a little, so it's not too likely that it will happen unless you bring a virtual stranger home.

Don't flash a wallet or purse with a lot of money and credit cards either, for the same reason. An experienced pickpocket can steal from you, even in public, and you won't even notice until it's too late.

A far bigger danger of financial rip-off, however, is that someone will gain your confidence and borrow money or only be charming you for what they can get out of you. People are most vulnerable to this scam when they are low in self-confidence, shy or lonely, newly out of a long-term relationship through divorce or breakup, or had a partner die, and thus are grieving.

While most of us wouldn't dream of taking advantage of a person in such a vulnerable state, a con artist seeks this kind of person out, flatters and soothes them, and then takes advantage.

If you doubt someone's sincerity, or he or she seems "too good to be true," be very careful. If your friends express doubts about your date, or if he or she is reluctant to meet your friends, or tries to come between you and your friends, be very suspicious. Too much charm and savoir-faire can be a warning sign.

Unless you know someone very well, and are absolutely certain they have a reliable money history, don't lend money, your car, or valuable possessions to them, no matter how acute their need seems to be. If you do lend something to a relatively unknown person or to someone whose financial history is unknown, assume you won't get it back.

Cheating/lying

There are two main reasons lovers lie. First, to coerce you into doing something you wouldn't do if you knew the truth (such as giving away money or putting up with cheating), and second, to prevent you from finding out something that will cause you to end the relationship.

"Liars, or people who conceal information, often succeed because the target of their lies makes it so easy for them," writes Paul Ekman, Ph.D. in *Telling Lies.* "Unless you are prepared to deal with the truth, you are very likely to overlook the subtle signs in a person's words and voice, face and body movements that signal deception. First meetings and rushed encounters are especially vulnerable to errors. People who you like instinctively and want to get closer to immediately, even before you know anything about them, are much more likely to get away with lies than dour, cranky personalities." This is exactly why it is essential to establish open communication before you're in a relationship. Knowing a person makes it easier to tell if he or she is trustworthy, and to tell when you're being told the truth.

Before you tell someone what you want to hear ("If I ever found out you were cheating on me, I'd leave you"), find out what they will say on their own. A liar will lie, no matter what threats you use—in fact, threats make lying more likely.

If you draw a person into conversation before you begin dating, and observe him or her around other people, you'll most likely see signs of a dishonest character. If your prospective friend lies to his boss about why he's not at work, and to his ex-wife about when he'll show up, he'll probably lie to you. If your date uses a phony excuse so she can break a date with her friend, and go out with you, she'll probably do the same thing to you one day.

Stalking and harassment

One of the biggest problems you can encounter in dating is the person who can't let go. The "Fatal Attraction" personality is someone with severe emotional problems, who finds security in possessing others, and regards anything less than total devotion to be a betrayal, deserving of punishment. These personalities can range from mildly annoying, pestering you and not taking "no" for an answer, to creepy and frightening, capable of violence and even murder.

The recent laws passed making stalking and harassment a crime in several states are an indication of how serious the problem can get. These laws have made it easier to get protection, because the rule used to be that the police would not get involved unless bodily harm was done, or at least damage to property. Now you can report a stalker, and the police regard the stalking and harassment itself as a crime.

Stalking is the ultimate expression of the controlling personality, which is why I have included so many warnings about noticing and breaking it off with someone who appears to want to control you. Possessiveness is not a compliment, although in the very early stages it can be flattering to be so desired. Soon, however, it becomes obnoxious and even frightening.

If you get involved with a person who won't let

go, be very careful not to encourage the behavior by "not wanting to hurt" him or her. The slightest kindness will be taken as encouragement by this sort of obsessive person.

Say "no" very clearly, and do not back down. The most dangerous thing you can do is to say "no" and then allow the person to talk you out of it, which teaches this kind of person that they can pressure you into giving in. If you set your boundaries early, the person might leave, but he or she most likely won't harass you further.

If, once you break the relationship off, the person continues to bother you by phone or in person, or shows up at your work or your home uninvited, say very clearly and firmly that the behavior is unacceptable, and you do not want to see or talk to him or her again.

If that doesn't work, get a restraining order (which means he or she can be arrested for coming too close to you anywhere) from the police department. If he or she violates the restraining order, do not hesitate to call the police. You must be extremely clear that you will not be coerced or bullied into giving in.

Emotional blackmail

In her book *Emotional Blackmail*, Harriet Lerner lists six symptoms of emotional blackmail:

1. **A demand.** If your date demands, rather than asks, for whatever he or she wants, (whether it's sex or more of your time) and expects you to comply simply because he or she wants it, pay close attention. The difference between a request and a demand is that a request will accept "no" for an answer.

2. **Resistance.** The nature of a demand is such that

Watch Out!
If you feel your date is frequently pressuring you for sex, more time, more attention, and/or is having temper tantrums or crying fits when you say no, be careful. Tell your date in very clear terms that you feel pressured and you want him or her to stop this behavior. If it doesn't stop, recognize the danger and break off the relationship.

you will probably resist it. You'll instinctively react to the pressure by objecting.

3. **Pressure.** Once you resist, the demanding nature of the request will become more obvious. Your date will not be willing to accept "no" for an answer.

4. **Threats.** If you persist in saying no, the situation will escalate, and your date will use threatening or coercive tactics: threatening to end the relationship, tears, rage, badgering.

5. **Compliance.** If you give in, you're setting a dangerous precedent. Your date now knows you can be pressured into giving in to him or her, and this will increase the intensity of what your date is willing to do to pressure you. For the moment, however, your date will be all smiles and affection—he or she has gotten his way, and is as delighted as a child.

6. **Repetition.** An obsessive person will go through the previous five steps over and over, wearing you down each time. The easiest thing is to be sure when you say "no," it means no.

Emotionally healthy people do not need to indulge these sorts of behaviors. Should you encounter emotional blackmail in anyone you date, recognize the behavior for what it is and refuse to go along. This is not someone you want to be spending much time with.

Verbal, emotional, or physical abuse

Although women sustain more serious and visible injuries than men during domestic disputes, they are just as likely to resort to physical aggression during an argument with a sexual partner. Such are the findings of Dr. John Archer, a researcher at the

University of Central Lancashire (Great Britain).

Partner abuse is a huge problem in this country. Men and women both lash out in rage at their nearest and dearest... sometimes verbally, sometimes physically.

If your date gets violent or abusive, shouts at you or at others, becomes verbally aggressive at other drivers on the road, hits the wall with his or her fist, throws things, gets upset, or otherwise throws tantrums, it's the first step on a path that leads to more and more anger and violence. Should you recognize that someone you're involved with has a problem with controlling his or her violent reactions, keep the following points in mind:

- Realize that it's not going to get better. If your partner flies into rage, or verbally or sexually abuses or batters you or your children, no matter what he or she may say, it isn't your fault, and you have no control over his or her behavior. Even the abuser has very little control. It is not just a one-time incident, it is an indication of a severely disturbed character, and it will *not* go away without *years* of intense therapy.

- Protect yourself and your children. The best way to do this is to tell the truth about your situation to family, friends, your minister, your doctor, your therapist, your co-workers, a domestic violence hotline, the police, and anyone else who will listen. There is no need for you to be ashamed, but there is an urgent need for you to get help. If it seems that no one is listening, consider that you might not be telling the whole truth—battering victims have a tendency to downplay and make excuses for

> " [W]omen visit emergency rooms for injuries caused by their husbands or boyfriends more often than for injuries from car accidents, robberies and rapes combined.
> —Gaven De Becker in *The Gift of Fear: Listening to the Intuition That Protects us from Violence.* "

the abuse. The best protection for you and your children is for your abuser's behavior to become public knowledge. The vast majority of abusers are cowards, who only prey on dependent, defenseless people. They like to believe they are in control, and they aren't as likely to lose control before witnesses.

- Once you have been witness to a rage, or you've been physically abused, do not be alone with the abuser again. This is another reason to tell everyone you know. You either need a place to go, or someone (perhaps several people) to stay with you until you are safe. You may also need financial help.

- If you are hit, call the police (911). They respond much better now than they used to, and the law is now on your side. When they come, press charges. Do not make excuses to yourself or anyone else. If your abuser gets away with it even once, he or she will get more abusive. Do not listen to pleas for sympathy, understanding, or forgiveness. You can forgive the abuser *after* he or she has gotten help, and *only* after you and your children are safe.

- If injured, get medical help. Tell the doctors and nurses the truth about how it happened.

- File a restraining or protective order. Volunteers at the police department will help you fill it out. With a restraining order, you can call the police as soon as the abuser gets close to you or your home. Without one, the police need evidence of the abuse to arrest anyone.

- If you've been a victim of violence before,

attend Al-Anon meetings. You will learn a lot of good information that will help you avoid being someone else's victim.

Suspicious?

Perhaps nothing bad has happened, but something doesn't feel right to you. If your hackles are up, and you have an uneasy feeling, if anything doesn't seem quite right to you, pay close attention to your feelings.

If you are feeling anything at all strange, or you find yourself feeling oddly reluctant to go on a date, or even if you're too excited, your body may be trying to tell you something. It's essential that you pay attention to these signs.

We all have an inner sense that picks up subtle, emotional and physical signals from people—unaware, we observe a tense jaw, a furtive glance, an angry response that we can choose to ignore with our intellect. But the body will notice and try to alert you. If it does, don't be too occupied with your thoughts to feel your feelings.

Investigating the truth

On the other hand, if you have no real evidence that anything is wrong, and you're enjoying time with your date, one thing that seems odd is not enough to jump to conclusions.

What you want to do is investigate your date until you find out the truth. Don't hesitate to look your date up on the Internet, in the phone book, to ask to meet his or her friends, to check out what you know about your date.

The longer you know someone, and the more you get to observe him or her, the more you'll find out about how trustworthy this person is.

Meet friends, family—pay attention

When you do get an opportunity to meet your date's friends, family, and children, pay attention to what people say. If they talk about a lot of other dates, or joke about what a "problem" your date is, don't just laugh it off, find out how true it is.

Stealth interview your date's friends and family just as you did your date—you'll find out plenty of information to tell you what kind of person you're getting involved with.

While one "bad sheep" family member is nothing to worry about, if your date's family and friends drink too much, or act inappropriately, it might be an indicator of what kind of person your date is, also.

Getting help if you need it

If you need to get some extra help to find out the truth, be sure you're interested enough in the person to go to all that trouble. If your suspicions are this intense, maybe it's not worth trying to find out

However, if you decide you really need to know, here are some kinds of help you can get.

Private investigations. A few years ago, there were a number of news stories about people hiring private eyes to spy on their partners—in the stories that made the news, we heard about the problems. Feeling suspicious enough to hire a detective is not a good sign about your relationship. Perhaps if you're this suspicious, you should just let the relationship go before it gets too serious.

If you decide to go through with it, be sure you find a reputable investigation agency that is licensed. If you have a lawyer you trust, perhaps you can get a recommendation there.

Enlisting friends. If you have concerns, ask your friends to ask around. Perhaps someone you know

Moneysaver
Find out what a private investigation will cost in advance—they can be very expensive. Also, remember that you can choose how much of an investigation you want conducted. Checking a person's history on the Internet, or checking for a criminal record only, is cheaper than a full-scale investigation.

knows one of your date's ex's—a great resource for all the negatives about your date. Or, perhaps your friends have heard rumors they are reluctant to share with you. Telling them you want to check out your date will give them permission to tell you whatever they know.

If you find out your suspicions are groundless, and your partner checks out fine, good! Be sure anyone you told of your suspicions knows they were unfounded.

Are you oversuspicious for a reason?

If your suspicions turned out to be wrong, were you oversuspicious? If you had a difficult past, you may indeed be too quick to suspect people. Because it is so important to protect yourself, it's better to be oversuspicious than too trusting. But if you find that over-caution is creating too much anxiety, or causing needless problems in your relationships, you may want to take the problem to your therapist.

If your fears turn out to be unfounded, you may want to clear the air between you and your date by confessing your suspicion, letting your date know you found out you were wrong, and apologizing for your suspicions. If your date is realistic about modern life, and cares about you, he or she should be able to forgive you, and it will be one more relationship hurdle you have overcome. In the long run, it will probably bring you closer.

If your suspicions were caused by a difficulty in communication, tell your date that, and work together to open up the conversation between you.

If your fears are related to your childhood or an earlier, abusive relationship, you may have emotional leftovers from your history. If this is true, your emotional traumas can distort your perceptions to the point that you'll be too afraid of the wrong things, and not worried enough about other things.

A survivor's group, Adult Children of Alcoholics, or therapy will help you to resolve the old traumas and learn to know when you can trust, and when you can't.

Coping with excessive suspicion

If you feel your fears are exaggerated, therapy will help you to figure out whether they are or not. Get a recommendation for a reputable therapist from a friend, or your doctor, if you can. If not, call a local hotline, for example the Suicide Prevention hotline, or the Rape hotline. They usually have reliable therapists they can recommend. Jewish Family Services and Catholic Charities are two nationwide organizations that offer low-cost, reliable therapy. You needn't be a member of the religion to use the services.

Find a therapist who handles issues similar to yours, whether it's child abuse, domestic violence, or anxiety, and ask what his or her experience is in these cases. Interview the therapist on the phone before making an appointment. Make sure that he or she has proper licensing and credentials, and that you feel comfortable with the approach he or she says he will use.

When your worst fears are verified

If your suspicions turn out to be right, you are very lucky that you paid attention and checked them out. Now, it's important that you act according to what you know.

Don't think you can change this partner; these problems are longstanding. If your partner does change, he or she can come and find you after the change has taken place, and see if there's anything still possible. But don't wait around. It could, and often does, take a lifetime to change severe personality problems.

If you find you have valid reasons to doubt this person, and there are real problems, such as lying, severe money problems, a history of alcohol abuse, violence, many past relationship problems, a criminal record, reports of illegal activities, or drug use, do not make excuses, and do not accept promises of change. Change is difficult, and will take a lot of time. Mere promises, no matter how well intended, are not sufficient.

Get out of this relationship before you are any more attached than you are now. If your partner decides to get help, let him or her do it because he or she knows they need it, not to get you back. That's not a strong enough motive to keep a person committed to change.

Reform is rarely an option
Don't fall into the trap of thinking you can change a severely problematic person on your own. If your date has a cold, needs a button sewn on, or a flat tire fixed, you can help—but problems this severe require more than you can provide, and your "help" may only postpone the real treatment this person needs.

Do both of you a favor and end the relationship, and don't look back. It may be appropriate for a spouse of years duration, with children involved, to go through the long struggle of helping a partner change, but a dating relationship is not the same kind of situation. Get out now. Forget any idea of a second chance. Go back to the search part of the dating process and find someone more stable.

Giving second chances to people who have severe problems merely keeps you from going on with your life, and sends you around the whole disappointing cycle again.

If you can't get out, get help—for yourself

If you find your partner has severe emotional problems, and has lied about it to you, and you have trouble getting out of the relationship, you have some problems of your own. This is called *co-dependency*. Get yourself immediately to a Co-Dependent's Anonymous or Al-Anon meeting to learn about why you're having trouble, and what you can do about it.

It's very easy to get hooked on a charmer who seems helpless to control him or herself. If you do, you're asking for months and years of anguish. Please find out why you are tempted to stay involved with someone who obviously has such severe problems that any kind of normal relationship would be impossible.

Couple problems

As your relationship develops beyond the early stages, the "rough edges" every couple has will emerge. Both of you will relax, and, as you get closer, the difficulties that every relationship has will emerge. A lot of this is very normal, but still needs to be handled well, or it can be made worse. For example, if you get stuck in bickering, accusing, and defending rather than communicating and negotiating, you'll start a downward spiral in the relationship, creating resentment and resulting in a shutdown of sexual activity, blocked communication, and power struggles.

Go for help early—while it's easy to solve

If problems arise between you, get help as soon as possible. Take a couples class or workshop, or go for counseling. I highly recommend "pre-commitment" or "pre-marital" counseling. It has been proven so helpful that many ministers, rabbis and other clergy have made it a pre-requisite to their conducting a wedding ceremony.

Early counseling can be to your marriage as the operation manual is to your computer software: If you just try to make it work by trial-and-error, you may succeed, but if you have the right directions to begin with, you'll be a lot more effective and efficient. An expert, objective counselor will ask you all the questions you, in your rosy glow of love, haven't considered, and help you correct any negative patterns that are beginning to form.

A few counseling sessions, a class or a workshop early in the relationship can teach you skills you'll use for the rest of your years together. These skills can make the difference between a smooth ride or a bumpy one, especially if the examples of relationships you grew up with were not good ones.

Problems are not necessarily tragedies

All relationships have problems—they are not tragedies unless they are handled badly. You are two extremely different people (no matter how *simpatico* you feel now), and blending those differences into a smooth team is not easy. You have personal differences, perceptual differences, and differences in how you handle money, time, friends, work, feelings, communications family and children—all of which need to be worked out.

In addition to all your personal differences, you have the (often intrusive) influence of your in-laws, friends, children, family and your past relationship history to deal with.

As if that were not enough, you have things like work and travel schedules, commutes, and personality conflicts at work which affect your moods and your availability to one another. Life changes, deaths of loved ones, illnesses, problems with children, and aging also have an impact on your relationship.

No couple can or should be expected to handle all of these dynamics alone, without help, or without having some problems. When problems arise, look on them as challenges that, if met and handled as a team, will strengthen and deepen your connection, and fill your relationship reservoir with an endless supply of good will, trust, and mutual love and respect.

What is routine, what requires help?

Any problem you can handle yourselves within a couple of days and without serious fighting is fine. But if a problem leads to dramatic fights, recriminations, and temper tantrums, or if a problem can't be solved and keeps coming back, you should get some help.

Once you establish a relationship with a counselor, he or she can be there like your family doctor, familiar with your history, and available to help you with a session or two, whenever you need it. It's a great support for your success as a couple.

Your support network

Just as "it takes a village to raise a child" it takes a cohesive group to support your relationship. Gather about you those members of your friends and family who can truly be supportive. You need people who can hear about a spat, not take sides, and offer wisdom from their own experience to help you.

Don't rely on people who "take your side" and agree with you when you're angry at your partner; rather, go to those who can be objective, sympathize, and still help you see where you, also, contributed to the problem.

Certainly never confide in those people who use the intimacy against you later, or who report it back to your spouse or to friends. You need a safe space to blow off steam, when you're frustrated or upset—someone who can take what you're saying in anger with a "grain of salt", and listen with compassion for both you and your partner.

People who can do this are fairly rare, so when you find them, cherish them.

Step-family problems

The most difficult task of all is building a step-family. The dynamics of blending a new family out of divorce or loss are tough, because the children and the parents have already experienced loss and stress, and there are divided loyalties. If you are a step-parent to your partner's children, the children may worry that their betraying their real parent by getting close to you. If the divorced parents don't get along, or play the children off against each other, the problem is even worse.

Do not attempt step-parenting without help and wise counsel. Preventive counseling is essential to helping you keep the dynamics straight. Understanding how this feels to the children, knowing when to set rules and use tough love and when to be sympathetic, as well as working out your partner issues, is more than you can do alone.

Breakups

No matter how carefully you've screened a date, and no matter how hard you try, all relationships do not work out well. If both of you are adult about it, you may simply be able to part as friends, on a mutual understanding. But if you discover that your date has severe problems, and have to leave, or if you get left

Bright Idea
When there are stepchildren involved, work out your coparenting strategy together *privately*. Then present a united front to the children.

by someone you care about, it's not so simple.

Breaking up begins your dating—again cycle over. Once again, you go through the process of grieving, analyzing what happened, learning from it, and meeting new friends and dating. However, if you followed the process outlined in this book, you have set up a network of new people, which will easily get you right back into circulation as soon as you're ready.

Keep in mind you've come through this already, survived it, and actually had a lot of good times doing it. Use what you learned last time to help you now, and put more energy into learning from this relationship experiment than in giving yourself a hard time about the breakup.

Getting support

The same people who supported you in this relationship will most likely support you in grieving it. Using your support network to help while you're grieving will make that phase easier. If you allow your grief to happen, and don't resist it, or compound it by blaming yourself for the whole breakup, or scare yourself that you'll never meet the right person, the grief will come and go easily for a while, until you feel over it enough to take a few more emotional risks.

If this episode brings up a lot of grief from earlier times, past relationships, or childhood traumas, it's a good thing to tell this to your therapist or counselor. If you're struggling to let go of the relationship, and obsessing on it, try a few Co-Dependents Anonymous meetings. You'll find being around others who struggle with the same feelings very supportive.

You can save a lot of time in therapy, whether it's

couple counseling or individual therapy, to work out problems, or to help you with grief, by bringing a list of what you think the problems are and what you want to accomplish to the first session.

Reading books related to your therapy will give you a lot of information, and thereby save time (and money) in your sessions, because the therapist won't have to explain the concepts you learn in the books—he or she can just help you apply them.

Regard therapy as teamwork—both you and the therapist work together to identify and solve the problems, rather than just sitting back and wanting the therapist to tell you what to do.

Being pro-active

Whether you handle your breakup well or have a lot of trouble, mobilizing yourself to accomplish something will help. Seek out support, read books about ending relationships or the specific problems you had in this relationship (for example, a book on anger and fighting, or one on self-esteem), and focus on what you need to do to move through the ending of the relationship and your grief.

Have supportive conversations with yourself about what happened, and what you'd like to do differently next time. Use your support system to help you express your grief, then move beyond it and focus on the future. Take a class or workshop in communication or relationship skills, to be better equipped for the next one. The more pro-active you are, the better you'll feel about yourself and the more hope you'll have for the future.

Breaking the news

One of the truly difficult things about breaking up is having to let everyone who thought of you as a couple know that it's over. This can be tough, but there

Watch Out!
When you break up you may want to rush right into a new relationship, but hold off! That's one way to repeat bad relationships choices—you need time to recover, first.

are ways to make it easier.

If you have e-mail, send a message to your friends and family (NOT business associates) that says something like: "After some heartfelt discussions about the future of our relationship, and finding our differences unsurmountable, Susie (or Sam) and I have decided to part. We will remain friends, and I have the highest regard for her (him), but we have decided it is in both of our best interests to look for someone else."

This puts the best light on things, and prevents you having to explain over and over to each person. When you talk to them individually, you needn't give further details unless you want to.

Of course, the people who are most involved with you as a couple deserve a face-to-face conversation or a phone call, and telling your children, depending on their ages, could take a number of long or short conversations.

The primary person you may have trouble telling that the relationship should end may just be yourself. If you know it's really over, it's bad for you, or it's just not working any more, but you're not bringing up the subject, you probably need to have a heart-to-heart with yourself.

Go over the pros and cons of the relationship, make a list if you need it to see things clearly. If you still have doubts about whether you want out, and if there's anything you haven't tried discussing with your partner, bring it up and see of you can work it out. If you think counseling is a possibility, try to get your partner to go—if your partner won't go, you can go by yourself.

If you know you've tried everything you can think of, and it's still not working, especially if you've discussed it with a therapist, admit it's over and make your decision to move on.

Telling your partner it's over

There's no really easy way to do this, but there is a responsible, reasonable way. If you must be the one to tell your partner it's over, do your best to be clear, definite and caring. Unless you're dealing with a controlling or stalking type (in that case, none of these suggestions apply—see above), you can be gentle and considerate about it.

Get together, in private, and tell your partner that the relationship is not working for you, and you need to withdraw. If the break has been coming for a while, this session can be a chance for both of you to thank each other for what you got out of the relationship.

If it will be a surprise to your partner, or something he or she suspected was coming, but didn't want, you may have to steel yourself for some angry or upset words from him or her. If that happens, just stay calm, and give the other person a chance to tell you how he or she feels about it. Remember, you've been working up to this for a while, and this person, who cares for you, hasn't.

There is no need to blame your partner, or even yourself, for why things aren't working. If you think your partner doesn't know, and will ask you, then think your answer out beforehand, so you have some acceptable things to say. Keep your remarks general, like "we're very different people," "I wasn't getting what I wanted," or "I'm not ready to focus on just one person."

Since you're the one breaking it off, give your (now ex) partner the room to say what he or she wants to happen next. If you want to be friends, make the offer, but let your ex decide if he or she is ready, and when to see each other again.

If your relationship has lasted long enough for your family and friends to know about it, you have to find a way to let them know it's over, also. If you and your ex are going to be friends, tell your family and friends that—if not, just tell them it's over, as simply as you can.

Children are a more difficult story. If you have kids who have bonded with your ex, it's important to take their feelings into consideration, too. If you can work it out, it's best if your ex doesn't suddenly disappear out of their lives. If your children have already been through a divorce, losing yet another adult they've gotten close to is really unfair. Of course, all of this also applies to your ex's children, if he or she has any. If the two of you can work together to make the changes easier on the children, it's worthwhile to do so.

Grief

You grieve to the extent that you loved, so if the relationship was an important one to you, you'll be grieving for a while. Also, this breakup may bring up all the grief of your past relationships, whether you wanted this one to end or not. Your grief will go through several stages, coming and going, fading for a time, and coming back.

As I said above, it's essential that you have support for grieving, especially if you must be a support system for your own children.

Self-recriminations

Because the grief involved in ending the relationship is painful, it's very easy to blame yourself and give yourself a hard time over it. This helps nothing, and intensifies the pain.

While it's important to evaluate what went wrong and the part you played in it so you can learn from it, you won't learn anything by blaming yourself for everything.

If you can't be constructive in evaluating what went wrong, get a therapist to help you. Don't prolong the agony by directing hostility toward yourself.

How to survive the loss of a love

You will survive this, and you'll learn from it, and you'll get another, better relationship after you get through the grief. If you really let yourself grieve and go through all the stages, you'll learn and grow as a result.

Unexpectedly, grief for a current loss can trigger any grief you've ever had. Don't be surprised if you find yourself reliving your grief for someone who died or who left many years ago, even back as far as your childhood.

As you let your grief out, you will experience an amazing array of feelings. Anger, jealousy, sadness, depression, giddiness, bitterness, silliness, and fear will all come up, in succession—some of the feelings more intense than others. You'll also re-experience the good memories of the relationship.

At times you'll feel peaceful, then be overwhelmed with anger, resentment, or hurt. These feelings will be very intense at first, but if you allow yourself to express them by talking to understanding friends, journaling, or talking to a therapist, you'll find they begin to subside rather quickly.

It's very helpful to put pictures and mementos away until your grief subsides. Pack up all the pictures, knickknacks, jewelry or other gifts, cards, letters and reminders and put them away for a while. Until your feelings settle down, you don't want to be

> **❝**
> The progression is from shock/denial to anger/depression and finally to understanding/acceptance. At the end of this progression are the rewards: the pleasures of freedom, the joys of growth and the sense of mastery derived from having dealt with a loss in a 'right proper way
> —Melba Colgrove, Peter McWilliams, and Harold Bloomfield, *How to Survive the Loss of a Love.*
> **❞**

ambushed by coming across such a reminder. Later, when your grief has healed, you can go through these mementos and decide which, if any, you want to keep.

But do not attempt to go through this all alone. Find a grief support group, go to therapy, talk to your clergy person, to friends and family. Do not keep your feelings to yourself.

Take a journal workshop or an art therapy workshop to get the feelings out. The more you express your feelings, the faster you'll get through this. Think of it as if you have X number of tears to shed, and the faster you get them shed, the better you'll feel.

You knew better, but. . .

Everybody does things that they should have known better than to do. It's easy to have a self-recrimination field day when this has happened, but try to learn from your mistakes, figure out what you'll do differently if you're ever in a similar situation, and then forgive yourself, and let it go. Causing yourself needless pain from self-criticism won't help a thing, and it will make you feel much worse. Here are a few of those "I *knew* I shouldn't have done that!" situations that you may encounter during your dating experience.

Dating ex's. If you went down in flames after trying to date an ex, simply learn from it, and don't let yourself be tempted again. Sometimes you just have to try it one more time to convince yourself that it won't work. You are a human being, and that means you'll sometimes make mistakes. You have to get over it and move on. Take a look at what you were thinking that allowed yourself to try it again (when you already knew it went bad before), and re-think it,

> 66
> If we are to know love, we must come to understand and use constructively *all* the feelings that both love's pleasures and love's disappointments arouse, not only the ecstasy, but also the hurt and pain, the anger and hate.
> —Jane Goldberg, Ph.D. in *The Dark Side of Love.*
> 99

so you're not vulnerable to this kind of mistake any more.

The never-ending divorce story. Getting involved with someone who keeps promising to get a divorce, and never does, is a very old trap. If you finally gave up on the person who was stringing you along, congratulate yourself, and be gentle with yourself about your grief and loss. Make yourself a promise that the next person you get involved with will really be available. You deserve to have a person who is all there for you, not half there.

Ex's who won't go away. If you got involved with someone who actually got a divorce, but still is so entangled with his or her ex that there was no room for you, and you finally figured that out, see the congratulations, gentleness, and promise instruction above.

Too entangled—too soon. This is probably the most common mistake made—getting emotionally bonded to someone, inviting him or her into your life, introducing him or her to your friends, family and children, before you knew who he or she really was. If you got too close to your ex too soon, and then you found out something about who he or she really was which meant you had to leave, again you have an opportunity to learn from your mistake.

You found out something awful. If you were fooled by someone who had a criminal past, a terrible drug habit, who turned out to be gay, or some other revelation that disqualified him or her as a legitimate partner, you'll naturally feel badly for a while. You may realize that you didn't get to know this person well enough, or, you may realize that anyone could have been fooled as you were. Either way, you need to forgive yourself, learn from your mistake, and move on.

If these kinds of revelations cause you to feel so guilty or angry at yourself that you can't forgive yourself or let go of it, or if you are filled with fear about resuming dating, then therapy is called for. Do yourself a favor and handle these negative feelings now, before they create further problems.

Most people have made relationship mistakes and had to learn from them—what we call the "school of hard knocks." Everyone has experienced painful relationships. While it's important to learn from your mistakes, first you have to make a correction and then let go and forgive yourself. Don't keep yourself away from a lifetime of fun because of the few things that go wrong.

The many faces of dating: From fun to happily ever after

You may be interested in dating again because you want to meet people, make friends, and simply have a good time, or because you want to find the love of your life. All of these reasons are legitimate reasons for dating.

If you follow all the guidelines in this book, you'll have a better chance of being clear about what you do want, finding others who have similar reasons, and getting together with someone who feels the same as you do will be easier and clearer.

No matter what you're looking for, I wish you well and hope you find the perfect date.

Just the facts

- Safety should be your first concern.

- Minimize or eliminate alcohol on dates—it's the most common reason for a dating situation to turn bad.

- Never let attraction overrule your common sense.

- If your date turns dangerous, don't hesitate to get help—and if the situation calls for it, file charges against an abusive date.

- Don't waste time attempting to "reform" a date with severe problems—the odds are high that you are simply not qualified.

- When breaking up a relationship, turn to your network of supportive friends to help you get through.

Resources

Tina Tessina:
http://www.lbcbn.com/Tessina

Rainbow World Directory:
http://www.rnbow.com/rwd/c740.htm

Long Beach Rainbow Net:
http://www.lbrainbownet.com/

E-mail: tinatessina@Compuserve.com
The Love Buzz with Dr. Romance:
http://www.OCNOW.com (entertainment section)

To Find Books By Dr. Tessina
On Amazon.com:
http://www.amazon.com/exec/obidos/generic-quicksearch-query/002-8157782-3960607

At University of California San Diego Library:
ttp://roger.ucsd.edu/search/aTessina+Tina+B/
-5,-1,0,B/frameset&aTessina+Tina+B&1,1

Through the Family Forum Bookstore:
http://familyforum.com/marriage.htm

Interviews with Dr. Tessina can be found in the following sites:
Concerned Counseling CCI Journal
http://www.concernedcounseling.com/ccijournal/conference/tessinarelationships.htm

Amazon.com Interviews Tina B. Tessina:
http://www.amazon.com/exec/obidos/show-inter-
view/t-t-essinainab/002-8157782-3960607

**Utne Cafe, where Dr. Tessina is host of the
relationships conference**
http://www.utne.com

**Love Life Radio (will archive interview in
November 1998):**
http://www.lovelife.com

Recommended Reading List

Booth, Richard, and Marshall Jung, *Romancing the Net: A 'Tell-All' Guide to Love Online*. Prima Publishing, 1996.

Calvo, Emily Thornton, and Laurence Minsky, *25 Words or Less: How to Write Like a Pro to Find That Special Someone Through Personal Ads*. NTC/Contemporary Publishing, 1998.

Carey, Sylvia, *"Jerk Alert."* New Woman (May, 1996).

Colgrove, Melba, Peter McWilliams and Harold Bloomfield. *How to Survive the Loss of a Love* Lion Press, NY 1976

Friedman, Sonya, *Men Are Just Desserts*. Warner Books 1983.

Goldberg, Jane, PhD *The Dark Side of Love* Tarcher/Putnam New York, 1993.

Jillson, Joyce. *The Fine Art of Flirting*. Simon and Schuster, 1989.

Keyes, Ken. *The Power of Unconditional Love*. Coos Bay, OR: Love Line Books, 1979.

Appendix B

Klein, Marty, *"Are you Sexually Normal?"* New Age Journal, September, 1985.

Lowndes, Leil, *How to Make Anyone Fall in Love With You.* NTC/Contemporary Publishing.

Martin, Judith. *Miss Manners' Guide for The Turn of the Millennium.* Pharos Books, 1989.

Perls,Frederick S. *The Gestalt Approach and Eye Witness to Therapy,* Science & Behavior Books, 1973.

Rabin, Susan, with Barbara Lagowski, *How to Attract Anyone, Anytime, Anyplace: The Smart Guide to Flirting,* Plume 1993.

Roberts, Denton, *Able & Equal.* Human Esteem Publishing, 1984.

Sills, Judith, Ph.D, *A Fine Romance: The Passage of Courtship from Meeting to Marriage.* Ballantine Books, 1993.

Smith, Riley K., and Tina B. Tessina, *How To Be a Couple and Still Be Free.* 2d ed. Newcastle, 1987.

Smith, Riley K., and Tina B. Tessina, *True Partners: A Workbook For Developing Lasting Intimacy.* Tarcher, 1993.

Tessina, Tina B. *Lovestyles, How to Celebrate Your Differences.* Newcastle, 1987.

Winokur, Jon, *A Curmudgeon's Garden of Love,* Penguin, 1989.

A

B

C

The *Unofficial Guide*™ Reader Questionnaire

If you would like to express your opinion about dating again or this guide, please complete this questionnaire and mail it to:

The *Unofficial Guide*™ Reader Questionnaire
Macmillan Lifestyle Group
1633 Broadway, floor 7
New York, NY 10019-6785

Gender: ___ M ___ F

Age: ___ Under 30 ___ 31-40 ___ 41-50
___ Over 50

Education: ___ High school ___ College
___ Graduate/ Professional

What is your occupation?

_____

How did you hear about this guide?
___ Friend or relative
___ Newspaper, magazine, or Internet
___ Radio or TV
___ Recommended at bookstore
___ Recommended by librarian
___ Picked it up on my own
___ Familiar with the *Unofficial Guide*™ travel series

Did you go to the bookstore specifically for a book on dating again? Yes___ No___

Have you used any other *Unofficial Guides*™?
Yes___ No___

If Yes, which ones?

_____

_____

What other book(s) on dating again have you purchased?

_____

_____

Was this book:
___ more helpful than other(s)
___ less helpful than other(s)

Do you think this book was worth its price?
Yes___ No___

Did this book cover all topics related to dating again adequately? Yes___ No___

Please explain your answer:

_____

_____

Were there any specific sections in this book that were of particular help to you? Yes___ No___
Please explain your answer:

_____

_____

On a scale of 1 to 10, with 10 being the best rating, how would you rate this guide? ___

What other titles would you like to see published in the _Unofficial Guide_™ series?

_____

_____

Are _Unofficial Guides_™ readily available in your area? Yes___ No___
Other comments:

_____

_____

_____

About the Author

Tina Tessina, Ph.D., MFT, can tell you everything you need to know about about dating and relationships. She is the author of *The 10 Smartest Decisions A Woman Can Make Before 40* (Health Communications, Deerfield Beach 1998), *Gay Relationships: How To Find Them, How To Improve Them, How To Make Them Last* (Tarcher, 1990), and *Lovestyles: How To Celebrate Your Differences* (Newcastle, 1987). She has co-authored (with Riley K. Smith) *Equal Partners* (Hodder and Stoughton, London, 1994), *True Partners: A Workbook for Developing Lasting Intimacy* (J.P. Tarcher, 1992), *The Real Thirteenth Step: Discovering Confidence, Self-Reliance and Autonomy Beyond the Twelve Step Programs* (J.P. Tarcher, 1991), and *How To Be a Couple and Still Be Free* (Newcastle, 1987). Dr. Tessina also writes "The Love Buzz with Dr. Romance," a weekly online column for OCNOW.com. She has been excerpted and quoted in *New Woman, Cosmopolitan, Ladies Home Journal, Time, Newsweek, Shape, First for Women, Women's World* and many other publications. Dr. Tessina also lectures and conducts workshops nationwide, and has appeared on all major television and radio shows, including *Donohue, Oprah, Geraldo,* and *Larry King Live.*

Dr. Tessina is a licensed marriage and family therapist with a private practice in Long Beach, California since 1978. These years of sessions with real people, coupled with the experiences in her own life and the issues confronted by her friends and acquaintances, provide the inspiration from which she writes her books.

Dr. Tessina lives with her husband of 17 years, Richard Sharrard, two dogs and a cat.